Banjo FOR DUMMIES®

by Bill Evans

BICENTENNIAL
1807
WILEY
2007
BICENTENNIAL

Wiley Publishing, Inc.

Banjo For Dummies®

Published by
Wiley Publishing, Inc.
111 River St.
Hoboken, NJ 07030-5774
www.wiley.com

Copyright © 2007 by Wiley Publishing, Inc., Indianapolis, Indiana

Published by Wiley Publishing, Inc., Indianapolis, Indiana

Published simultaneously in Canada

For general information on our other products and services, please contact our Customer Care Department within the U.S. at 877-762-2974, outside the U.S. at 317-572-3993, or fax 317-572-4002.

For technical support, please visit www.wiley.com/techsupport.

Wiley also publishes its books in a variety of electronic formats. Some content that appears in print may not be available in electronic books.

Library of Congress Control Number: 2007926013

ISBN: 978-0-470-12762-9

Manufactured in the United States of America

10 9 8 7 6 5 4

WILEY

About the Author

Banjo player **Bill Evans** is not to be confused with the deceased jazz piano legend or the very much living jazz saxophone player (or the Austin, Texas, real estate agent). *This* Bill Evans is a banjo player, performer, teacher, workshop leader, recording artist, composer, producer, record label owner, and American music historian. For a banjo player, Bill has an unusual amount of schooling. He earned his bachelor's degree in anthropology with a specialization in folklore from the University of Virginia as a DuPont Scholar and a master's degree in music with a specialization in ethnomusicology from the University of California, Berkeley. After completing coursework for the PhD at Berkeley with a specialization in American music and the music of Japan, Bill taught courses in ethnomusicology and American music history at San Francisco State University, Duke University, and the University of Virginia and was the Associate Director of the International Bluegrass Music Museum in Owensboro, Kentucky. A recipient of a Brown Foreman–Al Smith Artist Fellowship from the Kentucky Arts Council, Bill has also served as a consultant to the National Endowment for the Arts.

As a recording artist, Bill's CD *Native and Fine* (Rounder Records) earned an honorable mention for Acoustic Instrumental Recording of the Year from NAIRD. His CD *Bill Evans Plays Banjo* (Native and Fine Records), featuring all original instrumental compositions, was on many "best of" lists, including those of the *Chicago Tribune* and *County Sales*. Bill earned a nomination for "Recorded Event of the Year" from the International Bluegrass Music Association for his work as producer on Suzanne Thomas' CD *Dear Friend and Gentle Hearts*. As a performing artist, Bill has played with Dry Branch Fire Squad, Tony Trischka, David Grisman, Peter Rowan, Maria Muldaur, Jody Stecher, Kathy Kallick and Laurie Lewis, among others. He tours nationally with his solo show "The Banjo in America" in addition to leading his own band, the Bill Evans String Summit.

Bill is a long-time contributor to *Banjo Newsletter* magazine and co-hosts an annual banjo camp, the Sonny Osborne NashCamp Banjo Retreat, held each fall outside of Nashville, Tennessee. In addition, Bill participates in workshops all over North America, hosts several popular instructional DVDs for AcuTab Publications, and maintains an active private teaching practice at his home in Albany, California. His former students include Chris Pandolfi, Greg Liszt, Jayme Stone, and Eric Yates. He is the co-author of *Parking Lot Picker's Songbook: Banjo Edition* from Mel Bay Publications.

To learn more about Bill, visit www.nativeandfine.com.

Dedication

I'd like to acknowledge the support and love of my family: my wife Kathy and my children Jesse and Corey. I dedicate this book to you.

Author's Acknowledgments

I'd like to thank Jody Stecher, Brad Leftwich, and Eli Kaufman of the American Banjo Fraternity for their advice and assistance in the preparation of the clawhammer and classic banjo sections of this book.

I am indebted to Elderly Instruments of Lansing, Michigan for providing many of the photos. Many thanks to Elderly's Stan Werbin, photographer Dave Matchette, and gig bag model C. Misener for their time and energy. Thanks also to photographer Kelsey Vaughn at Gruhn Guitars for supplying photos of the Osborne Chief banjo. The rest of the photos in this book were taken by Anne Hamersky. Thanks, Anne, for your fantastic, inspirational work, and thanks to Anne's assistant, Caitlin Atkinson. I'm also grateful to have worked with Dix Bruce on the CD that accompanies this book. Thank you, Dix, for your guitar and mandolin playing and for your engineering and mixing talents. Thanks also to Larry Cohea, John Lawless, Gretchen Snyder, Erin English, Paul Hostetter, and Don Nitchie of *Banjo Newsletter* for their continued support and assistance.

I'd like to express my thanks to the team at Wiley Publications who cheerfully and patiently dedicated themselves to this project: my project editor Tim Gallan, my acquisitions editor Michael Lewis, copy editor Sarah Westfall, and Joyce Cullen. Thanks also to technical editor and good friend Jan Threlkeld, and to my agent Carole McClendon. A big salute also goes out to *Dummies* author Bob LeVitus (a.k.a. "Dr. Mac") for getting the ball rolling by answering my e-mail inquiry regarding life as a *Dummies* author.

I would like to take this opportunity to thank three individuals who have provided a lifetime of musical inspiration and have mentored me over many years of close friendship: Sonny Osborne, Ron Thomason, and Tony Trischka. Your influence is found on every page of this book.

Publisher's Acknowledgments

We're proud of this book; please send us your comments through our Dummies online registration form located at www.dummies.com/register/.

Some of the people who helped bring this book to market include the following:

Acquisitions, Editorial, and Media Development

Senior Project Editor: Tim Gallan

Acquisitions Editor: Michael Lewis

Copy Editor: Sarah Westfall

Technical Editor: Jan Threlkeld

Editorial Manager: Christine Meloy Beck

Editorial Assistants: Erin Calligan Mooney, Joe Niesen, David Lutton, Leeann Harney

Cover Photo: Anne Hamersky

Photographers: Anne Hamersky, Dave Matchette, Kelsey Vaughn

Cartoons: Rich Tennant (www.the5thwave.com)

Composition Services

Project Coordinator: Patrick Redmond

Layout and Graphics: Claudia Bell, Carl Byers, Denny Hager, Shane Johnson, Heather Ryan, Julie Trippetti

Anniversary Logo Design: Richard Pacifico

Proofreaders: David Faust, Betty Kish, Susan Moritz

Indexer: Sherry Massey

Special Help
Christine Williams

Publishing and Editorial for Consumer Dummies

> **Diane Graves Steele,** Vice President and Publisher, Consumer Dummies

> **Joyce Pepple,** Acquisitions Director, Consumer Dummies

> **Kristin A. Cocks,** Product Development Director, Consumer Dummies

> **Michael Spring,** Vice President and Publisher, Travel

> **Kelly Regan,** Editorial Director, Travel

Publishing for Technology Dummies

> **Andy Cummings,** Vice President and Publisher, Dummies Technology/General User

Composition Services

> **Gerry Fahey,** Vice President of Production Services

> **Debbie Stailey,** Director of Composition Services

Contents at a Glance

Table of Contents

Introduction

. . . .

Are you ready to play the five-string banjo? If so, get ready for a fantastic ride. So whether you're reading this book at home or standing in a bookstore aisle, hold *Banjo For Dummies* high and proud for all to see. I guarantee that this book is going to open the door to a life of musical fulfillment with one of the world's greatest instruments.

Although the title of this book is probably enough to raise a good chuckle from many self-proclaimed "music lovers," let me assure you right from the start that *Banjo For Dummies* isn't a collection of the world's best banjo jokes — or even the worst.

You probably have already come to the realization that no matter what you may have seen on television or in old movies, real banjo players aren't comedic rubes or country bumpkins. They're folks just like you and me from all walks of life who at some point heard the sound of a banjo and said to themselves "*That's* for me!"

And what a gloriously rambunctious and complex sound it is! The banjo is usually associated with bluegrass, folk, and country music, but these days, musicians play just about any kind of music on the banjo — from jazz to classical to rock and everything in between. You can use the banjo to accompany songs around a campfire or to play a Bach partita; what you do with the instrument is up to you.

If you're a total beginner to the banjo, *Banjo For Dummies* is the best way to get started on the five-string banjo. If you already play the banjo, this book can broaden your knowledge, enhance your playing ability, and deepen your love for the world's greatest instrument. You can begin to play the banjo at age 8 or 80, and if you don't think you have any talent for playing a musical instrument, then you've come to *exactly* the right place. The banjo is waiting to turn you into a musician.

About This Book

I've taught hundreds of banjo players of all ages in over 30 years of teaching, and for what it's worth, I even have a master's degree in music (how's that for blowing away a few banjo player stereotypes!). In the process, I've seen what works and what doesn't work, and I know the location of pretty much every nasty pothole along the old banjo-pickin' highway.

I've put all this experience to use in *Banjo For Dummies,* your complete guide to the five-string banjo. This book safely transports you from the most basic beginners' questions to performing intermediate tunes played in a variety of styles. I even sneak in a few advanced concepts for those of you who really want to be challenged. You can find clear, step-by-step explanations to each and every technique and discover shortcuts that are especially helpful to the adult student.

Although I'd like to think that this book makes for a gripping and powerful literary experience, don't worry about reading *Banjo For Dummies* cover to cover. Think of this book instead as a reference work that's designed for you to jump in and jump out at any point along the way. Take a look at the table of contents and start at the chapter or section that best matches your ability and interests the most. Don't forget to check out the index at the back of the book for an even more comprehensive listing of topics.

If you skim through the more than 130 musical examples in the book, you may notice that you can't find a speck of conventional music notation anywhere in *Banjo For Dummies.* Instead, you find banjo *tablature,* the universal form of written music notation for just about all styles of banjo playing. Tablature is easier to master than regular musical notation and clearly shows you exactly what to do with both hands. When combined with this book's excellent photos and the accompanying audio CD, not discovering the right way to play banjo is pretty darn impossible.

If you're new to playing, here's how to get the most out of this book:

- ✔ **Figure out the hand and finger positions by mimicking the photos and diagrams.** Finding a comfortable hand position — especially in the right hand — is crucially important in banjo playing. You can find plenty of pictures and detailed explanations showing you how to find the positions that work best for you throughout this book. *Chord diagrams* reinforce the photos by showing you exactly where your fingers need to go.

- ✔ **Listen to the CD.** Each musical example in the book is included on the CD that you find inside the back cover. I can't overemphasize how important listening is to becoming a good banjo player. If you have the sound of every note firmly in your head before you start to play, you can master each exercise, hot lick, and song much more quickly. And on many tracks, you can play along with the guitar and mandolin accompaniment. Don't pass that gig up!

- ✔ **Read the tablature.** Also called *tab,* tablature is a great way to represent what both hands do when you play a banjo tune. Tab shows you which strings to pick with the right hand and what to fret with the left hand (more on tab, picking, and fretting in Chapters 2 and 3). I show you how to read it, how best to use it, and even when best to set it aside.

Conventions Used in This Book

To make key terms and ideas more consistent and easier to understand, *Banjo For Dummies* employs the following conventions throughout the book:

- ✔ When I reference a Web site that I want you to check out, it appears in a very official-looking monofont type. (Believe it or not, even banjo players use the Internet.)

  Note: When this book was printed, some Web addresses may have needed to break across two lines of text. If that happens, rest assured that the publishers haven't put in any extra characters (such as hyphens) to indicate the break. Just type in exactly what you see in this book, pretending that the line break doesn't exist.

- ✔ I *italicize* words I define (words you may want to pay attention to) in regular text. I also use italics for emphasis here and there (as a banjo player, getting excited once in a while is just natural for me).

- ✔ Key words or phrases in bulleted lists and numbered steps are printed in **bold,** so you don't miss out on this important info.

- ✔ When I talk about the right-hand techniques, know that the *right hand* is the hand that picks or strums the strings, and the *left hand* is the hand that presses the strings down on the neck and does some of those fancy techniques that may have attracted you to the banjo in the first place. However, if you're left handed and already play a banjo specially made for left-handed players, please read *right hand* to mean *left hand,* and vice versa.

- ✔ This book often uses the terms *up, down, higher,* and *lower* to refer to where your left hand moves on the banjo *neck* (the skinny part with the strings). When you move up the neck on the banjo, you're moving your left hand towards the body (or *pot*) of the instrument and playing notes that are higher in pitch. Conversely, when you move down the neck, you're moving your left hand towards the banjo headstock, away from the pot, and playing notes that sound lower.

- ✔ I use numbers in different ways throughout the book (don't worry — no math skills required). The five banjo strings have number names (5th, 4th, 3rd, 2nd, and 1st), and I also refer to left-hand fretted positions using numbers (which can be from the first to the 22nd fret). Sometimes, numbers also describe the quality or sound of a chord, such as in D7.

- ✔ If numbers weren't enough, I also use letters throughout the book to instruct you in finger placements. You encounter letters standing for the right-hand finger that picks a string (*T* = thumb, *I* = index, and *M* = middle) and also for the left-hand finger that pushes a particular string against the fingerboard (*I* = index, *M* = middle, *R* = ring, and *P* = pinky).

    ✔ As in all *For Dummies* books, figures are numbered sequentially within each chapter. I number the tablature examples, or tab, separately. Many tab examples are on the accompanying CD, and the track number is provided in the tab's caption.

What You're Not to Read

If you're looking just for the need-to-know information and want to skip a few parts that aren't essential to knowing how to play or maintain the banjo, you can breeze right on by sidebars (the gray shaded boxes) and paragraphs tagged by the Technical Stuff icon. However, if you like knowing some banjo trivia or want some nonessential tips and tools, by golly, read it all!

Foolish Assumptions

I'm betting that because you've picked up this book you're interested in playing the banjo, but I don't want to assume too much more as I begin this banjo adventure with you. You may or may not own a banjo or have any prior experience on the banjo or any other kind of instrument, and I don't assume you come to this book knowing anything about music. I also don't assume you're interested in one particular style or way of playing the banjo over another (which is why I include more than one).

However, I *do* assume that you're going to be playing a five-string banjo instead of a tenor or plectrum banjo, which are actually different kinds of instruments (see Chapter 1). I also assume that you want to get started quickly and not waste time with unnecessary and overly technical information. If I've described you in one way or another, you've come to the right place.

How This Book Is Organized

Banjo For Dummies is organized so that you can get the information you want quickly without spending a lot of time digging for it. The chapters are grouped into the following seven parts that focus on different aspects of the banjo.

Part I: The Amazing Five-String Banjo

This part includes information that every beginner needs to know to get started playing the banjo, including the different kinds of five-string banjos and the various parts of the instrument. You also discover the correct body posture, how to tune the instrument to itself and to an electronic tuner, and how to fret your first chords. I also cover some of the basic elements of music, such as rhythm, meter, chord progressions, and banjo tablature.

Part II: Let's Pick! The Basic Ingredients

One of the things that makes *Banjo For Dummies* unique is that it covers *both* clawhammer and bluegrass styles in Part II. Although these techniques are the two most popular ways of playing banjo today, most *other* banjo books focus on either one way of playing or the other. That's not good enough! I cover both approaches within these pages.

I help you find a comfortable right-hand position and present the basic picking patterns used in bluegrass and clawhammer banjo playing. You also figure out in this part how to select fingerpicks and shape them to fit your right hand for bluegrass playing. You can then make your playing sound more authentic by incorporating left-hand slides, hammer-ons, pull-offs, and chokes, and even discover how to find a melody on the banjo and play it by using either clawhammer or bluegrass techniques. This part closes with beginners' bluegrass and clawhammer versions of four popular banjo tunes.

Part III: Playing Styles Past, Present, and Future

You move beyond beginners' material in this part and experience the historical roots of the banjo as well as explore the most recent stylistic and technical innovations. I take you back to the late-19th and early-20th centuries as you play two minstrel-style tunes and two classic-era pieces. You also get a more in-depth look at bluegrass style, exploring Scruggs, melodic, and single-string techniques and licks. And you can find a handful of great tunes scattered throughout this part, just ready for the playing.

Part IV: Buyer's Guide, Care and Feeding, and More

Don't have a banjo? Not sure how to keep your banjo in tip-top shape? No worries. I include a complete (and completely honest) buyer's guide and maintenance advice in this part. The buyer's guide can help you spend your money wisely on anything from a beginners' instrument to a professional-model banjo. I also cover those accessories you *really* need as well as those extras that are just fun to have around the house. I take time to focus on banjo maintenance and string changing as well, so you can unearth the secrets of what you can do to keep your banjo sounding and looking great. Finally, I help you find a good teacher, survive your first jam session, and expand your musical horizons through workshops, camps, and music festivals.

Part V: The Part of Tens

The Part of Tens is a *For Dummies* trademark section — and you don't want to miss out by not reading this part. In it, I present ten suggestions to make your practice time more fun and productive. I also include a select list of ten important banjo players who are well worth the listen.

Part VI: Appendixes

You can never grow tiresome when it comes to information on the banjo (at least I think so), which is why I've included some supplementary info in appendix form. In this part, you can find a handy chord digest. I also include some instructions about the CD that accompanies this book to ensure that you're getting the full multimedia experience.

Icons Used in This Book

In the margins of this book, you can often find the following friendly icons to help you recognize different types of information I've included:

This icon highlights the really good information worthy of your full attention. If you want to store away anything you read from this book, here's where you do it.

Expert advice and time-saving strategies that can make you a happier banjo player are the mission of the Tip icon.

You can consider information attached with this icon to be fun but not essential to playing the banjo. You can skip over it without causing harm to any living thing (whew!).

Exercise caution with text marked by this icon in order to protect yourself, your banjo, or your musical reputation!

Text next to this icon offers explanations on how to better utilize the examples on the CD as well as how to find the CD tracks for songs in each chapter.

Where to Go from Here

You're probably a banjo player on a mission, so you want to know where, when, and how you can get started. You can always read this book straight through, but the beauty of any *For Dummies* book is that you can direct your own course and dip into chapters as you need them.

As you create your own roadmap, I can offer you a few suggestions to point you in the right direction:

- ✔ If you need to purchase a banjo or you're interested in an upgrade, head to the buyer's guide at Chapter 9 first.

- ✔ If you're a beginner and want to start playing right away, proceed to Chapters 2 and 3, where you get your banjo in tune and play your first chords.

- ✔ If you're ready to start work on authentic banjo styles, roll up your sleeves and work through Chapters 4, 5, and 6.

- ✔ More experienced players can check out the historical styles covered in Chapter 7 and the modern techniques in Chapter 8.

Part I
The Amazing Five-String Banjo

The 5th Wave — By Rich Tennant

JELLY'S SALOON — Showing Nightly — Dueling Banjos

"Actually, they started out as just bickering banjos."

In this part . . .

I give you just about everything you need to know to get started playing the banjo, including the different kinds of five-string banjos and the various parts of the instrument. I also show you correct body posture, how to tune the instrument, and how to play your first chords. I also cover some of the basic elements of music, such as rhythm, meter, chord progressions, and banjo tablature.

Chapter 1

First Steps: Banjo Basics

In This Chapter

▶ Getting to know different kinds of banjos

▶ Exploring the banjo and all its parts

▶ Discovering how to be a good player

*1*f you take a trip, you'd probably like to know where you're going (after all, you don't want to end up like those guys in that *Deliverance* movie, do you?). If you're new to the banjo and don't yet own an instrument or if you're wondering about your eventual musical destination, this chapter is definitely the place to start your *Banjo For Dummies* trip. The key is in the ignition, so put this thing in drive!

In this chapter, you spread out your banjo road map and start planning what I hope will be a wonderful, lifelong musical journey with the five-string banjo. I discuss what makes the five-string banjo different from other kinds of stringed instruments, and you can also take a look at the various kinds of banjos available today. I name the parts of the banjo and summarize the musical skills you can master in this book on the way to becoming a good player.

Getting into Banjo

Something about the five-string banjo brings out strong feelings in people. Folks who like the banjo usually *really* like it. What is it about this instrument that inspires such passion, and how can you tell if you've been bitten by the banjo bug? This section explores the answer to these questions.

Loving that amazing sound

You know the sound of the banjo when you hear it: the bright, rhythmic waterfall of short, cascading notes that can conjure up just about any emotion (but usually *happy* first comes to mind for the typical guy on the street). The banjo is usually associated with folk, country, and bluegrass music, but these days, you can also hear the instrument in jazz, rock, and even classical settings.

Over the years, I've asked hundreds of amateur and professional players why they initially got interested in the instrument and the usual answer is "I fell in love with the sound." I think an equal attraction is the lure of hearing a lot of notes compressed into what seems like the smallest of musical spaces. In the hands of a skilled player, the banjo is an instrument that's capable of amazing virtuosity.

Becoming a true believer

Banjo players usually remember well the precise moment in time that they became hooked on the instrument. For me, growing up as a suburban teenager far from significant hills of any kind, that moment was when I was watching Roy Clark play banjo on *Hee Haw* and thinking to myself, "If I can somehow sit through this show every week, I think I can eventually learn 'Cripple Creek.'" I didn't especially like country music at that time, and I'd never heard of folk or bluegrass music — but I really loved the sound of the banjo.

Growing up in the 1970s, I could also hear the banjo as a background instrument on hit songs from the Eagles, the Doobie Brothers, Neil Young, and James Taylor. Hearing the banjo in these contexts made me believe that the banjo *must* be cool if those musicians used it on their recordings, despite what my friends thought about this disturbing turn in my musical tastes. And, of course, I was also influenced by the popularity of "Dueling Banjos" during these years (I didn't realize until years later *who* was depicted playing the instrument in this movie). I already knew a little about playing the guitar, and I decided that I wanted to try and teach myself to play banjo.

After enrolling in a community college beginners' banjo class, I discovered an entire musical subculture of folk and bluegrass music where the banjo was not only welcome, but was also pretty much the most revered instrument of them all. Getting to know others who felt the same way as I did about the banjo really helped to get me hooked.

Almost 40 years later, I'm happy to report that the banjo is more popular than ever. Musicians have continued to push the musical boundaries of the instrument, and these days, about the only folks who think the banjo is good for just one musical style are those television producers who still insist on having banjo music in the background of their pickup truck commercials.

My own youthful enthusiasm for the banjo evolved into a wonderful lifelong relationship that is still growing strong. I get a joyful feeling every time I play a tune on the banjo. I'm also amazed at how my love for the instrument has opened the door to many new and wonderful experiences (such as graduate school, international touring and teaching, and this book!) and is at the basis of many of my most cherished friendships. Even if you never become as obsessed about the banjo as I am, I believe that the banjo can improve your life and make you a happier person if you give it the chance.

Identifying Different Kinds of Banjos

Banjo For Dummies is your complete guide to musical adventure on the five-string banjo. I focus on the five-string banjo because this instrument is by far the most popular type of banjo being played today and is the kind of banjo that is used to play bluegrass, folk, and country music. The five-string banjo is also currently carving new niches in jazz, rock, and classical music.

However, in the first half of the 20th century, the most popular banjos were four-string tenor and plectrum banjos. These banjos are really different instruments and shouldn't be confused with the five-string banjo. Understanding the differences between banjos is important, because before you begin your adventure, you need to make sure you're traveling with the right kind of equipment.

In the following sections, I compare and contrast the different instruments in the banjo family, so you don't mistake one type of banjo for another.

Five-string banjo: The subject of the book

The short 5th string is what makes the five-string banjo different from other types of banjos and from just about every other instrument in the known universe. Most of the time, you know immediately that you're looking at a five-string banjo when you see a *tuning peg* (a geared mechanism that keeps the string in tune) that's sticking out almost halfway up the *neck* (the long narrow piece of wood where you fret strings with the left hand; for more on these terms, see a later section on the parts of the banjo). This tuning peg holds the 5th string of the banjo (see Figure 1-1).

The 5th string is a crucial distinguishing characteristic of the five-string banjo, both in the instrument's appearance and the sound of the music. The 5th string is not only shorter than the other four strings of the banjo, but this string is also the highest in sound (or *pitch*). The 5th string on a banjo lies within easy reach of the right-hand thumb, which you use to play this string in all kinds of banjo music. Having the highest-pitched string next to the string with the lowest pitch is unusual in comparison to how pitches are arranged on the strings of a guitar (as you can see in Figure 1-1), but this is one of the things that makes the banjo sound so great! This characteristic of the banjo is also one part of the instrument's ancient African ancestry (for more on this, see Chapter 7).

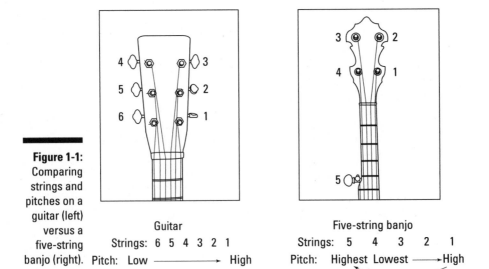

Figure 1-1:
Comparing
strings and
pitches on a
guitar (left)
versus a
five-string
banjo (right).

Guitar
Strings: 6 5 4 3 2 1
Pitch: Low ⟶ High

Five-string banjo
Strings: 5 4 3 2 1
Pitch: Highest Lowest ⟶ High

Tenor and plectrum banjos: Look for another book

In the early decades of the 20th century, folks loved the quality of sound of the banjo so much that they attached different kinds of necks to the banjo body to create new instruments with different numbers of strings. These hybrid instruments were tuned and played differently from the five-string banjo.

Tenor and *plectrum* banjos are examples of this phenomenon. These four-stringed instruments are commonly used in traditional jazz and Dixieland music, don't have the short 5th string, and are usually played with a flatpick instead of with the fingers.

Although these banjos have the same tone and general appearance as the five-string banjo, tenor and plectrum banjos use other tunings and playing techniques and are viewed as different instruments by banjo fans. These days, you may encounter a tenor or plectrum banjo when you hear a Dixieland band or the Preservation Hall Jazz Band, go to a mummers' parade, or catch an old Lawrence Welk rerun on television.

Don't confuse these types of banjos with the five-string variety! The five-string banjo is by far the most popular kind of banjo played today and its music is almost certainly what attracted you to the instrument. However, confusing the appearance of a five-string banjo with the four-string tenor or plectrum type of banjo is easy. You see, the bodies of these instruments are the same, but the necks reveal the difference (see Figure 1-2). You can't play five-string banjo music on a four-string tenor or plectrum banjo — these instruments aren't interchangeable! You need a five-string banjo to play five-string banjo music.

More banjos (with a twist)

In the early decades of the 20th century, America was mad for anything that sounded remotely like a banjo (amazing, isn't it?). Instrument makers took guitar and mandolin necks and attached them to banjo bodies, creating new kinds of instruments that had the sound of a five-string or tenor banjo but were played by using guitar and mandolin techniques.

Banjos with mandolin necks have eight strings and are called *mandolin banjos* or *mando-banjos*. These instruments are generally smaller than most five-string banjos. Banjos with guitar necks have six strings and are called *guitar banjos*. These instruments can be a bit larger than most five-string banjos.

Today, these more obscure branches of the banjo family tree are seen largely as novelty instruments and, like the tenor and plectrum banjo (see the section "Tenor and plectrum banjos: Look for another book" in this chapter), are considered to be a different kind of instrument than a five-string banjo. You may hear these types of banjos used occasionally in early jazz or blues or by a jug band.

Figure 1-2:
Comparing
a five-string
(a) and a
plectrum
banjo (b).

a

b

Knowing the Parts of a Banjo

Unlike a guitar, violin, or mandolin, a banjo is an amalgam of wood, metal, skin, and/or plastic held together by rods, nuts, screws, and brackets. You could call it the Frankenstein of musical instruments, but I like to think of it more like the *Bionic Woman*. All banjos share the common characteristic of having a replaceable membrane made of plastic or animal skin (called the *head*) that is stretched tightly across the body of the banjo (called the *pot*) to form the top of the resonating body of the instrument (see Figure 1-3).

Five-string banjos come in three basic different styles: open-back, resonator, and electric banjos. Musicians select the kind of banjo they play based on their musical style and their personal tastes. Chapter 9 explains the differences between these kinds of banjos, along with tips for making an informed purchase.

In the following sections, you get to know the banjo from head to toe. You also discover how the instrument captures the energy of a plucked string and turns it into that unmistakably great sound that banjo players love. You can refer to Figure 1-4 to see exactly where these parts are located on the banjo.

Looking at the neck

The neck is one of the two main sections of the banjo (the pot being the other; see the section "Checking out the pot"). The *neck* is the long piece of wood that supports the strings and tuners. Necks are usually made of maple, mahogany, or walnut.

To get a better feel for the banjo, take a look at the parts of the banjo neck:

- ✔ **Frets:** The thin, metal bars on the banjo neck that are positioned at precise intervals to give you the various pitches needed when fretting a string. (*Fretting* is what you do when you move a left-hand finger into position behind a fret to change the pitch of a string.) In the world of fretting, you use the term *up the neck* to refer to moving the left hand towards the pot and *down the neck* when you talk about moving the left hand towards the nut and peghead.

- ✔ **Fingerboard:** A thin, flat wooden strip glued to the neck that holds the frets and acts as the surface upon which the left hand produces notes and chords.

- ✔ **Peghead:** Also called the *headstock,* the peghead is the elaborately shaped end of the neck that holds the tuning pegs for the four lower strings of the banjo.

- ✔ **Tuning pegs:** Sometimes called *tuners* or *tuning machines,* these pegs are the devices that raise or lower the pitch of the banjo's strings with a turn of the buttons located on the backside of the peghead. The pegs for strings 1 through 4 are attached to the peghead, while the tuning peg for the 5th string is found at the top of the neck near the fifth fret.

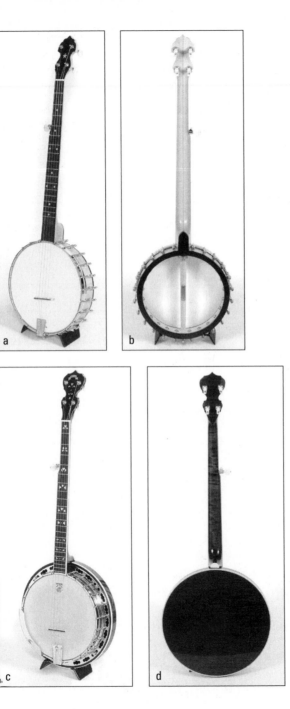

Figure 1-3:
Comparing
open-back
(a and b)
and
resonator
(c and d)
five-string
banjos.

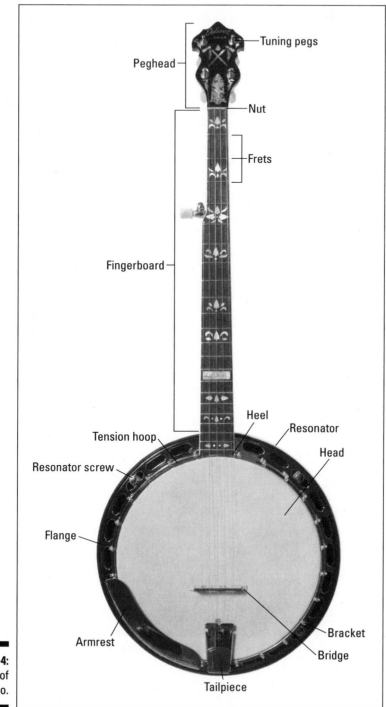

Figure 1-4:
The parts of
a banjo.

✔ **Nut:** A block of ivory, bone, or plastic that's glued to the end of the fingerboard where the peghead begins. Strings 1 through 4 pass through the grooves in the nut on their way to the shafts of the tuning pegs. The 5th string has its own nut, located near the fifth fret.

✔ **Heel:** The name given to end of the neck that's attached to the pot of the banjo.

✔ **Truss rod:** You can't see the truss rod, but it's an important part of the banjo neck. The *truss rod* is an adjustable metal rod that runs down most of the length of the banjo neck in a channel underneath the fingerboard. This rod helps to keep the neck stable and controls the amount of curve in the neck to keep the strings from buzzing when fretting. Most banjos have adjustable truss rods, which can be accessed at the peghead by removing the truss rod cover (a procedure best left to the pros).

Checking out the pot

The other major section of the banjo (other than the neck; see the preceding section) is the *pot,* the round lower body of the banjo including all of its constituent parts:

✔ **Head:** The plastic or skin membrane that acts as the vibrating top of the banjo. The head is largely responsible for the unique sound of your new favorite instrument.

✔ **Rim:** Sometimes called the *shell,* the rim is the circular wooden ring that is the centerpiece of the pot and is made from laminations or blocks of maple or mahogany. A well-made rim is essential to a good-sounding banjo.

✔ **Tone ring:** This part of the pot is a metal circular collar that is machined to fit on top of the wooden rim, and the head is stretched tight across its top outer circumference. Tone rings come in a variety of shapes and sizes. Together with the rim, the tone ring provides the fundamental shape and color to the banjo's tone. However, tone rings aren't found on all banjos and having one isn't absolutely necessary to having a good-sounding instrument. (See Chapter 9 for more on tone rings.)

✔ **Brackets:** Sometimes called *hooks,* brackets are ringed around the banjo pot and are responsible for tightening the head via the bracket screws that are attached to each bracket on the underside of the banjo.

✔ **Tension hoop:** Sometimes called the *stretcher band,* this circular metal ring fits over the outside edge of the banjo head and helps to uniformly stretch the head down across the top of the tone ring as the brackets are tightened.

✔ **Bridge:** The bridge transmits the vibrations of the strings to the head. Bridges range in sizes from ⅝" to ¾". They are movable, but are held fast to the banjo head with the tension of the strings.

✔ **Tailpiece:** This part holds the strings on the pot end of the banjo. Many tailpieces are adjustable in various ways that can subtly affect overall banjo tone. (For more on tailpieces, see Chapter 10.)

✔ **Armrest:** The armrest is attached to the pot of the banjo and extends over the top of the banjo head to make right-hand playing more comfortable while simultaneously protecting the head.

✔ **Coordinating rods:** Seen only from the back of the banjo, these rods are attached at opposite ends of the rim, parallel to the banjo strings. The primary function of the coordinating rods is to keep the neck securely attached to the pot. However, they can also be used to make slight adjustments to the height of the strings off of the fingerboard (called *string action*). Some banjos have only one coordinating rod.

✔ **Resonator:** The bowl-shaped piece of wood that's attached to many banjos, especially those used in bluegrass music, is the resonator. The resonator projects the sound out and away from the instrument. They're usually constructed from the same kind of wood as the banjo neck. *Open-back* banjos don't have resonators (see Chapter 9 for more on the types of banjos).

✔ **Resonator screws:** Three or four screws that keep the resonator attached to the rest of the banjo pot.

✔ **Flange:** A circular metal piece connecting the pot to the resonator that helps to keep the resonator in place.

Picking up string vibrations

When you strike a banjo string with a right-hand finger or thumb, the string starts to move back and forth. These vibrations move through the *bridge* (a piece of wood positioned on the banjo head) to the banjo head, which amplifies that sound. Banjo players frequently refer to right-hand playing as *picking* the banjo. You can read more about authentic right-hand banjo picking techniques in Chapter 4.

The *pitch* of any string (its sound as measured by how high or low it is) is determined by how much tension or tightness is in each string and how long or short it is. The tighter or shorter the string, the higher its pitch. You can change the pitch of a string in two ways:

✔ **Turn the tuning pegs.** A twist of a tuning peg in one direction or the other raises or lowers the pitch of a string. The direction is different for each string. (For more on tuning, check out Chapter 2.)

✔ **Fret the strings.** When you *fret* a string, you place a left-hand finger behind one of the 22 frets found on the fingerboard of the neck. As you fret, you're shortening the length of the string and raising its pitch. An *open* string is one that is unfretted in the left hand. A fretted string sounds higher in pitch compared to an open string or to that same string fretted on a lower fret (a lower fret is one that is farther away from the banjo body). For more on fretting with the left hand, see Chapter 2.

Becoming a Banjo Player

If the banjo is the first stringed instrument you've ever attempted to play, it may seem as if you have a million things to remember at this first stage. *Everything* feels so new and unfamiliar. Don't get discouraged! Banjo players tend to be perfectionists, so be careful not to let your desire to play things correctly overwhelm your love for playing (and remember that everyone learns from their mistakes — even banjo players). Having fun with the banjo is more important than playing everything perfectly.

When you're wanting to become more proficient on the banjo, you can't find a substitute for time actually spent playing the banjo — the more you play, the faster you progress. Focus on one new skill at a time and don't spend too much time on the Internet finding out what everyone else thinks about this or that aspect of banjo playing. Just *play* (and check out Chapter 13 for more great practice suggestions). After you've gained a few basic skills, find other musicians at your ability level to play with as soon as possible. Playing with others also significantly speeds up your progress.

In the following sections, I present just a few of the skills you should strive to master as a banjo player (and as you make your way through *Banjo For Dummies*).

Making wise purchase choices

These days, new players can find good starter banjos that are affordable and easy to play. The crucial first step in your purchase is finding an acoustic specialty store that really knows banjos and actually *likes* banjo players. And as you shop, keep in mind that your choice of instrument should be based mostly upon the kind of music you want to play (and, of course, how much money you have to spend).

I cover everything you need to know about what to look for in banjos and playing accessories and how to find them in Chapters 9 and 10.

Tuning and holding your banjo

Keeping your instrument in tune is something that you practice each time you play — and an absolutely essential skill when playing music with others. Tuning your banjo can be frustrating at first, but with careful listening to compare one pitch with another and some trial and error, you can have this skill mastered in no time.

After you're in tune, you want to adopt a comfortable playing position for both sitting or standing. You have a lot of individual options in this regard. Just remember to not raise the neck too high and try using a strap. If you follow these two suggestions, you can be well on your way to finding your personal comfort zone.

In Chapter 2, you can get comfortable holding the banjo, fitting the strap, and getting in tune with an electronic tuner or another instrument.

Fretting chords with the left hand

A *chord* is three or more notes sounded together. Chords support a melody and are the building blocks for accompanying other musicians. The best way to begin your playing adventures is to become familiar with well-used chords such as G, C, and D7. A comfortable left-hand position makes forming these chords much more fun. Let your thumb touch the top of the back of the banjo neck and be sure you're using the tips of your fingers to press the strings just behind the frets — now you're in business.

In Chapters 2 and 3, you can dig deeper into finding a comfortable left-hand position and get used to fretting chords up and down the banjo neck.

Playing authentic right- and left-hand patterns

Coordinating right-hand picking techniques with the left-hand work of making chords and creating new notes is a full-time job for banjo players! Mastering exercises that isolate what each hand does by itself lays the foundation for making great banjo music with both hands together.

In Chapters 4, 5, and 8, you take a look at these techniques, because you can use them in clawhammer and bluegrass banjo, create melodies, and accompany others with these patterns.

Practicing some real tunes

The real fun begins when you utilize your technique to play melodies on the instrument in a real banjo style. Melody notes can usually be organized as a group of notes, called a *scale*. Finding melody notes in a song becomes easier after you've mastered a few scales on the banjo neck, so I recommend that you start with the scales I outline in Chapter 6.

After you get the feel for the scales, you can then use the right- and left-hand techniques you've already mastered to capture as many melody notes as you can and create arrangements that sound good on the instrument.

In Chapters 6, 7, and 8, you can play beginner and intermediate versions of tunes in clawhammer, bluegrass, minstrel, and classic styles. Don't forget to listen to the CD to get the sound of these tunes in your ears before working through them by using the accompanying tablature.

Making music with others in jam sessions

Banjo players love to make music with other musicians — guitarists, fiddlers, mandolin and dobro players, and bassists. When you're playing your banjo with others, remember to play in a way that enhances the sound of the total group. Active listening and playing in good rhythm play a big role in your efforts to make other musicians sound their best.

In Chapters 3 and 12, I discuss the unique techniques and skills you need to accompany other pickers and singers on familiar bluegrass and old-time tunes in informal jam sessions. I also cover some of the unspoken ground rules of jam etiquette to make your transition into group playing go smoothly.

Meeting other banjo lovers

You may be amazed at how many opportunities you have to share your enthusiasm for the banjo with other like-minded players. From finding a teacher to attending a workshop, camp, or festival, you can have more fun with the instrument and become a better player faster by connecting with others who share your enthusiasm for the banjo. As a new player, don't wait until you've already acquired some playing skills before seeking help from others. You'll become a better player much more quickly by seeking out help at the very beginning of your banjo adventure. In Chapter 12, I talk about the world of banjo that lies beyond your doorstep.

Camps and workshops are often designed for all levels of students. If you already play, you can recharge your banjo-picking batteries at a regional camp or workshop where you can hang out with the banjo stars, make many new friends, and come away with new playing ideas that will keep your hands busy for months to come.

Keeping your banjo sounding great

Banjos are much more adjustable than other stringed instruments such as the guitar or bass. However, you don't have to become an accomplished, all-knowing instrument-repair person to keep your instrument in top shape.

 Keeping fresh strings on your instrument is the most important thing you can do to keep your banjo running right. After a few weeks or months of playing, your strings will inevitably become harder to tune — or they may even break. Keep an extra set of strings handy in your case along with a small pair of wire cutters and you'll be ready for all contingencies!

You may also want to check out all the movable parts on your banjo every couple of months. For example, keeping the head tight keeps your banjo sounding bright and loud, and checking to see that the bridge is in just the right place on the banjo head keeps your fretted notes in tune. I cover everything you need to know about these topics, as well as determining when you need to seek out professional advice, in Chapter 11.

Chapter 2

Meet Your Banjo

In This Chapter

▶ Understanding banjo terms

▶ Sitting and standing with the banjo

▶ Using the left hand to fret chords

▶ Finding different ways to get the banjo in tune

▶ Reading a chord diagram

▶ Playing the G, D7, and C chords

*Y*ou've brought your new banjo home and cleared a corner of the house to practice, far enough out of the way to not disturb the unbelievers in your household. As you sit down and open the case, that wonderful new banjo smell fills the room. Go ahead and savor this moment! Pat yourself on the back for taking the plunge and making the commitment to become a banjo player. But now what?

This chapter answers that question for you. I help you liberate the banjo from its case, attach a strap, and get comfortable holding the banjo when you're both sitting and standing. I show you several different ways to keep the banjo in tune and how to work on a good left-hand position for fretting chords. You finish up by discovering how to play the G, D7, and C chords, the three chords you'll play frequently in hundreds of banjo songs.

Talking Banjo Talk

As with any culture, you must be familiar with the language before you can get to know the people. The banjo is very much the same; you need to know banjo speak if you're going to be a banjo player. Plus, you may find *Banjo For Dummies* a little clearer if you know some of the basic terms I use throughout this book.

So, hold on to your hat, and familiarize yourself with the following words:

✔ **Left hand:** When I give you any instructions regarding the left hand, I'm referring to the hand you use to push the strings against the fingerboard to make chords (you do this with the tips of your fingers, of course, not the entire hand). You also use the left-hand fingers to create new notes on the banjo by using slides, hammer-ons, pull-offs, and chokes (slide on over to Chapter 5 to discover more about these special techniques).

✔ **Right hand:** The right hand is the hand that strikes the banjo strings. In *Banjo For Dummies,* you first use the right-hand thumb to strum across all the banjo strings, but soon enough you utilize techniques where the right-hand thumb and the index and middle fingers each play a different role in producing authentic right-hand banjo styles (you can find these techniques in Chapter 4).

✔ **Frets:** The metal strips that run along the top surface of your banjo fingerboard below your strings are the frets. Most banjos have 22 frets with each fret assigned a number. The first fret is the fret that's closest to the nut and the 22nd fret is located the closest to the banjo head.

✔ **Fretting:** The act of pushing one or more left-hand fingers against the fingerboard just behind a fret to shorten the length of a string is called *fretting*. Fretting changes the sound (or *pitch*) of a note. The shorter the length of a string, the higher that string's pitch — and the higher up the neck you're fretting. (For more on fretting, you can check out the section "Fretting with the Left Hand" later in this chapter.)

✔ **Open:** You call an unfretted string an open string. In Chapter 3, you're introduced to *tablature,* the written form of banjo music. In tablature, an open string is indicated with the number 0.

✔ **Strings:** Yeah, I know you know what strings are. But banjo players are so methodical that they assign numbers to each string so they can talk about them easier. Remembering the order of strings as expressed through these numbers is crucial to understanding banjo tablature and in interpreting a *chord diagram,* which is a representation of how a chord is fretted.

The 5th string is the short string on your banjo. If you're holding the instrument in a playing position (see the following section, "Positioning Body and Banjo"), the 5th string is the string that is the closest as you look down at the strings. If someone were looking at you and your banjo from across the room, they'd say that the 5th string is the top-most string. From the 5th string, the strings are then numbered 4, 3, 2, 1 across the banjo. The 1st string is the farthest away from you as you look down on the instrument (or the bottom string if someone is looking at you).

✔ **Sharp and flat:** You use these terms in reference to getting the banjo in tune. If a note you're playing on your banjo is *sharp,* its pitch is higher than the note you're trying to tune to; if its pitch is lower, your banjo note is *flat.*

If you're left handed, you may be tempted to turn the banjo upside down and fret with the right hand and strike the strings with the left. However, I don't recommend spending much time playing in this way. The strings are then in a different orientation to your picking hand and executing the right hand patterns (that you can encounter later in this book) is physically impossible. The bottom line is that you need *both* hands to play banjo well. I'm left-handed, but I learned to play using the standard right-handed orientation. I'd like for you to try this too — especially if you've already purchased a regular banjo.

Positioning Body and Banjo

Picking up a banjo and trying to play for the first time may seem a little awkward if you don't know how to hold or position the instrument. To get the most enjoyment out of your practice time and to be ready for anything when playing with others, you should be comfortable both sitting and standing while playing the banjo. In either case, being as relaxed as possible is a good idea.

So how are you supposed to play in these positions with ease? Take a deep breath and don't worry — this section gives you the foundation you need to comfortably strike a banjo player pose.

If you've never played banjo before, you may not be quite ready for all the advice in this section. You may need to first become comfortable with your left- and right-hand positions on the banjo, which I discuss later in this chapter and in Chapter 4. After you have a good grasp on your hand positions, feel free to come back to this section and devote a bit of time again to finding a comfortable posture sitting and standing with the banjo.

Strapping on your banjo

You've probably already discovered that banjos can be heavy. Even if you have a more lightweight, open-back banjo, the distribution of weight on your banjo may very well be uneven, with much of the mass at the peghead concentrated where the four tuning pegs are located.

Take a moment and sit in a chair with your banjo in a playing position, with the pot of the banjo resting on your legs and the neck extending to your left at about a 45-degree angle. If you remove your left hand as a support, does the neck move downward? If so, start using a strap even when sitting. You need the left hand free to fret chords, not supporting the weight of the banjo neck.

Find a real banjo strap to use on your instrument and not a guitar strap. Both kinds of straps look pretty much the same except for what's at either end. Most banjo straps have hooks, ties, or screws at both ends that you use to attach the strap to the banjo pot. A guitar strap more often has just holes punched into the leather or plastic at either end and nothing else — providing no way to easily attach it to the banjo. (For more info on picking out the right strap for you, see Chapter 10.)

Getting used to holding the banjo and working with the strap is a bit like breaking in a brand new pair of shoes — it takes a bit of time, but soon enough everything fits like a glove. The following sections provide all you need to know to fit the strap on the banjo and the banjo on you.

Attaching the strap

Some inexpensive banjos have hooks on the banjo body that are designed to hold a strap. However, these hooks usually aren't located in a position that provides the most comfortable support. You want to instead attach each end of the strap to one of the brackets that encircle the banjo head.

Many players attach the strap to brackets located underneath the neck and the tailpiece of the banjo, as shown in Figure 2-1. This position seems to provide a good deal of support and control, but you want to experiment by using different strap lengths and brackets to see what feels right to you.

Figure 2-1: For a comfortable fit, try attaching the strap below the neck and the tailpiece.

If you attach the strap to the banjo in this way, you shouldn't have to remove it when you need to put the banjo away in its case. You should have plenty of room within the case to wrap the strap around the banjo pot (see Figure 2-2).

Fitting the strap

Although some players wear the strap across the right shoulder (like the renowned bluegrass player Kenny Ingram in the bottom photo of Figure 2-3), most players adjust the length of the strap so that it wraps over the left shoulder, around the back, and underneath the right arm (like banjo legend J. D. Crowe in the top photo of Figure 2-3).

As you fit the strap to the banjo, you need to properly adjust its length. The length of your strap determines the vertical placement of the banjo in relation to your body. Although you can't find any hard-and-fast rules, I like to have just enough length to the strap so that when I sit down I can feel the strap exerting upward pressure keeping the banjo neck in place, but I'm also able to rest the banjo on my knees when sitting down to relieve the pressure from the strap on my left shoulder.

After you've found a strap position that seems to work when sitting, try standing up with the banjo to see how the strap feels. You need to use the same strap length for both sitting and standing, so experiment to find a strap fit that works well for both situations.

Figure 2-2:
Getting the strap out of the way when it's time to put the banjo in its case.

Figure 2-3: Bluegrass banjo greats J.D. Crowe (a) and Kenny Ingram (b) illustrate two different ways to wear a strap.

Making three or four adjustments as you try to find the right strap position for your banjo isn't unusual. You may have to take the strap off the banjo each time to adjust its length until you find what feels just right. This is a minor hassle, but after the strap is set, you won't have to worry about it any more. You can then move on to playing music with a more comfortable left-hand position.

Sitting down to play

How you hold your banjo while sitting down is determined by how much you need to see the banjo fingerboard while you're playing. Some players discipline themselves to use the position dots on the top side of the banjo neck to keep track of where they are on the banjo neck, but most players prefer to actually see the banjo fingerboard.

Another aspect of finding a comfortable playing posture is to experiment with different neck angles (the banjo neck that is, not *your* neck!). New players are often so concerned with seeing the fingerboard that they raise the neck to bring it closer to their eyes. Too much of this can lead to some technique problems in both the left and right hands. My advice is to angle the neck such that the peghead is no higher than eye level.

You also want to find a chair around the house that allows you to comfortably sit upright, provides you with some back support (if you need it), and allows your arms to move freely (no recliners allowed unfortunately). Around the house, I like to use an adjustable office chair with the side arms removed. As you sit, position the banjo so that you're able to see the fingerboard and the banjo head, but don't let the banjo be so low that you have to reach far around the neck to fret with the left hand.

After you've actually started to play banjo, take a look at photos of some of your favorite players and experiment with different neck angles and chair positions to see what works the best for you. Figure 2-4 shows three different ways of holding the banjo while sitting. Note that the middle player, Jody Stecher, rests the banjo on his right knee and doesn't need a strap at all. Erin English (left) and yours truly (right) prefer straps on our heavier resonator banjos.

Figure 2-4: From left to right, Erin, Jody, and Bill show three different ways to enjoy playing banjo while sitting.

Don't let "Dunlap's disease" get you down

If you're in the prime years of your life like me, you may suffer from Dunlap's disease. What's that, you innocently ask? Well, Dunlap's disease is when your belly is so big that it "done laps" over your belt! If you suffer from this common malady, you may prefer to position the banjo a bit to the right side of your body, whether sitting or standing (see the section "Standing with your banjo" in this chapter). Many players position the banjo squarely on their right knee and may not need a strap to support the banjo at all while sitting. When standing with a strap, you want to position the banjo in a similar way at the right side of your body. If you're a Dunlapper like me, don't be afraid to move your banjo around until you find a position comfortable for you.

Standing with your banjo

The key to being comfortable while standing with the banjo is to adopt a position that's similar to the position you use when sitting. If you've found a good sitting position (see the preceding section), stand up with the banjo and watch what happens. Try adjusting the strap length so that you have little to no change in the position of the banjo for both your sitting and standing positions.

Note also the relationship of your hands to the instrument as you both sit and stand. You want these to be as close as possible to one another whether you're up or down. Keep your arms relaxed and your elbows bent while standing and remember not to raise the peghead above eye level. Your left hand should easily be able to fret at any point along the banjo fingerboard, and your right hand should have easy access for striking the strings.

Figure 2-5 shows three different ways of standing while playing banjo. Erin (on the left) holds the banjo a little lower and off to the side of her body. Jody (in the middle) angles the banjo neck a little higher and holds the banjo a bit more off to the side while yours truly (on the right) holds the banjo higher on the body and more out in front. All are fine ways to take a stand for better playing.

I spend almost all my time practicing sitting down and even though I've been playing for over 35 years, I still have to make a subtle mental adjustment every time I stand up to play. A day or two before a performance, I devote a share of my practice time to playing standing up so that I'll feel more comfortable playing with others on stage. At a bluegrass festival, you spend a good deal of your time standing in a circle of musicians at jam sessions, so practicing while standing up is a great idea every now and then (and don't forget to bring a comfortable pair of shoes to wear to your next festival!).

Figure 2-5:
From left to right: Erin, Jody, and Bill use straps for standing while playing.

a   b   c

Fretting with the Left Hand

The left hand's job is to change the pitches of the banjo strings to get all the notes you need for chords and melodies. The left hand accomplishes this task by pressing the tips of the fingers against the fingerboard just behind a fret, as needed, to shorten the length of a string and make its pitch higher. This technique is called *fretting*.

Fretting individual strings and chords on the banjo is a breeze after you've adopted these few simple tips for properly attaching the left hand to your banjo neck. Here's a step-by-step guide:

1. **Rest your left hand on your leg and totally release all body tension from your hand and arm, just as if you were asleep (see Figure 2-6a).**

   Your hand should assume a relaxed shape in which all the fingers are slightly bent in towards your palm.

2. **Keeping the wrist relaxed but straight, place the left-hand thumb on the upper part of the back of the banjo neck, opposite the space between the first and second frets (see Figure 2-6b).**

   Remember not to support the weight of the neck with the left hand and try to keep your hand and fingers relaxed, as in Step 1.

3. **Relax your shoulder, arm, and elbow, bringing your elbow down and in towards your body and causing your left-hand fingers to position themselves more directly over the banjo fingerboard.**

4. **Move your left-hand middle finger just behind the second fret of the 3rd string and push down on the string, fretting it with the tip of your finger (see Figure 2-6c).**

    Don't fret on top of the second fret but position the finger as close behind the fret as you can. Try to maintain a vertical position with the fretting finger so that the adjacent strings are able to ring freely.

5. **Try playing the 3rd string with the thumb of your right hand.**

    The goal is to get a clear, ringing sound out of the note you've just fretted with no buzzing.

If the new note sounds good, congratulations! You've accomplished the first necessary task to becoming a great banjo player, and you're now officially playing the banjo!

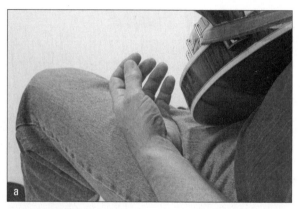

Figure 2-6: Getting a good left hand position: Relaxing the left hand (a), positioning the thumb to get ready to fret (b), fretting the third string at the 2nd fret (c).

Now lift up the fretting finger and play the open (or unfretted) 3rd string with your right-hand thumb. As you lift the fretting finger, don't bring it too far up above the string; position your finger just above the string so that you're ready to fret again. Now fret the 3rd string again at the second fret and strike the string with the right-hand thumb to check for clarity. Alternate between the open and fretted positions until the movement of your left-hand finger becomes second nature.

Remaining relaxed while fretting is important, so every now and then, do a quick mental check to make sure your arm, elbow, and hand are as comfortable as possible. However, creating tension by using *too much* pressure with the left-hand fingers when fretting isn't unusual for new players. You want to use as much fretting pressure as it takes, but no more.

You can find out just how much pressure you need by placing a finger in a fretted position, just barely touching the string. Now gradually apply more pressure on the string with the left-hand finger, striking it repeatedly with the right hand as you go. You literally hear the sound come into focus as you fret. After you've passed the threshold where the sound is clear, note how much pressure you're applying with the left-hand finger. If you're like most people, you may be surprised at how little effort it takes to cleanly fret with the left-hand fingers.

If you want to check out some more advanced left-hand techniques such as the slide, hammer-on, pull-off, and choke, turn to Chapter 5 with your right hand as soon as possible.

Tuning Up

Question: "What's the difference between a banjo and a motorcycle?"

Answer: "You can tune a motorcycle."

This unfortunate but frequently recited banjo joke speaks to a greater truth: Many banjo players are a bit lazy in their tuning habits.

Playing in good tune is an absolutely necessary component to becoming a socially acceptable banjo player. You simply *have* to know how to tune the banjo to itself so you can practice at home without driving your loved ones insane. And when the time has come to start making music with others, those around you will be thankful that you took the time to figure out how to get your banjo in tune with other instruments.

To tune the banjo, you raise or lower the amount of tension of each string to match the sound of another banjo string or to match a reference note provided by another instrument or an electronic tuner. You adjust each string by turning its corresponding tuning peg. In this section, you discover what it means for your banjo to be in tune, and I introduce you to several different methods to tune your banjo.

Like all other elements of banjo playing, tuning is a skill that gets easier with practice and the passage of time. Being able to distinguish one note from another isn't a mysterious psychic ability that you either are or aren't born with — tuning is a learned skill. No excuses! Keep actively listening to how the sounds of the strings change as you turn the pegs. Don't be afraid to ask others for advice if you're unsure about whether or not a string is in tune.

G tuning: Getting your strings in order

Although banjo players use a variety of tunings to play different kinds of songs and to create different moods on their instrument, the most frequently used tuning is called *G tuning* (which is also the type of tuning I use in this book). With this tuning, the five open strings of the banjo are tuned to the notes of a G major chord (a *chord* is a collection of three or more notes played together; I talk more about chords in Chapter 3).

Here are the pitches used for each string in G tuning:

- ✔ **5th string:** G
- ✔ **4th string:** D
- ✔ **3rd string:** G
- ✔ **2nd string:** B
- ✔ **1st string:** D

Note that only three different pitches are used in G tuning: G, B, and D. These three notes make up the G major chord. The 1st-string D and 5th-string G are one octave higher in pitch than their 4th- and 3rd-string counterparts. Your ears hear the two D notes and the two G notes as being essentially the same, but you can also hear that the 1st and 5th strings are higher in pitch. Musicians long ago decided to assign the same letter name to pitches that you hear in this way, but they also recognized that the two D's and the two G's aren't *exactly* the same pitch. They're one *octave* apart, with the octave being the point where that same note is repeated again but at a higher pitch.

Figure 2-7 shows the pitches of each string in G tuning along with a fretboard image summarizing the relative tuning relationships between the strings (which I cover in the next section).

Figure 2-7:
To tune the banjo in G tuning using relative tuning, you fret a string as shown to match the pitch of the next highest open string.

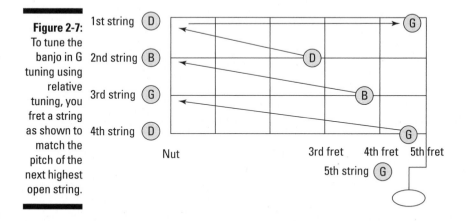

Relative tuning: Tuning the banjo to itself

Relative tuning involves using one string as a reference to tune the other strings of your banjo. That string doesn't really have to be in tune with any outside source, because in this case, you're just getting the banjo strings in tune with one another so that you can play by yourself.

With each new string you tune in relative tuning, you then fret that string to create a new reference note that you use to tune the next highest string. Relative tuning is the most useful way to tune the banjo, because you need nothing but your banjo and your ears to get your instrument in tune. You've got a banjo, now you can get to work on training your ears!

Even pro players follow up on their initial pass at relative tuning by trying different pairs of strings to hear what they sound like together and tuning the adjacent pairs of strings a second time. If one or more strings are severely out of tune to begin with, you definitely need to repeat the processes I describe in the following sections once or twice until the banjo is in good tune.

From low to high

When tuning from low to high, you begin with the lowest-pitched 4th string and work your way up to the 5th string, the highest-pitched string. Using the following instructions, tune the remaining four strings up from the 4th string, using the left-hand middle finger to fret each reference note. For now, try striking (or *picking*) each string with a downward motion from your right-hand thumb.

1. **Pick the 4th string fretted at the fifth fret and compare its pitch to the open 3rd string.**

   You may need to strike the fretted 4th string first, wait a moment to hear its pitch, and then strike the 3rd string to listen to its pitch. Does the 3rd string (the second note you play) sound higher or lower than the 4th string? Try singing the two pitches to *feel* whether the pitch rises or falls.

2. **If the open 3rd string sounds higher in pitch, the string is *sharp,* and you want to adjust the tuning peg for that string in the direction that brings its pitch down (usually clockwise for most banjos). If the 3rd string is lower in pitch, that string is *flat;* in this case, rotate the peg in the direction that causes the pitch of the string to rise (counterclockwise for most instruments).**

   When the pitches of the two strings match each other, the 4th and 3rd strings of your banjo are in tune.

3. **Pick the 3rd string fretted at the fourth fret and match the open 2nd string to this sound.**

   You use the same process as Step 2. After these strings sound the same, you have the 4th, 3rd, and 2nd strings of your banjo in tune.

4. **Pick the 2nd string fretted at the third fret and tune the open 1st string to this sound.**

   On most banjos, you turn the tuning pegs on the 2nd and 1st strings in the opposite direction than you did for the 4th- and 3rd-string pegs. Turning the pegs of the 1st and 2nd strings clockwise should raise the string's pitch, and turning counterclockwise should lower it.

5. **Pick the 1st string fretted at the fifth fret and tune the open 5th string to this sound.**

   Remember that the 5th string is the short string on your banjo that's situated on the opposite side of your 1st string. Some banjos have 5th string tuning pegs that are difficult to turn without causing wild fluctuations in pitch. Don't worry if it takes a bit more time to get the 5th string in tune.

Even if you follow my instructions carefully, I'm sure that you may discover the following frustrations when tuning the banjo in this way (but don't "fret" — you aren't alone):

- ✔ **Your reference point is always a fretted string when tuning from a lower- to higher-pitched string.** You need to lift the left hand up to adjust the tuning peg of the string you're attempting to tune and then fret it again on the lower string to play the reference pitch.

- ✔ **If you make a slight error at the beginning of this process, that mistake is exaggerated as you proceed to try and tune the rest of the strings.** You may have to start all over.

From high to low

Similar to the instructions from the preceding section, you can also tune your banjo by starting with the highest-pitched string (the 5th string) and moving down to the lowest-pitched 4th string. If you tune the banjo in this way, the string you're trying to get in tune is also the string that you're fretting. The open string is now your reference point.

For example, you can use the 5th-string G as a reference note to tune the 1st-string D. However, this time around, you fret the 1st string at the fifth fret to match it to the pitch of the open-5th string. You have to now lift your fretting hand off of the 1st string to turn the first string's tuning peg and then refret again at the fifth fret until the both strings' pitches are matched.

If you're having difficulty determining whether a string is sharp or flat, tune it down until the string is obviously below the pitch of your reference note. Then gradually bring the string you're trying to get in tune up in pitch to match the reference note.

Reference tuning: Getting a little outside help

Relative tuning is great when you're playing by yourself or to use as a quick touch up to a string or two in the middle of a practice session. However, when playing with others (or with the CD that accompanies this book), you need to get accustomed to tuning your banjo using one or more outside reference notes as provided by an electronic tuner, a CD, or another instrument. I show you how to tune by using reference notes in the following sections.

If you're practicing on your own, it doesn't matter from where you get your reference pitches — the important thing is to have the banjo in tune with itself. If you're playing with others, everyone should use the same reference pitch, whether it's coming from an electronic tuner or an instrument.

Utilizing an electronic tuner

Tuners provide a reference for you to tune individual strings, played one at a time. When you play a string, the tuner "hears" the note and gives an indication of the note's pitch by showing a letter name for the note closest to it in pitch, with an accompanying ♯ (sharp) or ♭ (flat) sign, if needed (for instance, if the note you're playing is closest to an F♯ in pitch, the tuner reads F♯). The tuner also indicates whether your string is sharp (too high) or flat (too low) to your reference note via a meter or a row of small LED lights. (Check out Chapter 10 for a discussion of how tuners work and of the different types of tuners currently available.) An electronic clip-on tuner is shown in Figure 2-8.

If the string is significantly out of tune, the tuner may assign an alphabet letter that isn't a G, B, or D (check out the section "G tuning: Getting your strings in order" earlier in this chapter for the skinny on the notes used in this tuning). I've been avoiding it up to now, but so you aren't thrown off by these various letters, you should know the following order of notes in music:

G / G♯ *or* A♭ / A / A♯ *or* B♭ / B / C / C♯ *or* D♭ / D / D♯ *or* E♭ / E / F / F♯ *or* G♭ / G

Figure 2-8:
Using an electronic clip-on tuner makes tuning easier.

Here are a few tidbits of info that may help you better understand this series of notes and how they relate to tuning your banjo:

- You may notice that some notes in the preceding series have an *or* between them. Without getting too boring, just remember that a G♯ is the same pitch as an A♭, an A♯ is the same as B♭, and so on. These equivalent notes are found at the same fret on your fingerboard.

- As you move to the right in the order of notes, you're naming higher-pitched notes; as you move to the left, the notes are lower pitched. If you move one note in either direction (for instance, going from a C♯ or D♭ note to a D note), you move a *half step*. If you move two notes in either direction (for instance, going from an F to a G or from a C to a D), you move a *whole step*.

A half-step movement corresponds to a change of one fret up or down on your banjo fingerboard, and a whole step equals a movement of two frets from one note to the next. For example, if you're playing an open string and you want to move up a half step, you would fret the first fret of that same string. If you wanted to move up a whole step from an open string, you would fret the second fret.

To use an electronic tuner, you turn the tuning pegs until the readout matches the note that string should match. For example, if you're trying to tune your 3rd string to a G and the tuner gives you an F♯ reading, you know from the preceding order of notes that your 3rd string is far enough below a G pitch that the tuner hears the note as an F♯ — the pitch that's one half step below G.

To get your 3rd string in tune, continue striking the 3rd string with the right hand and slowly move the tuning peg to raise the string's pitch. At some point, the tuner's readout should change from an F♯ to a G note, but at this point the tuner tells you that your 3rd string is a *flat* G note instead of a *sharp* F♯. Continue raising the pitch of the string until the tuner indicates that the string is exactly in tune to a G note. You use the same process for each of the strings, raising or lowering their pitches until the tuner indicates that you've reached the desired note.

Don't strike the strings too hard when using an electronic tuner. A light touch is best for the tuner to give the most reliable reading. Also, the meter on some tuners shifts slightly to the left or right as it responds to ever-so-slight changes in pitch that occur as a string continues to vibrate. If this happens to you, tune the string to the pitch that the indicator "sits on" for the majority of the time that the tuner is registering its pitch. This approximation gets you close enough to do a touch up on that string by using relative-tuning techniques (see the previous section on this topic for instructions).

Tuning with an electronic tuner at a jam session

When musicians come together to make music, they first take some time to make sure that their instruments are in tune with one another before they start to play. Just before a jam session begins, you may see musicians off in different corners or with their backs turned momentarily from the main group, as they get in tune by using electronic clip-on tuners (see preceding section for the how-to). In this case, the participants use the reference notes provided by their tuners to get as closely in tune with each other as they can (and if the participants have their backs turned because they're talking to their agents, find another jam session!).

Don't hesitate to borrow another musician's tuner whenever you need one in a group session. Believe me — everyone wants you to be in tune just as much as you do!

If your jam session is taking place outside, as often happens at a music festi-val, chances are good that all the instruments gradually drift out of absolute tuning in reaction to the sun, the humidity, and the warm temperatures. If you're joining a jam session that's already in progress, the musicians may be in tune with each other but not with your tuner. In these situations, get a reference pitch from another instrumentalist and tune your banjo, using the relative tuning techniques outlined earlier in this chapter (I describe how to do this in the next few sections).

Using another instrument as a reference

If you don't have an electronic tuner or you want to be in tune with others in a jam session, you can use pitches from other instruments to get your banjo where it needs to be. In general, ask another musician to play a certain note on her instrument. Then, try to get your string to match that pitch by turning the tuning pegs. After tuning each open string to the corresponding note, you can then double-check your tuning by using relative tuning techniques (see the section on this topic earlier in this chapter).

Don't be surprised if the instrument you're using isn't exactly in tune with an electronic tuner. Remember that you aren't aiming for perfect pitch at this point, but rather, you're wanting your banjo to be in tune with itself and with others you may be playing with.

Promote world peace: Use a banjo mute!

If you're one of those folks who live in a crowded household or a college dorm or if you have to catch your practice time late at night or very early in the morning, you need to find a way to ramp down the volume of your banjo. Try these quick solutions to temporarily tame your savage banjo beast:

✔ **Place a mute on the bridge.** A *banjo mute* fits onto the top of your banjo bridge and soaks up the musical energy that the bridge normally transmits from a vibrating string to the banjo head. (See photo a in the accompanying figure.) Mutes dramatically reduce your banjo's volume and can change the tone quite a bit too, lending a sweet sustaining sound to your banjo that makes it sound almost like a harpsichord. You can buy a banjo mute at an acoustic specialty store (but don't let them talk you into believing that a ball-peen hammer is a real mute — that's a more permanent solution!). In lieu of a store-bought mute, you can also use a couple of clothespins, snapped to either end of the bridge (shown in photo b). This solution works just about as well!

✔ **Just stuff it!** Cram a hand towel or a T-shirt into the back of the banjo, in the space between the head and the closest coordinating rod (shown in photo c). If your banjo has a resonator, you need to remove it first to get to the back of your instrument. The more firmly you position the cloth against the underside of the head, the more it absorbs the energy of the head and the quieter your banjo will become.

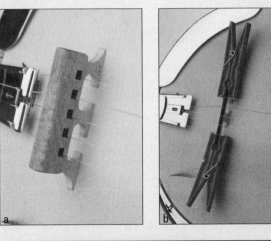

Here's how you can use various instruments to tune your banjo:

- ✔ **Guitar or dobro:** The 4th (D), 3rd (G), and 2nd (B) strings of the guitar are tuned to the same pitches as the corresponding strings in G tuning on the banjo (see the section on G tuning earlier in this chapter for more info). The dobro's top four strings are tuned to the same pitches as the top four strings on your banjo, so you can use these instruments as reference points to tune your banjo.

  I usually try to tune my 3rd-string G first, and then I move down in pitch to tune the 4th string and up to tune the 2nd, 1st, and 5th strings. When I have a break in between songs, I ask the guitar or dobro player to play a 3rd string open, or the fretted equivalent if she has a capo on, so I can make sure my banjo is in tune with the other instruments. If I'm out of tune, I make adjustments on each string until my strings' pitches match the pitches on the guitar or dobro.

- ✔ **Piano:** If you have a piano or an electronic keyboard around the house, that's another great source for getting reference notes to tune your banjo. Tune each banjo string to the corresponding piano note (see Figure 2-9).

- ✔ **Fiddle or mandolin:** If you're playing music with just a fiddler or a mandolin player, you can still get in tune with them by asking for their G note. A fiddle is tuned to the same pitches as a mandolin. The open G notes on these instruments are an octave higher in pitch than your 3rd-string G.

  However, you can still use this note to tune your G string, and then you can tune your remaining strings using relative tuning techniques or you can ask for the other pitches you need to get the other strings in tune (see the section "Relative tuning: Tuning the banjo to itself" earlier in this chapter for more help).

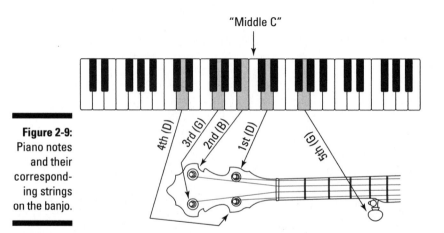

Figure 2-9:
Piano notes
and their
correspond-
ing strings
on the banjo.

The tone of the other instrumentalist's notes are going to be different than the notes on the banjo, but remember you're comparing the pitch of each note, not the tone. When in doubt about your own tuning, don't hesitate to ask another musician for help.

Enlisting the help of this book's CD

Last but not least, you can pop the CD that's in the back of the book into a CD player and proceed directly to Track 1, where I name and play all the open strings on the banjo in G tuning. These pitches should be very close to what you'd get when using an electronic tuner (for more on these techie tuners, check out the section "Utilizing an electronic tuner").

Checking Out Chord Diagrams

Looking for an easy way to remember how to fret a chord with your left-hand fingers? A *chord diagram* not only communicates which strings are fretted for a particular chord but also where on the fingerboard you put those fingers and which left-hand finger you use to fret each string.

Chord diagrams aren't the same as banjo *tablature,* which is the written form of banjo music that I explain in Chapter 3. Chord diagrams show you *how* to fret a chord with the left hand, but they don't tell you *what* to play with it. However, when you play with others, you use chords all the time. Chords are also the basic building blocks of just about every melody, so getting comfortable reading chord diagrams is a good idea, which is just what I intend to help you do in the following sections.

Reading a chord diagram

If you're already familiar with reading chord diagrams for the guitar, you find that banjo players use the same system. If you turn your banjo around so that the fingerboard faces you, that's how the banjo neck is represented in a chord diagram (check out Figure 2-10 to more fully break down the parts of a chord diagram):

✔ From left to right, the vertical lines represent the 4th, 3rd, 2nd, and 1st strings on your banjo. Most banjo chord diagrams don't include the 5th string, because you rarely fret it, especially when you're just beginning to play.

✔ The top horizontal line represents the banjo nut. The *nut* is what guides the strings from the fingerboard to the peghead. One way to think of the nut is as a "0" fret, because your banjo strings are open at this location on the neck.

✔ The second line from the top stands for your banjo's first fret, and the line below that represents the second fret, and so on.

✔ The black dots that appear on the vertical string lines indicate behind what fret and on what strings on the banjo fingerboard you should fret.

✔ The letters located underneath the chord diagram indicate the left-hand finger you use to fret each string. For the left hand, I = index finger; M = middle finger; R = ring finger; and P (or sometimes L) = ring finger. Some books use the numbers 1 through 4 to represent the left-hand fingers in the same way.

Figure 2-10:
Chord diagrams show which left hand fingers fret which strings as well as where to fret. Here's the chord diagram for a C chord.

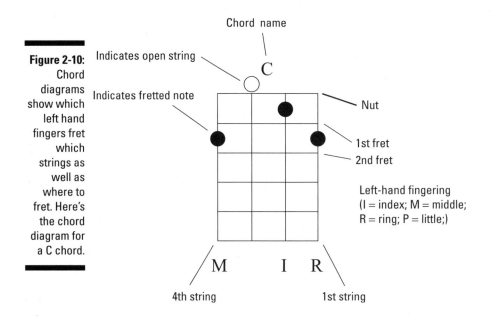

Chord name

Indicates open string

Indicates fretted note

C

Nut

1st fret

2nd fret

Left-hand fingering
(I = index; M = middle;
R = ring; P = little;)

M   I   R

4th string   1st string

Interpreting up-the-neck chord diagrams

As you become more proficient, you can fret chords all up and down the neck of your banjo. To represent a chord that's played above the fifth fret, a chord diagram includes a number that appears to the right of the diagram — either next to the top fret line or adjacent to the uppermost fretted note in the chord. This number indicates exactly where you need to position your left hand on the banjo neck (see Figure 2-11).

If you need to fret the 5th string as part of a chord, a fifth vertical line is added to the left side of the chord diagram to represent this string. The 5th string is often fretted up the neck with the left-hand thumb, which is represented with the letter *T* in a chord diagram.

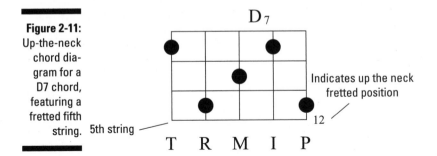

Figure 2-11:
Up-the-neck
chord dia-
gram for a
D7 chord,
featuring a
fretted fifth
string.

Fingering G, D7, and C Chords

The first time you discover how to fret a chord on your banjo is a very big moment in your burgeoning playing career. If the world suddenly seems like a much better place after you've successfully fretted each of the chords in this section, that's a good indication that you were born to be a banjo player.

Figure 2-12 shows chord diagrams for the three most important chords you play on the banjo: the G, D7, and C chords.

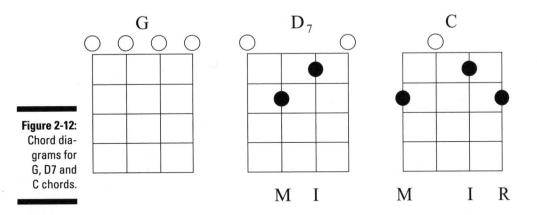

Figure 2-12:
Chord dia-
grams for
G, D7 and
C chords.

After you practice the chords as described in the next three sections, try moving from one chord to the next, in any order that strikes your fancy. Strum with a downward right-hand thumb motion across all five strings a few times for each new chord and strive for a clear, unmuted sound from each string for all three chords. This stuff is pretty exciting, isn't it? Take a listen to Track 2 on the CD to see whether your chords sound like the ones that I demonstrate. You can put these chords to use in Chapter 3.

Try to keep the tips of your left-hand fingers close to the neck and pointed towards the fingerboard at all times as you move from one chord to the next. At first, you may have to move one left-hand fretting finger at a time as you work the different chord fingerings into your motor memory. However, in the long run, fretting all the strings you need for a chord at the same time is more efficient. After you've mastered this skill, you can switch between chords with greater speed and accuracy.

The G chord: Real easy

Although people very seldom associate the banjo with Zen, you really *don't* have to fret anything at all to play the G chord, grasshopper! A G chord is just the sound of your right hand strumming the open strings in G tuning (see the section "G tuning: Getting your strings in order" earlier in this chapter for more info). That's why this chord diagram includes no black dots at all — your five open strings do all the work! You could use your left hand to wave to your adoring fans, but I think it may be a little early for these kinds of grand gestures.

The D7 chord: A little harder

For the D7 chord, you place your middle finger just behind the second fret of the 3rd string and your index finger behind the first fret of the 2nd string. Try strumming down across all five strings with your right-hand thumb, starting with the 5th string and striking each note down to the 1st string. Try a slow strum to check the accuracy of your fretting on each individual string, but then don't be afraid to go wild with some fast strumming to strut your stuff!

The C chord: More challenging still

The C chord is a bit harder than the D7 chord (see preceding section), because you use one more left-hand finger to fret this chord. Here, the left-hand index frets the 2nd string, first fret — just as with the D7 chord. However, now you move your middle finger to the 4th string, second fret, and you also need to fret the 1st string at the second fret. Be careful that you fret the 4th and 2nd strings with enough of a vertical angle with your left-hand fingers so you don't block the sound of the open 3rd string.

Your hand should look something like Figure 2-13 when you fret the D7 and C chords:

Chapter 3

Playing by the Rules: Not Enough Theory to Hurt

*I*f you've worked through Chapter 2, your banjo is in tune and you're comfortable fretting a few chords, so you're just about ready to play some real music. For most new banjo players, going from learning a chord or two to actually playing an entire song is a pretty big leap.

In this chapter, I cover everything you need to know to make this transition as easy and painless as possible. You'll soon be strumming along with songs and be well on your way to having more fun with the banjo than you ever thought possible!

This chapter unlocks the mystery of playing music by helping you understand two of the basic building blocks of a song: *rhythm* and *chord progressions*. You also become acquainted with banjo *tablature,* the written form of music for the banjo, and you discover a great way to accompany others using something called the *pinch pattern.* This chapter also examines the different roles that the banjo takes in a band and helps you understand how to be a cooperative team player when playing music with others.

You can return to the tools and skills covered in this chapter each time you work on a new song or take out your banjo to join in a jam session.

Breaking Down the Parts of a Song

How is it that some banjo players can play along with just about any song that comes up, even something that they've never heard before? I can tell you from personal experience that you aren't simply born with this skill — it's something that's nurtured. Songs are like roadmaps, and if you can follow the signposts correctly, you eventually make your way through just about any bluegrass or old-time tune. The more songs you learn, the more you can get around Banjo Town without getting lost.

Although every song has something that makes it different from any other song (even if it's just the title!), most bluegrass and old-time songs share many of the same underlying musical characteristics. If you understand how songs are put together, you have a much easier time getting started down the road to becoming a great banjo player.

Songs are made up of rhythm, chord progressions, and melodies. However, at this first stage of playing, your goal is to play a song by strumming the correct chords in the proper rhythm, which is what I cover in the following sections; you can worry about playing melodies a little later (see Chapter 6 to begin to unlock this mystery).

Rhythm: Catching the beat

One of the things that separates music from random noise is that time is organized (in some way) within a piece of music. When talking about music, *rhythm* can refer to several different things: You can refer to the rhythm of a particular musician or band (as in "That banjo player really plays with a lot of drive!" or "I think those guys' rhythm needs some work!") or the rhythm of a particular piece of music ("I like that song — it's really bouncy!"). For now, I use the word *rhythm* to refer collectively to all the different aspects of music that have to do with time and duration.

The most important aspect of playing the banjo well — both as a beginner and as an advanced player — is to play with good rhythm. Although your biggest worry at first may be about fretting chords and hitting the right strings (see Chapters 2 and 4 on these topics), you eventually want to put a lot of effort into playing a song all the way through in a steady rhythm without stopping — no matter what! Playing without stopping is especially important when playing music with others or along with the CD that accompanies this book. If you start to work on this skill right now at the earliest stages of your playing, you can soon be comfortable playing songs with others, even as a beginner.

Rhythm is something that everyone is born with — it's in the steady pulse of your heartbeat and in the measured cadence of your steps as you walk. If you can keep a steady beat or pulse by tapping your foot or clapping your hands, you've got rhythm. You can apply that natural sense of rhythm to playing songs on the banjo.

On the other hand, finding the rhythm in music may not be natural for everyone. If you struggle finding the rhythm of a song, you can break down the elements of rhythm, and you can practice to keep pace with any song. I get you started in the following sections by introducing a few key terms you need to know. However, I'm with Pete Seeger who once wrote that he's willing to learn just enough formal music to get by as long as it didn't hurt his banjo playing, so I cover only a few terms that all musicians use to talk about rhythm in music — and I guarantee you won't lose any self-respect as a banjo player in the process.

To count or not to count: It's all in your head

Have you ever watched the feet of your favorite musicians while they're playing on stage or in a jam session? Even though they may actually be *playing* in perfect time together, musicians often don't tap their feet in the same rhythm or even in a way that has any discernable relationship to the beat of the music.

What's with that? The answer lies in the fact that what you're seeing in all the fancy irregular footwork isn't necessarily how a musician is keeping time. Musicians often count out the rhythm just before starting a piece to give the other players an idea of the tempo, but after a song has started and everyone is playing along, most musicians rely on their internal sense of rhythm by listening to what's happening around them while simultaneously keeping track of the rhythm in their heads. Most musicians don't keep an actual count going after a song has started, but they do actively keep track of the tempo and where the beat falls.

Although most people (even beginning banjo players like you) can establish a consistent beat in their heads, keeping that beat going while trying to play banjo is usually more difficult. That's when a good outside source for keeping the beat can come in handy. A metronome, a device that keeps a steady beat for you, is a great way to play in good rhythm when practicing by yourself (see Chapter 10 for a discussion of how to play with the metronome).

However, when playing with others, keeping good time is everyone's shared responsibility. Listening and adjusting to the rhythm of the other musicians as you play is just as important — if not more important — than following the beat you've established in your head. Keep one ear on what others are playing and the other one on your own picking, and you'll soon be playing all your music in good time!

Beats, tempo, and meter

I use the term *beat* to refer to a musical unit of measure. To understand what a beat is, try singing one of your favorite songs and tapping your foot in rhythm to your singing. For example, the song "Will the Circle Be Unbroken" would sound like this (try tapping your foot with each capitalized syllable and tap indication): "WILL the CIR-CLE [tap] BE un-BRO-KEN [tap], BY and BY LORD BY [tap] and BY [tap] [tap]." Each foot tap is a beat. In all the music you play, each beat is equal in duration to every other beat.

Check out the words to the old favorite "Red River Valley" on Track 3 of the CD (Tab 3-1). You can see slash marks above the lyrics, which indicate where the main beats occur. Try singing along with the CD, clapping on these beats as indicated.

G

From this   val - ley they   say   you are   going_____   We will

6   D7

miss   your bright eyes   and sweet   smile_____   For they

10   G   C

say   you are   tak -   ing the   sunshine_____   That has

14   D7   G

bright - ened our   path - ways a   while.

Tab 3-1: Singing and clapping to "Red River Valley" (Track 3).

The idea of playing along with a steady beat is central to good banjo playing. The word *tempo* refers to how fast you're tapping (or clapping or playing) that beat. Although classical musicians use a lot of fancy Italian words such as *presto, largo,* and *fuselli* to refer to different tempos (okay, fuselli is actually the name of a pasta), banjo players use terminology such as *slow, fast, real fast,* and *really, really fast.* Most of the time, banjo players actually just start playing at whatever tempo feels right, and everyone else joins in when they've grabbed hold of that steady beat.

You can organize beats into groups of two, three, or four beats for most banjo music (and if you're playing Irish music, you sometimes group beats into units of six and even nine beats). Musicians use the word *meter* to refer to any recurring cycle of beats.

Time signatures, measures, and downbeats

A *time signature* indicates the meter and the kind of count you use for a particular song. The time signature usually appears at the very beginning of a written piece of music and is shown as two numbers positioned one on top of the other (like a fraction without the horizontal line). As you can see in Figure 3-1, the top number in the time signature indicates the number of beats in a cycle, while the bottom number stands for the kind of note that equals one beat.

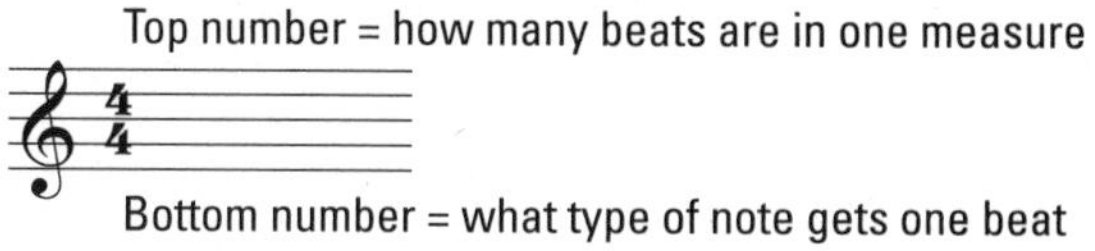

Figure 3-1:
4/4 time
signature.

Top number = how many beats are in one measure

$\frac{4}{4}$

Bottom number = what type of note gets one beat

Just like the song in Figure 3-1, 4/4 time (spoken "four-four time") is the meter used most frequently in printed music for bluegrass and old-time banjo music. With this time signature, you have four beats in each cycle and a quarter note equals one beat (I discuss note values a little later in this chapter). The count that goes along with this time signature is "one-two-three-four, one-two-three-four," and so on. Most waltz-time banjo music is in 3/4 time with three beats per cycle and a quarter note signifies one beat. The count that goes with 3/4 time is "one-two-three, one-two-three."

A *measure* (or *bar*) marks off a single rhythmic cycle. In written music, a measure is indicated by a vertical line that extends through the *staff*. In banjo tablature, the *staff* consists of five horizontal lines that represent the five strings of your banjo (more on reading tablature later in this chapter).

The first beat of each measure is called the *downbeat*. The downbeat of each measure is usually emphasized when counting but isn't necessarily played louder. The initial *downbeat* (the first beat of the first full measure of a song) is an important moment when you're playing with other musicians, because that's usually the time when the other players join in. When it comes time to change chords in a song, you most often (but not always) move to the new chord on a downbeat of a new measure.

Chord progressions: Playing your first songs

The *chord progression* of a song is the part of your musical road map that indicates what chords you play, in what sequence these chords occur, and how long each chord lasts before you move on to play the next one as you play a song. Although you can find about as many different chord progressions as you can songs, you can count on some predictability in how chords follow one another in most songs you play on the banjo, making figuring out and remembering new chord progressions easier as you encounter them in a new piece.

Many songs use only the G, C, and D7 chords (which I present in Chapter 2). However, the more chords you know, the more quickly you can play along with new songs.

You want to become familiar with the chord progression of a new song just as soon as you begin to work on it. The chord progression not only lays out the form of the piece, but also provides the foundation you use later on for playing (and remembering!) the melody and for improvising. The chord progression is also what keeps everyone on the same page as you play a song with others in a jam session. In this situation, everyone plays through the chord progression repeatedly until all the players agree that it's time for the song to come to an end.

A little musical knowledge need not be a dangerous thing. The time has come to put all these concepts and terms to work as you play your first piece. You're now on the entrance ramp to the banjo interstate!

Progressing from chord to chord

When you're working through a chord progression, try strumming with an even downward motion of your thumb across all five strings of the banjo, striking all five strings in an even sweeping motion with the thumb. In the next few chapters, you find more interesting things to play as you accompany a tune, but for now, strumming is just fine! You're working on the crucial new skill of changing chords in the left hand without losing the beat with your strumming in the right hand, which takes a lot of coordination! If you don't get it at first, simply take your time and keep trying.

Take a look at "Red River Valley" (Tab 3-2). In this example, I've added a tab staff, a time signature, measures, a chord progression (indicated above the staff) and the song's lyrics (indicated below the staff). You can hear the strumming on Track 4 of the CD.

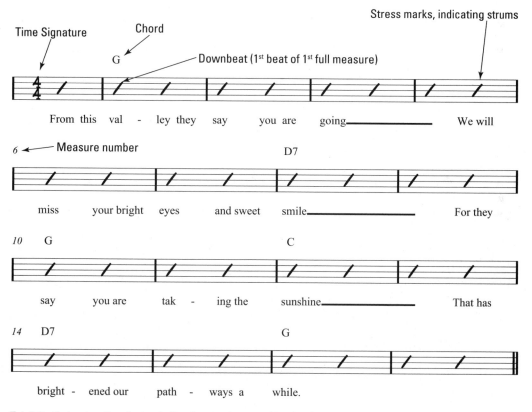

Tab 3-2: Understanding rhythm indications and strumming chords to "Red River Valley."

The time signature to this piece is 4/4, which means that every measure has four beats. This piece has sixteen measures all together. The chord progression to "Red River Valley" consists of six measures of G, two measures of D, two measures of G, two measures of C, two measures of D, and two measures of G.

Note that in this particular tune, the chords change at the start of a new measure. I've also added a label to show where the *downbeat* occurs. Note that you don't start "Red River Valley" on this downbeat. Your first strum and your singing begin at beat three of the preceding measure. This happens a lot when beginning a song, so no need to worry!

Your assignment (should you decide to accept it) is to play the chords to "Red River Valley" with two right-hand strums per measure on the first and third beats of each measure (the stress marks indicate a strum). You can also listen or play along to this song on the CD, Track 4.

Changing chords quickly

Most new players find that the hardest part of strumming along to a song like "Red River Valley" (see Tab 3-2) is going from the G to the C chords smoothly without interrupting the right-hand strums. When you run into difficulties at a particular point in any song, try to isolate that problem and practice it over and over again.

Smooth sailing

Trying to get the feel for a new song isn't always the easiest of tasks; however, here are a few practice tips that you can use when you begin any new song:

✔ Don't worry about speed when learning a new song; just try to keep the strums steady and fret each chord as cleanly as you can (for more on fretting, see Chapter 2).

✔ Listen to the CD track first to get an idea of what the song or technique is supposed to

sound like, then try practicing it on your own. Finally, try playing along with the CD track.

✔ Try to memorize the chord progression as quickly as you can. This will free up your visual attention to look at your amazing left hand fretting maneuvers instead of your eyes being tied to the written music.

✔ Don't worry about singing while you're playing - but if you eventually feel comfortable doing this, by all means go for it!

For example, you can practice moving back and forth between just the G and C chords by creating an exercise where you shift from one chord to the other with each right-hand strum. You aren't playing the entire song at this point, but you're working on that "problem" moment in the song where you have to fret the C chord, by practicing this move over and over again. In the long run, you save a lot of time and energy by focusing on problem areas rather than playing through the entire tune and slowing down at the trouble spots.

Keep the tips of your left-hand fingers pointed towards the banjo fingerboard even if you aren't using them at that moment to fret. When playing the G chord, you can position the left-hand fingers you use for the C chord just above their fretted positions, a technique called *ghosting*. These fingers are then ready to move into position and push down (or *fret*) the strings behind the appropriate fret (Figure 3-2 shows how to ghost and fret a chord). Even when you aren't fretting anything at all in the left hand, it's still a good idea to keep the tips of your left-hand fingers pointed towards the fingerboard. You can be sure that you'll need them sooner or later!

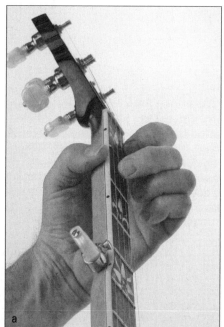
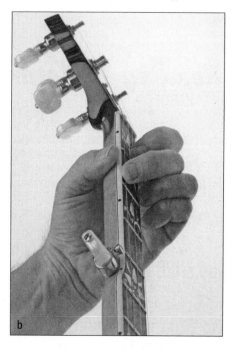

Figure 3-2:
Ghosting the
C chord
(a) and
fretting the
C chord (b).

You can now try strumming along to a new song, "Boil Them Cabbage Down," that uses the same G, C, and D7 chords as "Red River Valley," but requires you to change from one chord to another more quickly (see Tab 3-3). "Boil Them Cabbage Down," which is Track 5 on the CD, moves to a new chord with each measure (with the first change coming to the C chord, which you've thoroughly practiced by now, right?). In measure seven, you play *two* chords, strumming a G chord on the first beat followed by a D7 chord on the third beat in the same measure.

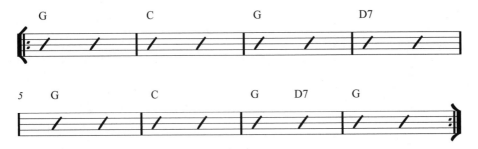

Tab 3-3: Strumming chords to "Boil Them Cabbage Down" (Track 5).

Reading Tablature

Tablature (or *tab* for short) is the written form of music for the banjo. Although tablature uses quite a few elements that are also found in conventional music notation, tab imparts information that's specific to the banjo such as what string you play and whether that string is open or fretted. Tablature is a part of almost every instructional book and CD set. And although tab never replaces being able to play by ear, it enables you to cover ground more quickly when learning a new piece of music and allows you to double-check what you've learned by ear. Therefore, take a little time to get acquainted with reading tablature in the following sections.

Finding notes

The big difference between banjo tablature and standard music notation is that although both use five horizontal lines on the staff, the lines on the banjo tab staff represent the five strings of your banjo. The top line corresponds to the banjo's 1st string and the bottom line represents the banjo's 5th string, with the second, third, and fourth lines from the top standing for the 2nd, 3rd, and 4th strings on your banjo (see Tab 3-4).

1st string

2nd string — 4th string

3rd string — 5th string

Tab 3-4: The five lines on the banjo tab staff represent the five banjo strings.

Need help in remembering which tab lines stand for which banjo strings? Note that the visual orientation of the strings on the tab staff is the same as what you see as you look down on the strings while playing. From this point of view, the 1st string is the string that is farthest away (and is "on top" of the tab staff) and the 5th string is the closest (and "on bottom" of the tab staff).

In banjo tablature, you also see numbers on each line. These numbers represent the notes you're being asked to play, as shown in Tab 3-5. The line that the number sits on indicates which string you play and the numeric value tells whether you're to play an open (unfretted, indicated with "0") or fretted string.

2nd string – 1st fret — 1st string – open (zero fret)

3rd string – 2nd fret — 5th string – open (zero fret)

Tab 3-5: Numbers on the tab staff lines show open and fretted notes.

And Tab 3-6 displays what the G, C, and D7 chords look like in tablature. The "b" below the tab staff indicates a right-hand brush.

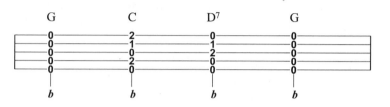

Tab 3-6: Tablature for G, C, and C7 chords.

Tracking down the rhythm

Banjo tablature expresses rhythm in much the same way as it is in conventional music notation, in terms of measures and time signatures (see the section "Rhythm: Catching the beat" for more info). Banjo players typically think of a single measure of tab in 4/4 time as a rhythmic space that's waiting to be filled by a maximum of eight notes (or an equivalent combination of fewer notes with longer duration).

Each note on the tab staff has a stem attached that indicates the duration of the note. The three note values that you encounter most frequently in banjo tablature are the quarter note, the eighth note, and the sixteenth note.

Each of these notes has a vertical line extending down from the note that is called the *stem*. An eighth note has added to it either a curled or horizontal line attached to the bottom of the stem, while the sixteenth note has two horizontal lines. These lines are called *flags* and distinguish one rhythmic value from another on the tab page. Each note value also has a corresponding *rest* sign, which indicates a corresponding number of beats where no note is played. Tab 3-7 shows these three note values with their corresponding rests as they appear on a tab staff.

a

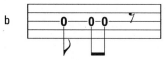

Quarter note/rest
equals "1 +"

b

Eighth notes/rest
equals "1" or "+"

c

Sixteenth notes/rest
1/2 count each

Tab 3-7: Quarter, eighth and sixteenth notes and rests in banjo tab.

Determining the value of a note in tablature is just like using grade school fractions: two sixteenth notes take up the same amount of musical space or time as one eighth note, and two eighth notes occupy the same amount of space as one quarter note. A measure in 4/4 time needs to be filled with the equivalent of four quarter notes. Tab 3-8, which is Track 6 on the CD, shows just a few of the many rhythmic combinations that will meet this requirement.

In the beginning, it may be helpful to count out loud (or in your head) "1 and 2 and 3 and 4 and" for each measure of 4/4 time as you play through a piece, letting each note last for its appropriate rhythmic duration. For example, if you're counting along in the example in Tab 3-8, you can see that an eighth note takes up the space of one count (either a number *or* an "and"), while a quarter note takes up the space of two counts (a number *and* an "and"). And playing songs along with the CD is an even better way to internalize these rhythms.

```
0   0   0   0   0 0 0 0 0 0 0 0   0   0   0 0 0 0   0 0 0 0 0 0 0
1   2   3   4   1 + 2 + 3 + 4 +   1   2   3 + 4 +   1 e + 2 + 3   4
```

Tab 3-8: Combining quarter, eighth, and sixteenth notes (Track 6).

Playing Pinch Patterns

After you have a feel for how to figure out the notes and rhythm in tab (see preceding section), you're now ready to put all this musical knowledge to work by getting acquainted with the pinch pattern. The *pinch pattern* gets its name from the right-hand motion you use to play the strings. With the pinch pattern, you strike the strings with a downward motion with the thumb and with an upward motion with the right-hand index and middle fingers all at the same time. In other words, you're *pinching* the banjo strings with your right hand!

The pinch pattern is great for beginning players to use when following chord progressions and accompanying songs. For now, you can play this pattern without any fingerpicks on your hands, and don't worry too much about your right-hand position (I cover that more thoroughly in Chapter 4).

Here's a step-by-step guide to playing a pinch pattern for an open G chord (all strings are unfretted):

1. Pick the 3rd string with a downward motion of the thumb.

2. **Strike the 5th string with the thumb, the 2nd string with the index finger, and the 1st string with the middle, playing all three strings at the same time.**

   You should hear the sound of three notes together. Remember that the pinch pattern always uses a downward motion with the right-hand thumb and an upward motion with the index and middle fingers every time you pick a string.

3. **Pick the fourth string with the thumb.**

4. **Repeat Step 2 by playing the 5th, 2nd, and 1st strings simultaneously with the thumb, index, and middle fingers.**

You can see in Tab 3-9 what the pinch pattern looks like in tablature for the G, C, and D7 chords. Also, be sure to listen to Track 7 on the CD to hear the pinch pattern in action on these same chords. In the example, "t" stands for the right-hand thumb, "i" for index finger, and "m" for middle finger.

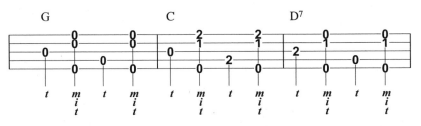

Tab 3-9: Playing the pinch pattern with G, C, and D7 chords (Track 7).

Note that the numbers on the tab staff change with each new chord in Tab 3-9, but that the right-hand picking pattern remains the same in each measure. As you read through any banjo tab, don't forget to follow the chord progression as you play. More often than not, if you fret the chord that's indicated above the tab staff, then you also have the fretted positions you need to match what the tab staff line numbers indicate to play. For instance, in Tab 3-9, you see a C chord above the tab staff. The lines on the tab staff (remember, these lines stand for the strings of your banjo) indicate that you need to fret the 1st string at the second fret, the 2nd string at the first fret, and the 4th string at the fourth fret. If you fret all three of these strings at the same time at the beginning of the second measure, following the C-chord indication that you see above the staff, you're also fretting everything that's indicated on the tab staff for this measure.

You can now try playing the pinch pattern with "Red River Valley" (Tab 3-10) and "Boil Them Cabbage Down" (Tab 3-11), which are Tracks 8 and 9 on the CD, respectively. You can check out Chapter 2 and the section on chord progressions earlier in this book if you need to get more familiar with the G, C, and D7 chords and the chord progressions to both of these tunes. If you're comfortable playing the pinch pattern, you may not need to look at the tab at all to play these tunes along with the CD.

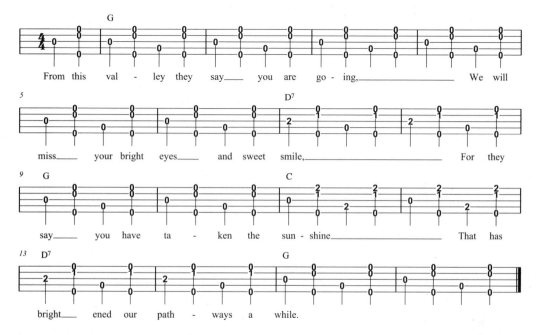

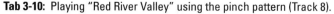

Tab 3-10: Playing "Red River Valley" using the pinch pattern (Track 8).

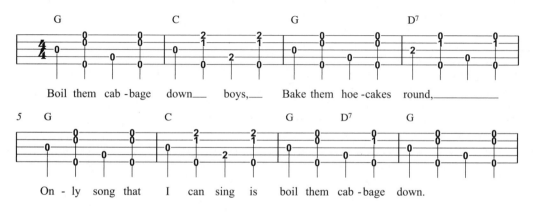

Tab 3-11: Playing "Boil Them Cabbage Down" using the pinch pattern (Track 9).

Being a Great Team Player

One of the primary reasons that many people want to learn to play the banjo is to have fun making music with others in bands and in jam sessions. There's nothing quite like a banjo, guitar, mandolin, fiddles and bass grooving along to an old lonesome-sounding ballad or burning up a hot, fast instrumental. At a music festival, seeing amateur musicians who have never played together before open up their cases, take out their instruments, and start playing tunes together as if they've been doing it for years isn't unusual. Musicians call these impromptu get-togethers *jam sessions*.

Musicians can play together in such a spontaneous way because they share a similar repertoire of songs and have internalized and put into practice some rules for effective group music making. If you listen closely to a great bluegrass or old-time band performance, you can hear that the roles of the different instruments seem to change from one moment to the next. At times, the banjo is out front and the center of attention, other times when the banjo is very much in the background, and then you recognize those moments when the banjo is somewhere in between these two extremes. When playing with others, you assume different musical roles with your banjo as you play a song from beginning to end.

In this section, I talk about some of the most important rules for playing with a group and discuss how you can put them to use as a brand new banjo player.

Perhaps the two most important aspects of playing with others are to maintain a great rhythmic groove that makes the band sound good and to control your volume. The easiest way to achieve good rhythm is to play simple things well. Your right hand not only controls your volume, but also communicates the heart and soul of your playing. Simplicity and drive in your playing creates musical space for others to play their best and for you to express your own emotions most powerfully. A successful jam session is one in which every musician feels that they're successfully contributing to the overall sound of the group.

Lead playing: Shining the spotlight on yourself

Lead playing has to do with those times when you're the center of attention in your band or during a jam session. If you're playing a well-known banjo instrumental like "Cripple Creek" or "Foggy Mountain Breakdown," you'll probably start the song by setting the tempo and playing all the way through the tune one time before handing off the lead to the next willing instrumentalist. If you've kicked off an instrumental, you're most likely to be the last one to play it as well, so have some kind of ending ready if you've chosen (or *called*) the tune in a jam session.

If you're playing a song with vocals, you may get the chance to play a banjo solo only once during the tune, either at the very beginning of the song or after a chorus. That's okay! You can have just as much fun in vocal tunes by playing banjo backup and singing your heart out on the choruses!

When you play lead (also called *taking a solo* or *break*), you call on everything you know as a banjo player to make your playing sound its best. At first, successfully playing a short, memorized arrangement of a song is enough of an accomplishment. As you become a more skilled player, you rely on the chord progression of the song to create new ways of playing a solo right on the spot (this creative process is called *improvisation*). Musicians spend an entire lifetime becoming great improvisers, so don't necessarily expect this to happen to you for a little while. The best journeys with the banjo are taken one step at a time!

When playing a solo, playing at full volume is fine, but don't forget to keep track of the rhythm of those around you as you play. Because banjo players play so many notes in comparison to the other players in the band, you may find yourself tending to push the tempo when you get excited (which usually occurs when you're playing lead). Racing away from the rest of the band is easy if you aren't careful, so as you're shredding through a great solo, keep an ear on the ongoing rhythm of the song and try your best to play in good time!

If you can't hear the other instrumentalists when they're playing lead, you're probably playing with too much force. In this case, reduce your volume until you can hear what everyone else is playing. By doing this, you can enjoy what others are playing a lot more, and in turn, others will enjoy playing music with you!

Backup playing: Allowing others to stand out

For every moment that you're the star of the show, you'll have many more occasions when you give it everything you've got to make those around you sound *their* best. *Backup playing* includes all the different techniques that a banjo player uses to accompany others and is perhaps the highest achievement of great banjo playing.

Because the banjo can so easily overpower other instruments during a jam session or in a band, a simple chording technique is sometimes the best way to allow others to be easily heard, especially if a singer is singing quietly or if you're playing backup to a guitar or mandolin solo (which never seem to be able to pick up as much volume as the beloved banjo). Bluegrass musicians call this chording technique *vamping*.

At other times, you want to keep a steady flow of notes going with the banjo, changing chords at the same time as other musicians. With this kind of backup (which sounds especially good when accompanying a singer or a fiddle solo), you're keeping the energy flowing by doing what the banjo does best with roll patterns and basic accompaniment techniques. To read more about these ideas, you can flip over to Chapters 4 and 8.

Part II
Let's Pick! The Basic Ingredients

The 5th Wave   By Rich Tennant

"Now this little plant is called Emma.
Emma blooms best to the melodic roll
patterns of Earl Scruggs."

In this part . . .

Clawhammer and bluegrass styles are the two most popular ways of playing banjo today, and I cover both approaches in this part. I help you to find a comfortable right-hand position and present the basic picking patterns used in bluegrass and clawhammer banjo playing. You can then make your playing sound more authentic by incorporating left-hand slides, hammer-ons, pull-offs, and chokes, and even discover how to find a melody on the banjo and play it by using either clawhammer or bluegrass techniques. This part closes with beginners' bluegrass and clawhammer versions of four popular banjo tunes.

Chapter 4

Getting Right with the Right Hand

In This Chapter

▶ Getting authentic banjo sounds with the right hand

▶ Understanding the right-hand basics of clawhammer and bluegrass techniques

▶ Accompanying songs in clawhammer and bluegrass styles

*T*he right-hand positions and basic playing techniques for the clawhammer and bluegrass styles are the two most popular banjo playing styles in use today. Most players from amateur to professional use these same techniques to make banjo music of all kinds.

These right-hand techniques are unique to the banjo and sound different from what you would hear on instruments like the guitar and mandolin. You may notice an immediate difference in your playing after just a few minutes of practice with these patterns. After you become comfortable with the exercises in this chapter, you can put your new skills to work by playing along with two tunes. You'll be well on your way to becoming a good banjo player!

Whether it's clawhammer or bluegrass, playing the banjo makes you part of a living and ever-evolving musical tradition. Each new generation of players, amateur and professional alike, makes its own unique contribution. Now it's time for *you* to start making your contribution by getting out your banjo and practicing the right-hand basics of clawhammer and bluegrass banjo.

Clawhammer and Bluegrass: Down-Picking and Up-Picking

When you're talking about the banjo, the terms *clawhammer* and *bluegrass* refer to two different ways of striking the strings of your banjo with the right hand. I describe these different approaches in the following:

> ✔ **Clawhammer** technique is sometimes called a *down-picking* approach to banjo playing because the right-hand fingers strike the strings in a downward motion. Clawhammer is the older of these two ways of playing the banjo, with historical roots that can be traced back several centuries to the African ancestry of the banjo (for more on these historical roots, check out Chapter 7).
>
> ✔ **Bluegrass** is known as an *up-picking* approach, because the right-hand index and middle fingers strike the strings in an upward motion, with the right-hand fingers moving in towards the palm of your right hand and the thumb moving in a downward direction. North Carolina banjo player Earl Scruggs is largely responsible for creating the bluegrass banjo style, bringing it to national attention in the late 1940s and early 1950s.

Both the clawhammer and bluegrass styles draw attention to the high-pitched 5th string in some way. Within easy reach of the right hand thumb, the 5th string is a big part of what makes banjo music sound unique. As you work through this chapter, take note of how the 5th string is used in each style and also how the melody of a song is played, and you can be well on your way to understanding what banjo music is all about.

Clawhammer Right-Hand Basics

Clawhammer banjo combines melody and rhythm in a way that makes people want to get up and dance. This playing style sounds unlike anything else in American music! The exact origin of word *clawhammer* is unknown. However, the term seems to describe the desired shape of the right-hand thumb when playing this technique — mimicking the "claw" of the top part of a standard nail hammer (hence clawhammer).

Other musicians relate the term to the hammer-like downward movement that's used to strike the strings. Many West African-type banjos (see Figure 4-1) have been played in similar ways for centuries, but the specific rhythms, techniques, and sounds of clawhammer banjo were developed in the southern United States from the mid-19th to the early-20th centuries. When you play clawhammer banjo, you're connecting to a very deep current of musical world history!

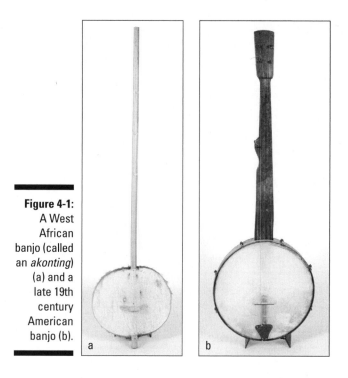

Figure 4-1:
A West African banjo (called an *akonting*) (a) and a late 19th century American banjo (b).

Finding a good right-hand position

Good right-hand technique is the most important aspect of clawhammer playing. Finding a comfortable and stable right-hand position to enable your fingers and thumb to do their work is the first step towards this goal. Here's a step-by-step guide to finding a position that works for you:

1. **With your palm and wrist parallel to the banjo head, grab the top of the 5th string with your right-hand thumb over the banjo head, not too far from where the neck joins the banjo pot.**

2. **While still holding the thumb against the 5th string, bring your right-hand fingers into your hand and make a fist; relax the fingers just a bit, keeping them flexed at such an angle that the fingernails are parallel to the banjo head and the fingers are no more than one or two inches above the strings.**

   Your hand should now look like the hand in Figure 4-2a.

3. **Play the 3rd string by moving down and across it with your right hand index finger, moving the hand from the wrist (see Figure 4-2b).**

Strike the string with enough downward force so that your index finger comes to rest against the 2nd string (as seen in Figure 4-2c). Some players also use their forearm in addition to their wrist to get a more forceful hand motion. Note that the right-hand thumb stays in contact with the 5th string throughout this exercise.

Your fingers should maintain the same position as your hand moves down to allow the index finger to strike the string — don't let the fingers flip out as they meet the strings. The fingers need to stay fairly stiff so that the index finger can provide resistance against the string, but you don't want to be *too* tense. Likewise, keep the wrist unlocked but not actually loose. The more you practice the techniques in this chapter, the more you can get the hang of playing clawhammer style with the "loose stiffness" that you need to get a good sound.

Figure 4-2:
Resting the right-hand thumb against the 5th string (a); Striking the 3rd string with the right hand index finger (b); Letting the finger come to rest against the second string (c).

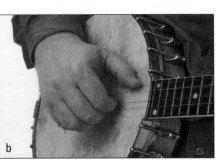

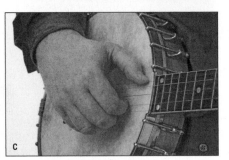

Playing your first clawhammer notes

After you've got a good hand position (see preceding section), it's time to try a few exercises to get used to striking the strings in the clawhammer style. Clawhammer is very much an individualized approach to banjo playing. Even the best players play in a personalized way, doing what works best for them.

Although I set some general guidelines for you here, experiment with different ways of doing things to see what works best for you. Seek out other players for advice whenever you can, but go for what sounds good and feels the most natural to you.

You can work up to playing the basic clawhammer strum by first getting comfortable striking individual notes. In the exercises to follow, I suggest that you use the right-hand index finger for playing melody notes (as indicated with the small letter *i* underneath each note in the banjo tab). However, the right-hand middle finger is another option preferred by many players. Try playing both ways and go with what feels best to you.

Here are some tips for developing good right-hand clawhammer technique:

- ✔ Having your finger knock the head after striking the string is okay (the *head* is the round, white top surface of the banjo; for more on banjo parts, check out Chapter 1). Remember, clawhammer is a percussive and rhythmic approach to playing the banjo. Don't be afraid to make some noise!

- ✔ Most players use their index or middle fingernails to get a good clawhammer sound. In lieu of fingernails, you can use fingerpicks as an extension of the fingernail but be sure to place the pick so that it covers the nail, not the pad of the finger as in bluegrass technique (see the section "Choosing and fitting thumbpicks and fingerpicks" later in this chapter).

  Try playing without picks first to see what kind of sound you get, and then play with picks if you think your fingernails aren't long enough to get enough contact with the strings.

- ✔ Remember that your finger is moving both *down* into the string and *down* towards the floor. Work towards developing a quick, decisive movement from the wrist that keeps your hand in control.

- ✔ When your index or middle finger plays the 2nd, 3rd, or 4th strings, it usually comes to rest against the next highest string.

- ✔ Some players bend their thumb at the joint to get that "claw" effect of hooking the finger underneath the strings. Other players extended the thumb outward. Again, try both and see which works best for you.

Melody-note exercises

Try playing individual notes on the 1st, 2nd, 3rd, and 4th strings with your right-hand index or middle finger (see Tab 4-1, which is Track 10 on the CD). As you slowly play these individual notes, focus on your hand position and technique. Are you moving from the wrist? Are you practicing with good economy of motion (no swooping right hand like guitar player Pete Townsend)? Does your finger maintain its bent shape when it meets the string?

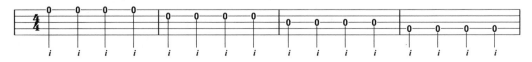

Tab 4-1: Clawhammer right hand melody note exercise 1 (Track 10).

As you get more comfortable with this first melody-note exercise, try playing different strings in succession in whatever order comes to mind. Tab 4-2 (Track 11) shows some examples.

Tab 4-2: Clawhammer right hand melody note exercise 2 (Track 11).

Brush exercise

The brush follows the melody note in basic clawhammer banjo technique. In banjo tab, the right-hand indication for the brush is the letter *b*, found below the corresponding notes in the tab staff.

With the brush, you get to choose which right-hand finger (or fingers) to use and how many strings to strike, but you don't have to decide exactly how you're going to do brush right now. Just keep trying different combinations and in time, you'll decide upon the way that works best for you. However, if you aren't sure where to start, first try brushing across the top two or three strings with just the middle finger by itself. Next, add the ring finger, using both fingers to brush across the top strings. Now try the index finger by itself.

All part of the old-time way

Clawhammer banjo is also known as frailing, rapping, or banging on the banjo. In the mid-19th century, this way of playing was called *stroke style* in banjo instructional manuals. These terms are all strange to use to describe a way of playing a musical instrument, but in this case, they're good ones because they all describe what the right hand is doing when playing the banjo in this way.

Clawhammer banjo is also frequently called old-time banjo, but these terms aren't synonymous.

Old-time refers to a wide variety of folk-based, non-bluegrass banjo techniques. Record companies in the 1920s used the term *old-time* as a descriptive label on 78 rpm recordings to refer to songs or artists with some kind of rural connection. The term stuck and today *old-time* now applies to a wide variety of string band music with guitars, fiddles, mandolins, and banjos. Clawhammer is one type of old-time banjo playing, but many other ways of playing banjo are also called old-time by the musicians who play them.

Whatever fingers you use, try striking just the 1st string alone for the brush. Then try the top two, top three, and finally all four strings (that is, excluding the 5th string) with any combination of right-hand index and middle fingers. Although the brush is most commonly played across the top two or three strings (all four is uncommon), you need to get used to the feel and sound you get with each brush. Don't forget to maintain a consistent, bent finger shape as you hit the strings. Try playing Tab 4-3 and listen to Track 12 on the CD.

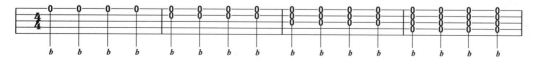

Tab 4-3: Clawhammer right-hand brush exercise (Track 12).

5th-string exercise

After you have a good feel for the brush (see the preceding section) try combining the brush with the 5th string. This time, as you play the brush with a downward motion of either the index or middle fingers, remember to bring the thumb against the 5th string as you complete the brush (as shown in

Figure 4-3a). You're now ready to play with the 5th string with a downward and sideways motion from the thumb. Don't be afraid to really snap this note with your right-hand thumb, bringing the right hand above the strings after the thumb has done its work (as shown in Figure 4-3b).

Figure 4-3:
Bringing the thumb to rest against the 5th string after the claw-hammer brush (a); Raising the hand off of the banjo head after striking the 5th string (b).

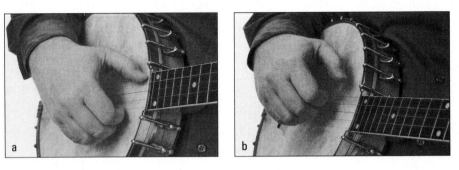

Listen to Track 13 and try the exercise in Tab 4-4.

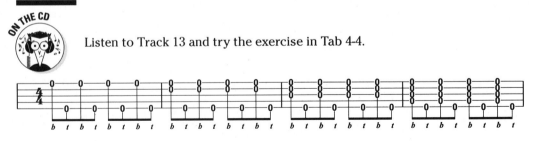

Tab 4-4: Clawhammer right-hand brush and 5th-string exercise (Track 13).

Putting it all together: Melody note + brush + 5th string

If you combine the three movements from the preceding sections, you get the basic clawhammer right-hand technique. The first note that you hit is the melody note, played on either the 1st, 2nd, 3rd, or 4th strings. This step is followed by the brush and ends with the thumb striking the 5th string. The first note lasts twice as long as the brush and 5th-string notes.

Players often describe the rhythm that they're after like this: BUM - dit - ty / BUM - dit -ty, with the emphasis on the "BUM" (sorry, no offense intended!). Tab 4-5 shows what this rhythm looks like, and you can hear it on Track 14 of the CD.

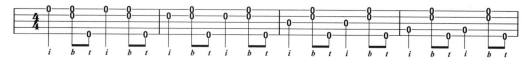

Tab 4-5: Basic clawhammer technique exercise 1 (Track 14).

Each measure begins with a different melody-note string, so try practicing one measure over and over again before going on to the next. When you're comfortable starting with any of the four strings, you can then begin to mix up the melody notes, as shown in Tab 4-6 (Track 15).

Tab 4-6: Mixing up melody notes: basic clawhammer technique exercise 2 (Track 15).

To go one step further, you can try the basic clawhammer technique with the G, C, and D7 chords (see Tab 4-7, which is Track 16). Although I suggest that you use particular index melody notes for each chord, try as many different string options as you can, from 1st to 4th, on each beat. (You need all of these choices when you play melodies in Chapter 6.)

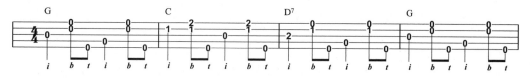

Tab 4-7: Using clawhammer technique for the G, C, and D7 chords (Track 16).

Using clawhammer banjo as accompaniment

Basic clawhammer technique is great to use as an accompaniment to all kinds of songs.

The first note that you strike in basic clawhammer technique (which I call the *melody note* in the previous sections) is dependent on the chord that you're playing (more on this in Chapter 6).

For now, follow the guide in Tab 4-7 in choosing the melody notes for the G, C, and D7 chords and play along to the following tunes in Tab 4-8 (Track 17) and Tab 4-9 (Track 18).

Tab 4-8: "Red River Valley" with clawhammer accompaniment (Track 17).

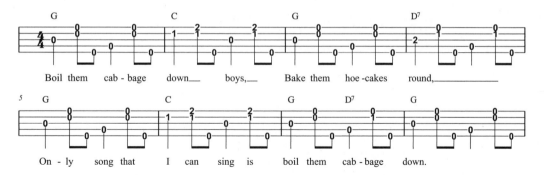

Tab 4-9: "Boil Them Cabbage Down" with clawhammer accompaniment (Track 18).

Bluegrass Right-Hand Basics

Bluegrass style banjo originated with the innovations of Earl Scruggs, who burst upon the national scene in the mid-1940s. The bluegrass style is characterized by a flurry of fast, brilliant-sounding notes and is the sound behind all-time banjo classics such as Scruggs' "Foggy Mountain Breakdown" and "Dueling Banjos." Although this way of playing the banjo is at the foundation of the bluegrass style, banjo players such as Béla Fleck and Alison Brown have used this approach as a starting point for incredible musical journeys into classical, jazz, and rock styles.

Bluegrass banjo playing uses the thumb, index finger, and middle fingers of the right hand and (for this reason) is sometimes called *three-finger picking*. Because banjo players always go for the shortest description, the term *three-finger picking* has stuck over the years even though it would be more accurate to call it a "thumb and two finger" style. Whether you call it bluegrass or three-finger style, this sound is most frequently heard on recordings and is the most widely played around the world today.

Just like when you're figuring out how to play clawhammer banjo (see previous sections), the biggest challenge with the bluegrass style is in getting a comfortable right-hand position that enables you to play clearly and quickly. And because bluegrass banjo players use picks on their thumbs and index and middle fingers, part of being able to play bluegrass comfortably is finding the right picks. In the following sections, you can select and fit the picks you need and find a right-hand playing position that works well for you.

Before Earl, 19th-century musicians played the banjo by using fingerpicking techniques borrowed from the guitar. Later, early 20th century rural musicians, such as Uncle Dave Macon and Charlie Poole, featured simplified (at least compared to Earl!) two- and three-finger picking techniques on their early country recordings.

Choosing and fitting thumbpicks and fingerpicks

Bluegrass banjo players use metal fingerpicks on their right-hand index and middle fingers and a plastic thumbpick on their thumb. Initially, you may find that getting used to the feel of these picks is a struggle. It may feel like you're wearing a coat of armor over the ends of your fingers, and you may hear a lot of scratchy sounds when you first start to play. However, just about everyone gets used to the feel of the picks after a few weeks, and you'll appreciate the extra volume and drive that the picks lend to your playing.

A visit to a music store can reveal numerous kinds of picks available for the thumb and fingers. In the following sections, I describe what you want to look for when you're picking up some picks.

The thumbpick

A *thumbpick* consists of a flat striking surface and a bent section that wraps the pick around the thumb. Most players prefer thumbpicks made from plastic, but a few players prefer the fit and sound of a metal thumbpick. In either case, choose a thumbpick that fits as snugly as possible, with the blade facing in towards your right-hand fingers.

Don't mistake a thumbpick for the more common flatpick, which is a pick used by guitarists and mandolin players. A *flatpick* is held in the right hand by the thumb *and* fingers. You can see the difference between the two in Figure 4-4. Don't be afraid to ask a music store employee or fellow musician to lead you in the direction of the thumbpicks.

Thumbpicks come in different sizes, thicknesses, and striking surface *(blade)* angles (see Figure 4-5), so try as many different brands as you can to see what feels the most comfortable to you. If you're like most players, you end up trying many different kinds of thumbpicks, and your preferences change as time goes on. There's nothing wrong with this! As in so many other aspects of banjo playing, you can't find one right answer. However, many professional players prefer a thumbpick that isn't too thin and doesn't have too short of a blade.

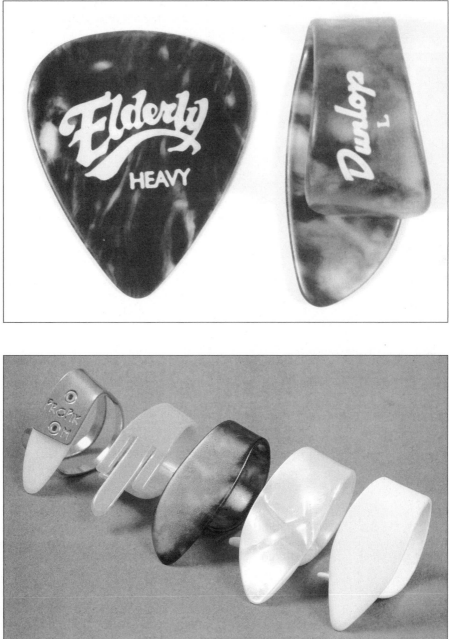

Figure 4-4:
Comparing
a flatpick
(left) and a
thumbpick
(right).

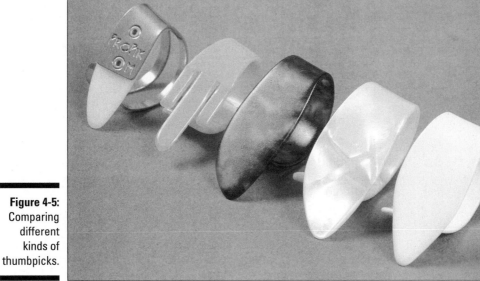

Figure 4-5:
Comparing
different
kinds of
thumbpicks.

As you fit the thumbpick onto your thumb, don't push it too far up your thumb — about halfway between the first joint and the end of your thumb is about right for most players (you can check out this placement in Figure 4-6).

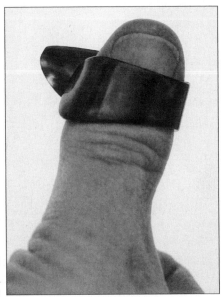

Figure 4-6:
Proper
placement
of thumbpick
on right
hand thumb.

If your thumb is too small for your favorite pick to fit tightly, don't be afraid to add surgical or duct tape to the inside of the pick to make it fit more snugly. Some players even place their thumbpick in boiling water for a few seconds to soften the plastic. You can then shape the pick to fit tighter after carefully removing the pick from the water. Do I have to tell you not to fetch the pick out of the water with your hands? Of course not! Banjo players are smarter than the average human being.

At prices around $1 to $4, thumbpicks aren't expensive, so go ahead and purchase a bunch of different kinds to see which one suits your playing best. Look for thumbpicks by Dunlop, Golden Gate, National, Propik, and Zookies, among others, for good sound and playability.

The fingerpick

Like thumbpicks, metal *fingerpicks* consist of a blade-shaped striking surface joined to a collar that holds the fingerpick around the end of the finger. You want to fit the picks on your index and middle fingers so that the striking surface is on the opposite side of your hand from your fingernail (as shown in Figure 4-7).

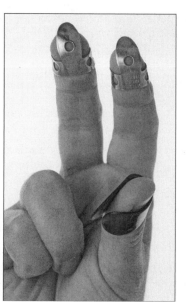

Figure 4-7:
Fitting the fingerpicks on the right-hand index and middle fingers.

You can find many different kinds of fingerpicks on the market today (you can have a look at a few of them in Figure 4-8). They vary in size and thickness and also in metal composition. Some fingerpicks have more of a curved striking surface while others have a flat blade. Some have holes in them and others don't. Your best bet is to experiment with different fingerpicks to see which ones fit the most comfortably and — most importantly — sound the best to you.

Fingerpicks tend to be more expensive than thumbpicks, ranging in price from $3 a pair to $35 for a pair of handcrafted stainless-steel picks. Look for metal fingerpicks from Propik, National, Dunlop, Showcase 41, and Sammy Shelor, among others, for the tone preferred by bluegrass players.

Figure 4-8:
Comparing different kinds of fingerpicks.

You need to bend the fingerpicks to get a good fit, because they don't usually come straight from the store ready to use without modification. Here's how you do it:

1. **Place the pick on the end of your finger with the collar placed between the end of the finger and the first joint.**

   Don't place the collar at the joint itself because that's too far up the finger.

2. **Grasp either side of the collar with your left-hand thumb and index finger and squeeze it so that the fit is snug but not too tight on the end of your finger.**

   Remember that you want the blade of the pick extending just past the end of your finger. If your pick fits well, you can stop here, but most players also like to bend the blade back a bit to match the natural curve of the end of the finger, which I explain in the next step.

3. **If your pick isn't too heavy, you should be able to successfully bend the blade by pushing down on the pick against a table top or another hard surface (as shown in Figure 4-9).**

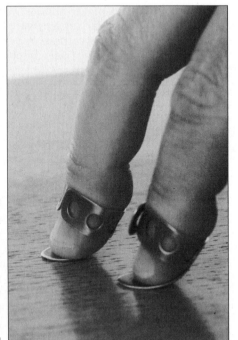

Figure 4-9:
Adjusting
the bend
of the
fingerpick
blade by
pushing on
a table top.

One last modification that some players make to their fingerpicks is that they fit the pick on the finger at a slight angle, so that when the finger strikes the banjo string, the pick will then meet the string at more of a straight, or parallel, angle. This modification can result in a fuller, more-pleasing tone as well as added volume. You don't need to worry about this right now, but you may want to try angling the fingerpick as you gain more experience playing.

Acquiring a good right-hand position

I bet that one of the main reasons that you love bluegrass banjo music is that it's so incredibly *fast* and *loud*. Me too! In order to play at those tempos that approach the speed of sound, you need to find a right-hand position that provides a stable foundation for the thumb and fingers to do all that incredible picking.

Relaxation is key to great right-hand bluegrass technique, so remember to constantly check for tension from your shoulder to your fingertips as you work through the following steps to find a comfortable right-hand position.

Getting set

Here's a quick way to get your right hand set in a good bluegrass playing position. I've used this method successfully with hundreds of players, and it can work for you too. Try the following steps while sitting comfortably in a chair without arms, with your feet resting on the floor (for info on the parts of the banjo I mention in this section, see Chapter 1):

1. **Relax your right arm and hand, letting the arm dangle loosely at the side of your body (see Figure 4-10a).**

2. **Bring the right hand up, resting it on your right leg and keeping your arm relaxed (see Figure 4-10b).**

   Note the position of your right hand: When the hand is fully relaxed, it should assume a cupped position with all the finger joints slightly bent.

3. **Place your right forearm against the armrest (or against the side of the banjo, if your instrument doesn't have an armrest), positioning the right hand to be over and above the banjo strings (see Figure 4-10c).**

   You don't want to position your right hand either too high or too low in relation to the strings. If your right-hand ring and pinky fingers are touching the banjo strings, your right hand is positioned too high. On the other hand, if you feel you're having to reach in quite a bit to play the 3rd string with your index, your hand is probably positioned too low in relation to the strings.

4. **Slide your right forearm back along the armrest until the ring and pinky finger come to rest on the banjo head close to the bridge, but aren't actually touching it (see Figure 4-10d).**

By completing Step 4, your right-hand thumb, index, and middle fingers should be set in a good playing position. You may have to move the right elbow out just a bit to allow your fingers to contact the head. As you anchor the right hand with your ring and/or little fingers, arch your wrist slightly so that your wrist and forearm don't touch the banjo head.

An arched wrist is just about essential for getting the right-hand fingers in a good position for playing. However, falling into the bad habit of bending the wrist in the opposite direction, towards the banjo head, is a common problem with many new players. This position only adds tension to your right hand, forearm, and shoulder, and makes it difficult for the thumb to easily reach all the strings that it needs to play.

Some players arch their wrists just a little and others a lot. You can work out the fine details of your wrist arch as you continue to practice. For now, try to remember to keep at least a bit of an arch in the wrist, and you'll be fine!

Putting your thumb and fingers to good use

With your hand positioned over the strings and ready to play (see the preceding section), you're ready to take a look at how the thumb and fingers actually strike the strings in bluegrass style:

✔ The thumb is the most active of the three striking fingers, and you need it to be in position to play the 5th, 4th, 3rd, and 2nd strings as needed.

✔ Your index finger plays the 3rd and 2nd strings.

✔ Your middle finger plays the 1st string.

Refer back to that cupped hand position that you used in Step 2 in the preceding section to set your right hand on the banjo head. That's your starting point as you begin to play. Working from this relaxed position, you want to strike the strings by sweeping the thumb across the strings, using the joint that's closest to the hand. If your wrist is arched, the thumb should move across and slightly up as you strike each string. You want to avoid hitting the adjacent string with your thumb.

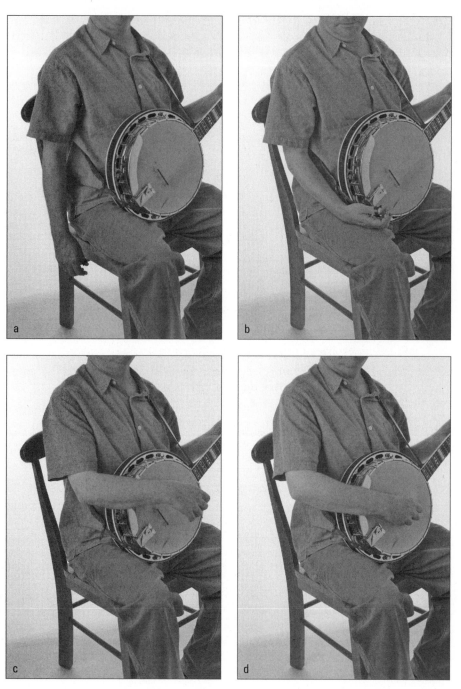

Figure 4-10:
Follow these
steps to find
a good
right-hand
bluegrass
position.

Now try playing the 5th through the 2nd strings with your thumb, playing each string four times slowly in succession before moving on to the next string, as indicated in Tab 4-10, which is Track 19 on the CD. Listen carefully to the result. Does the note ring clearly? Is there enough volume? Is your hand relaxed as you pick the string with the thumb? If so, good work!

Tab 4-10: Right-hand thumb bluegrass exercise (Track 19).

After you have your thumb movement down pat, you must move on to play notes with the index and middle fingers (be sure to refer to Tab 4-11 and Track 20 as needed). You want to use primarily the first joint — the one that's closest to the hand — to play strings with your index and middle fingers:

1. **Try playing the 3rd and 2nd strings with your index finger and the 1st string with your middle finger.**

   By using mostly the first joint to move the end of the finger pick across each string, you will almost feel as if you're pushing down on the string.

2. **Move the index or middle finger straight towards the palm of your right hand after picking a string.**

3. **After the follow-through in Step 2, simply relax the finger so that it can return to its original position.**

   Don't deliberately sweep it outward from your palm.

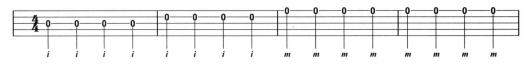

Tab 4-11: Right-hand index and middle finger bluegrass exercise (Track 20).

I know that these steps can sound quite complicated! However, I'm actually describing in great detail what usually occurs quite naturally after your hand is properly positioned on the banjo head. Don't think too hard about this process (after all, we *are* banjo players, aren't we?). Go for what feels effortless and natural and for what gives you the best tone and most volume.

Figure 4-11 shows my hand position when using the right-hand thumb to play the third string, the right-hand index to play the second string and the right-hand middle to play the first string. If your fingers and hand look close to mine, you're on the right track!

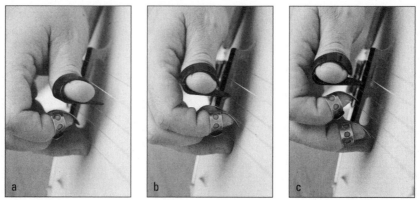

Figure 4-11: Picking with the right-hand thumb (a), index (b), and middle fingers (c).

Staying relaxed while picking with the right hand is important. If you're moving on to the exercises in the next few sections, try to imagine that your fingers are doing all the work, while your shoulder, arm, wrist, and top of your hand stay loose and relaxed.

Playing roll patterns

Roll patterns are repeated right-hand sequences of notes that are the basic building blocks for the rippling, fast sound of bluegrass banjo. While guitarists, fiddlers, and mandolin players practice scales, bluegrass banjo players work on roll patterns. You can use roll patterns as the foundation for accompanying other players and singers and for playing solos and melodies on the banjo.

Roll patterns are made up of both specific sequences of repeated right-hand finger movements as well as the actual strings that are played (these aren't always the same, because you can play different strings, using the same pattern of right-hand fingers). For most songs, roll patterns are made up of repeated phrases of eight notes that are equal in length. You usually won't use the same right-hand finger twice in a row or strike the same string twice in succession in playing a roll pattern.

94

Part II: Let's Pick! The Basic Ingredients

TECHNICAL STUFF

The great debate: One anchor finger or two?

One of the raging controversies in the bluegrass banjo world over the last several decades is whether it's best to anchor the right hand with both the ring and pinky fingers or whether it's alright to anchor with just the pinky finger. Most beginning players have trouble keeping the ring finger anchored on the head, especially when playing a note with the middle right-hand finger, because the muscles of these two fingers are interdependent and playing a string with the middle finger often causes the ring finger to move in tandem with it.

The majority of professional players have figured out how to anchor both the right-hand ring and pinky fingers on the banjo head (see the accompanying photo a), but several outstanding

players anchor just the pinky finger (see photo b), letting the ring finger move with the middle finger. I've taught many beginning students to anchor both fingers by urging them to play for a few weeks by using just the ring finger for an anchor. After this finger is trained to stay on the banjo head, having the pinky finger join it is a relatively easy matter. A proper arch to your wrist should really help in training the ring finger to stay on the banjo head.

The bottom line? My advice is to try supporting the right hand by using both fingers if you can, but if it feels better to use just the pinky finger for support, go for it! If you stay relaxed and you're finding you're getting a good sound, you can play well either way!

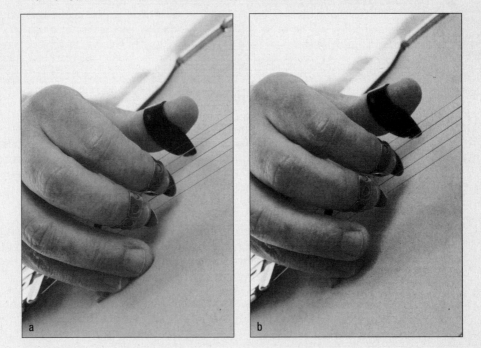

a

b

The alternating-thumb roll, the forward-backward roll, and the forward roll are the basic roll patterns that get you into the fast lane on the bluegrass banjo highway, and I explain them in the following sections.

Alternating thumb roll

The *alternating thumb roll* is sometimes called the *thumb in-and-out roll*. Whatever you call it, the right-hand thumb plays every other note in this eight-note roll, and you alternate using your index and middle fingers in between using your thumb. Note that this roll is actually made up of a four-note sequence that's repeated.

Here are the details on how the alternating-thumb roll works:

- ✔ The order in which you use the right-hand fingers is as follows: thumb, index, thumb, middle, thumb, index, thumb, middle.

- ✔ A common string sequence for this roll is: 3rd string, 2nd string, 5th string, 1st string, 4th string, 2nd string, 5th string, 1st string. In tablature, the alternating thumb roll played with the G, C, and D7 chords looks like what you can see in Tab 4-12, which is Track 21 on the CD.

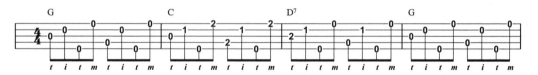

Tab 4-12: The alternating thumb roll with G, C, and D7 chords (Track 21).

As you play this roll, try to pick each note clearly, making sure that your index and middle fingers are producing enough volume in comparison with the thumb. Play the roll slowly and evenly and try not to stop as you change from the G to the C and to the D7 chords.

The forward-backward roll

The *forward-backward roll* is also known as the *forward-reverse roll* or the *reverse roll*. All of these labels suggest that this roll begins with the fingers moving in one direction but then doubles back in the opposite direction — and that's exactly what happens here:

- ✔ The order of right-hand fingers for this roll is: thumb, index, middle, thumb, middle, index, thumb, middle.

- ✔ A typical string sequence is as follows: 3rd string, 2nd string, 1st string, 5th string, 1st string, 2nd string, 3rd string, 1st string.

You can see what the forward-backward roll pattern played with the G, C, and D7 chords looks like in tablature in Tab 4-13, which is Track 22.

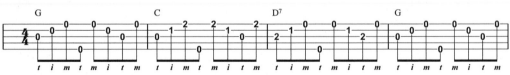

Tab 4-13: The forward-backward roll with G, C, and D7 chords (Track 22).

The forward roll

The *forward roll* is the pattern that gives bluegrass banjo its rhythmical and hard, driving sound. This pattern is a bit more difficult than the two rolls in the previous sections because this roll gathers notes into groups of three. You can find several different variations on the forward roll.

Here's a standard way of playing this roll:

- ✔ The order of right-hand fingers is thumb, middle, thumb, index, middle, thumb, index, middle.

- ✔ The string sequence for the G and D7 chords is: 3rd string, 1st string, 5th string, 3rd string, 1st string, 5th string, 3rd string, 1st string. Note that for the C chord, you substitute the 2nd string for the third string in this series. See Tab 4-14 and listen to Track 23.

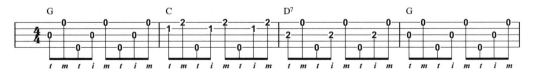

Tab 4-14: The forward roll with G, C, and D7 chords (Track 23).

Using bluegrass rolls as accompaniment

A great way to accompany other musicians or a singer is to use the rolls presented in the preceding section interchangeably in a song. Remember that you aren't really trying to play the melody of the song, but you're using the roll patterns to create a flowing accompaniment in the same way that a guitar or mandolin player strums his instrument.

Try accompanying "Red River Valley" (see Tab 4-15, which is Track 24) by using just the forward roll and "Boil Them Cabbage Down" (Tab 4-16, Track 25) by using the alternating thumb, reverse, and forward rolls interchangeably.

As you master these arrangements, feel free to mix and match the roll patterns in whatever way sounds good to you. As long as you stay in rhythm and start a new roll pattern on the first beat of each measure, you can't go wrong! If you make a mistake while practicing or playing along with the CD, that's okay. Just stop for a moment and join back in at the beginning of a new roll pattern as soon as you can.

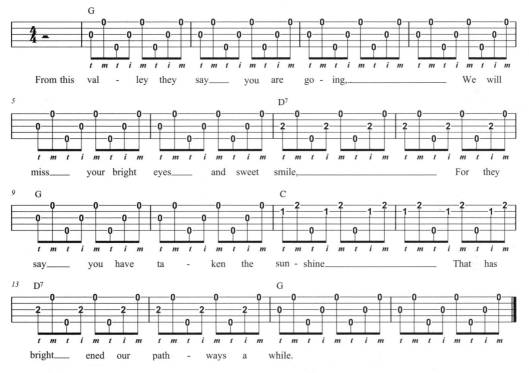

Tab 4-15: Accompanying "Red River Valley" using forward rolls (Track 24).

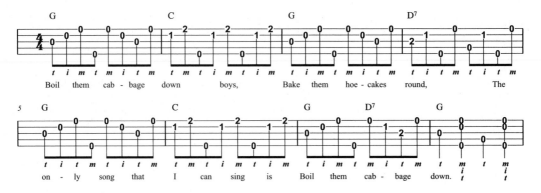

Tab 4-16: Accompanying "Boil Them Cabbage Down" using forward-backward, forward, and alternating thumb rolls (Track 25).

Chapter 5

Sliding, Hammering, and Pulling: Adding the Left Hand

In This Chapter

▶ Playing slides, hammer-ons, pull-offs, and chokes

▶ Using left-hand techniques in clawhammer and bluegrass banjo

*W*hether you're moving up or down the strings while fretting, coming down on the string to create a higher pitched note, snapping off the string to sound a lower pitched note or bending a fretted note up in pitch, the left hand has a lot to say in the world of banjo music. You can hear a big difference in your own playing after you can make the left hand not only talk the talk but also walk the walk!

In this chapter, you're introduced to the left-hand techniques that all banjo players use to make melodies flow more smoothly and sound more interesting and varied. All the techniques in this chapter focus on how the left-hand fingers can create notes that embellish what your right hand is picking. These left-hand techniques are similar for both clawhammer and bluegrass banjo and, when combined with the right hand, are the building blocks for both ways of playing the banjo.

You don't have to worry about playing the techniques in this chapter on the 5th string. The function of the 5th string in both clawhammer and bluegrass banjo is to provide a steady, high-pitched *drone* (a *drone* is a repeated pitch; bagpipes typically have low pitched drone notes while the banjo has a high pitched drone). Stick to strings 1 through 4 with these left-hand techniques and you'll be picking fine in no time!

As you gain mastery over each new left-hand technique presented in this chapter (the slide, hammer-on, pull-off, and choke), don't forget to have some fun with these ideas as you perfect them. Mix them up and play the different techniques at random to get used to moving from a slide to a hammer-on or a pull-off to a choke on different strings.

Approach the exercises in this chapter as if you're learning the vocabulary of a new language. As you gain more experience in playing, you'll encounter many more new phrases and gain greater skills in how to combine these phrases into meaningful musical expressions. If you've mastered the techniques in this chapter, you're off to a great start in "talking banjo," and you can confidently go on to the next step — learning some actual banjo tunes (which you can do in Chapter 6)!

Slipping into the Slide

You can't find anything quite like the sweeping sound of a well-played slide on the banjo, just like the ones you hear at the beginning of "Cripple Creek." *Slides* add emphasis to a melody note by moving to that note from another pitch. They can add a bluesy feeling to your banjo playing, resembling the sound of the lonesome wind, a baying hound, or even a speeding train.

To play the slide, you use a left-hand finger that's already fretting a string to sound a new note by moving up or down the banjo neck along the same string to a new fret. The left-hand technique you use is the same regardless of the string you're on. However, the frets that you begin and end each slide on vary according to which string you're playing.

In this section, you're introduced to the basic mechanics of the slide (using the 3rd string) and then move on to playing other slides on the 3rd string before going wild with additional slides on the 4th and 1st strings. (I don't include 2nd-string slides because they aren't as common.)

The secret to a good-sounding slide is to maintain enough fretting pressure with the left hand so that the sound isn't cut off.

Getting down the slide: The basics

To play a slide, check out each of the following steps (I use the 3rd string for the sake of example; you play slides on other strings too, starting and stopping at different frets, but use these basic mechanics for all strings):

1. **Press down (or *fret*) the 3rd string at the second fret with the middle finger of your left hand.**

   I tend to use the middle finger of my left hand for all the slides on all strings in this section, because I feel like I have the most control with this finger. However, depending upon what's happening with your left hand at a particular moment in a song, you may sometimes need to use another left-hand finger to execute a slide. The left-hand index finger is another good choice for any of the slides you encounter in this section.

2. **Pick the 3rd string with your right hand.**

   If you're playing clawhammer, move down across the string with your right-hand index finger (or your middle finger, if you've decided to use this finger for melody notes). If you're picking bluegrass, play the note with the right-hand thumb pick by moving down across the string.

3. **After the note has sounded, slide the left-hand middle finger along the 3rd string from the second fret to the fourth fret.**

   Keep exerting the same amount of pressure with the fretting finger as you originally used to fret the string and stop the finger just behind the fourth fret. You want to hear a continuous sound as your left-hand finger moves from one fret to another.

4. **Keep the left-hand finger fretted at the fourth fret and let the new note ring.**

Congratulations! You've just successfully played your first slide.

Just like you don't need a whole lot of pressure for the left-hand fingers to get a clear sound on a fretted note, you may also find that you don't need to exert much pressure with your fretting finger to get a good sound out of your slides. Experiment to find the least amount of fretting pressure you need to still maintain the ringing sound of the picked note as you slide from one fret to another.

Keep reading to find more slides you can play not only on the 3rd string, but also on the 4th and 1st strings too.

Trying 3rd-string slides

If you can play a slide on the 3rd string moving from the second to the fourth fret (I show you how in the preceding section), it's time to try two more 3rd-string slides, once again by using the left-hand middle finger.

You can tackle these 3rd-string slides in a few different ways. Both of these slides paint a banjo blues mood:

> ✔ **Slide from the second fret up to the third fret:** You can follow the same basic steps of a slide from the preceding section; just remember that you don't slide all the way to the fourth fret.

> ✔ **Slide from the third fret down to the second fret:** You carry out this slide in the same way as a slide that starts lower and moves higher. You're simply going in a different direction.

In banjo tablature, the *s* indication lets you know that you're supposed to slide. For example, you can see what these three 3rd-string slides look like in banjo tablature in Tab 5-1 and listen to Track 26.

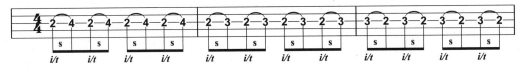

Tab 5-1: Playing 3rd-string slides: second to fourth fret; second to third fret; and third to second fret (Track 26).

Undertaking 4th-string slides

After conquering third-string slides (see preceding sections), you're ready to move on to the brave new world of the 4th-string slide. The 4th string is the lowest pitched string on your banjo. If you strike it with some force before you move your left-hand finger for the slide, you can get a booming slide that you can feel all the way into your belly (this is good, by the way).

The 4th string is thicker and heavier than your 3rd string, so don't be surprised if you have to fret a bit harder with your left-hand finger to sustain the sound of the note with your 4th-string slides.

Follow the basic instructions in the section "Getting down the slide: The basics" presented earlier in this chapter for the mechanics of the slide and don't forget to use your left-hand middle finger to fret the string for the following 4th-string slides (note that both of these slides end at the fifth fret):

> ✔ **Slide from the fourth fret up to the fifth fret:** You don't have far to go on this slide, but remember to apply the appropriate pressure so you can get the sound you're looking for.

✔ **Slide from the second fret up to the fifth fret:** Although this slide moves impressively three frets up the neck, other slides cover even more fretted territory. Remember that you don't want to hear all the pitches that lie between the beginning and end points of your slide. Make it a smooth, continuous swoop, and you'll be playing it the way that other banjo players like to hear it.

Check out the tablature for these two 4th-string slides in Tab 5-2, and listen to Track 26 on the CD.

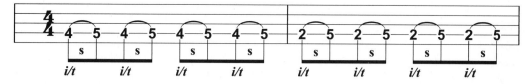

Tab 5-2: Playing 4th-string slides: fourth to fifth fret; and second to fifth fret (Track 26).

Focusing on 1st-string slides

You may need some slides on the 1st string every now and then to catch some high melody notes. You may notice that the following 1st-string slides are very similar to the 4th-string slides (you're just on a different string):

✔ **Slide from the fourth fret up to the fifth fret:** Because the 1st string is lighter in weight than the 3rd or 4th strings, sustaining the sound of this slide shouldn't take much pressure at all.

✔ **Slide from the second fret up to the fifth fret:** You're covering a greater distance with this slide, so use more pressure with the left-hand middle finger to sustain the note.

To get a feel for these 1st-string slides in tablature, take a look at Tab 5-3 and listen again to Track 26.

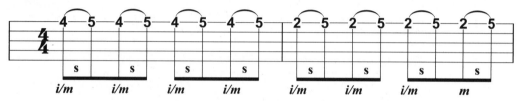

Tab 5-3: Playing first string slides: fourth to fifth fret; second to fifth fret (Track 26).

Nailing the Hammer-On

An aggressive and well-played hammer-on, like you hear at the very beginning of "Foggy Mountain Breakdown," can be one of the most exciting moments in banjo music. This technique lets everyone in the room know you've got a banjo, and you know how to use it! Hammer-ons can crack like a whip, its sound hitting you like a hair-raising blast of freezing-cold air. Hammer-ons are an important part of banjo music — and they're a heck of a lot of fun to play.

With the *hammer-on,* you create a new note with the left-hand fretting finger by bringing it down with some force on a string that's just been played by the right hand. You aren't moving *along* the string as you do with the slide (see the section "Slipping into the Slide"), but you're coming straight *down* on it with the tip of your finger — like a hammer. Like the slide, you use the hammer-on to embellish or emphasize a melody note — the note that's being "hammered on."

You can hammer-on either from an open string to a fretted string or from one fretted string to another, which I show you how to do in the following sections.

Playing open-string hammer-ons

You can get a feel for the open-string (unfretted) hammer-on by following these step-by-step instructions (for the sake of this example, go ahead and begin on the 4th string; you use the same procedure for different strings as well):

1. **Play the 4th string open with either the index finger of the right hand if you're a clawhammer player or the right-hand thumb if you're a bluegrass player.**

2. **Let the note ring for a moment.**

3. **While the open string is still sounding, push the string into a fretted position just behind the second fret with the left-hand middle finger (like a hammer).**

   You need to use enough speed with the left-hand finger so that the sound isn't cut off as your finger moves down to fret the string. You should hear an uninterrupted sound from beginning to end of the hammer-on, just as you do in the slide.

That's all there is to it. You've just played a hammer-on! Now you can try the same hammer-on on the 3rd and 1st strings, moving from the open string to the second fret on either string. Banjo players prefer to use fretted hammer-ons (see the following section) instead of open hammer-ons for the 2nd string, so you don't need to worry about this string right now!

You can check out what these three hammer-ons look like in tablature (the *h* indication tells you to play a hammer-on) by looking at Tab 5-4. And listen to Track 27.

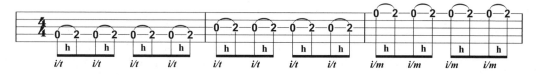
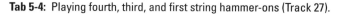

Tab 5-4: Playing fourth, third, and first string hammer-ons (Track 27).

Although you use some force to get your hammer-ons sounding right, try not to raise your left-hand finger too high above the fingerboard to achieve this (it's not like you're a baseball pitcher in a wind up — after all, it's just a hammer-on!). Keep your finger just above where you want to play the hammer-on, with the finger in a position that's fairly close to the banjo fingerboard (see Figure 5-1). When it's time to play the hammer-on, you can have more accuracy if your finger has to travel just a short distance to the fingerboard.

Giving fretted hammer-ons a chance

Fretted hammer-ons are a little trickier than open-string hammer-ons (see preceding section), because you're coordinating the movements of two left-hand fretting fingers. To get started, I want you to try one of the most awesome maneuvers you'll ever play on the banjo: the world-famous "Foggy Mountain Breakdown" 2nd-string hammer-on, and be sure to pay attention to the mechanics because you use this same technique for fretted hammer-ons on other strings:

1. **Fret the 2nd string at the second fret with the index finger of the left hand.**

2. **Play the 2nd string with either the index finger of the right hand (in clawhammer banjo) or the right-hand index finger or thumb (in bluegrass).**

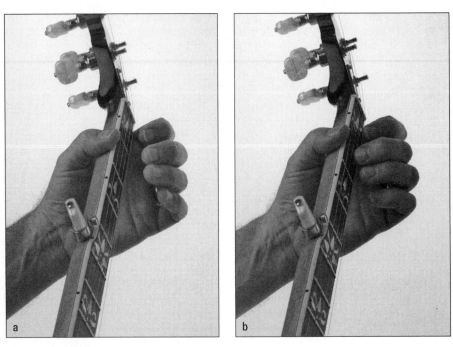

Figure 5-1:
The wrong (a) and correct (b) way to position your left-hand finger for a hammer-on.

3. **Let the note ring for a moment.**

4. **Bring down the left-hand middle finger just behind the third fret of the 2nd string, using enough force to sound a new note, and hold the middle finger down behind the third fret to let this string ring for a moment also.**

Give yourself a round of applause. You've just played two notes *exactly* like Earl Scruggs plays them — just 99,999 to go! (For more info on Earl Scruggs, check out Chapters 8 and 14.)

When you use this technique in bluegrass, you often play two of these hammer-ons right in a row. Try practicing the fretted hammer-on on the 2nd string many times in succession, keeping the left-hand index finger that's fretting the second fret down the entire time.

Now try this same hammer-on technique on the 3rd and 4th strings, again moving from the second fret to the third fret. (Although you can also play fretted hammer-ons on the 1st string, you don't need to worry about it to play any of the tunes in this book.) Check out the written fretted hammer-ons on the 2nd, 3rd, and 4th string in Tab 5-5, and listen to Track 28.

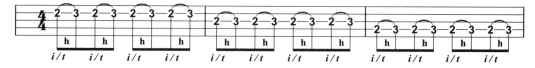

Tab 5-5: Playing fretted hammer-ons on the second, third and fourth strings (Track 28).

Pulling Off the Pull-Off

Like the hammer-on (see preceding section), the *pull-off* is another left-hand banjo technique that carries a lot of potential firepower. A pull-off can explode like a firecracker on the Fourth of July, be as mournful as a scorned lover's sigh, or as rhythmical as a horse's gallop. It's the most percussive of all the left-hand techniques and is generally used to connect a higher melody note to a lower note.

With the pull-off, the left-hand finger is already fretting a note on the banjo fingerboard. You create a new note by giving the string a slight sideways pull or push, either up or down (some folks use the term *push-off* for the latter kind of pull-off, but I use the term *pull-off* in this book to refer to both kinds). As your left-hand finger moves across the string, it snaps off the string literally sounding a note that can have as much power as a note played by a right-hand finger.

In this section, I show you how you can play pull-offs either from a fretted to an open string or from one fretted note to another on the same string. You can also use the pull-off in a special way that's unique to clawhammer style. I cover it all in the following section!

For most folks, pull-offs are a bit trickier than slides or hammer-ons. If you lift straight up off the string with your left-hand fretting finger, you likely won't snap the string with enough force for a strong enough pull-off note. The trick is getting used to the very small sideways movement that's also required of the fretting finger to pluck the string. Keep reading for more on this movement.

Digging into open-string pull-offs

You can start by taking the open-string pull-off step-by-step (I show you how to do it on the 1st string, but you can use this same technique on the 3rd and 4th strings):

1. **Fret the 1st string at the second fret with the middle finger of your left hand.**

2. **Play the 1st string with your right hand.**

   Use the index finger if you're playing clawhammer or your middle finger if you're playing bluegrass.

3. **Let the fretted note ring for a moment.**

4. **Pull the string with your left-hand finger to sound the open string.**

   Your left-hand finger should move both *sideways* (to pluck the string) and *up*.

Listen to the (hopefully) clear and beautiful sound of the open 1st string!

Banjo players don't use pull-offs often on the 2nd string but nothing is holding you back from trying this same pull-off on the 3rd and 4th strings, transitioning from the second fret to the open string, just as you did in the steps on the 1st string.

In banjo tablature, the letter *p* lets you know that a pull-off is in your very near future, as you can see in Tab 5-6. Give it a listen on Track 29 of the CD.

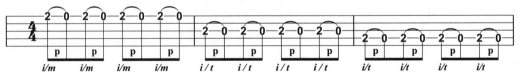

Tab 5-6: Playing open-string pull-offs on the 1st, 3rd, and 4th strings (Track 29).

Mastering fretted pull-offs

In addition to playing a pull-off to an open string (see preceding section), you can also play a pull-off to another fretted note. With fretted pull-offs, you want to make sure that you use your left hand to fret both notes at the same time before executing a pull-off.

The 3rd-string pull-off from the third to the second fret is a defining characteristic of the sound of bluegrass banjo. Here's how you "pull-off" a 3rd-string fretted pull-off (and be sure to note the technique, because you use this procedure for other strings as well):

1. **Fret the 3rd string at both the third fret with the left-hand middle finger and the second fret with your left-hand index finger (see Figure 5-2a).**

2. **Pull the string, moving both sideways and up, to avoid the 2nd string; as you pull-off with the middle finger, keep the index finger in place on the second fret (see Figure 5-2b).**

3. **Let the new note ring!**

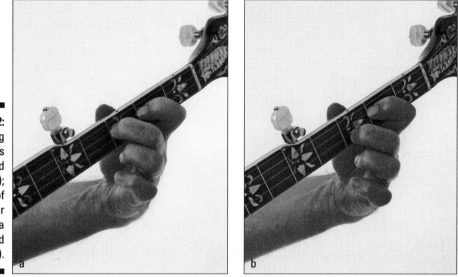

Figure 5-2:
Positioning
the fingers
for a fretted
pull-off (a);
position of
fingers after
playing a
fretted
pull-off (b).

Now try this fretted pull-off on the 1st and 4th strings (using the 2nd string isn't common), pulling off from the third to the second fret as you did on the 3rd string. You can take a gander at the tab for fretted pull-offs on the 1st, 3rd, and 4th strings in Tab 5-7, and listen to Track 30 on the CD.

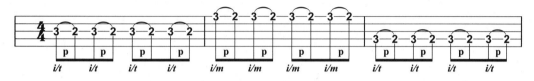

Tab 5-7: Playing fretted pull-offs on the third, first and fourth strings (Track 30).

Headbanger's banjo: A heavy metal lick

You can play *anything* on the banjo — including rock and roll! Listen to Track 31 on the CD and check out the signature heavy-metal banjo lick shown in Tab 5-8, which consists of a fretted hammer-on followed by a pull-off. Repeat for as long as possible or as long as your audience can stand it (whichever comes first).

Note that you use only the right hand for the first note of this lick, freeing up the right arm to make lots of sweeping big stadium rock hand gestures. This endless (and some might say *mindless*) lick can be played anywhere on the neck (but probably shouldn't really be played *anywhere*).

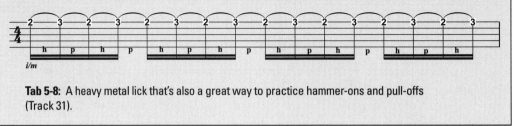

Tab 5-8: A heavy metal lick that's also a great way to practice hammer-ons and pull-offs (Track 31).

Sizing up special clawhammer pull-offs

You may want to use the pull-off in a way that's unique to clawhammer banjo. The technique is similar to what you play for an open string pull-off (see the section "Digging into open-string pull-offs" earlier in this chapter), but in this case, you don't play the string with the right hand at all. The sound is created *only* by the left hand moving across the string. This kind of pull-off is played almost always on just the 1st string. Here's a step-by-step guide on how to do this special clawhammer pull-off:

1. **Fret the 1st string at the second fret with the middle finger of your left hand.**

2. **Without striking the string with the right hand, pull off the first string with the middle finger of your left hand.**

This pull-off emphasizes just the sound of the open string. Because a note isn't actually fretted, many players simply grab the string with their left-hand finger (without actually bringing their finger all the way down to the fingerboard) and pull down from the 1st string.

Bending the Chokes

When you've got a serious case of the blues on the banjo, you're going to be playing some *chokes* on your instrument. This left-hand technique involves pushing or pulling on a fretted note to raise its pitch and then releasing the pressure to lower it back again. A choke is sometimes called a *bend*. (I could have called this section "Choking the Bends," but that sounded even worse than what I came up with, don't you think?) Blues and rock guitarists utilize this technique all the time to imitate the cry of the human voice, but it sounds equally great, if not better, on the banjo too, in my humble opinion. You can discover how to play a choke in the following sections.

Playing the Foggy Mountain choke

The classic choke for bluegrass banjo players is once again from Earl Scruggs' "Foggy Mountain Breakdown." The Foggy Mountain choke is way up at the tenth fret of the 2nd string. Here's a step-by-step guide to a Foggy Mountain choke:

1. **Place your left-hand index or middle finger at the tenth fret of the 2nd string (see Figure 5-3a).**

   Using either finger is fine; try both and see which one is strongest for you.

2. **Play the 2nd string with your right-hand index finger.**

3. **While the note is still ringing, push the 2nd string towards the 3rd string with your left-hand finger while still maintaining enough fretting pressure to hear a continuous sound (see Figure 5-3b).**

   This movement is called the *choke*. Remember that the pitch goes up as you choke the string.

   Most banjo players like to raise the pitch of this Foggy Mountain choke the equivalent of almost two frets. You have to really bend the string to do this — so much that the left-hand fingernail should come into contact with the 3rd string and push it out of the way.

4. **Release the fretting pressure from the left hand to mute the note and return back to a normal fretted position, but don't lift the left-hand finger up off the string.**

   You're now ready to repeat the sequence. Playing two or three chokes in rapid succession in a song isn't unusual, but this requires a lot of coordination! The trick to playing one choke after another smoothly is to release the left-hand fretting pressure when a choke is done. This quickly returns the string — and your left-hand finger — back to the starting position and readies you to play another choke.

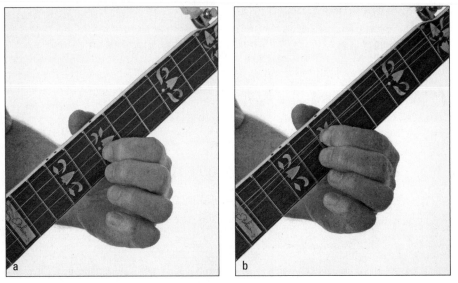

Figure 5-3:
The finger positions before (a) and after (b) playing a Foggy Mountain choke.

In tablature, a Foggy Mountain choke is indicated with an upward arrow, as you can see later in Tab 5-9.

Experimenting with choke variations

You can also try playing the standard Foggy Mountain choke in almost the same way I describe in the preceding section, but this time, keep *downward* pressure on the string as the finger returns to the normal position. This technique is called a *choke and release.* You should hear the pitch go up with the choke and then come back down again with the release.

Another way to add expression to your playing with chokes is to bend the string *before* striking it with your right hand, and then bring the pitch back down to its normal fretted sound by releasing the choke (but still keeping enough fretting pressure to sound the string!). This technique is called the *pre-choke,* for obvious reasons.

In tablature, a choke and release is indicated with an arched arrow going up and coming back down again, but a pre-choke is indicated with a line going straight up from the note with an arched arrow moving downward, as you can see in Tab 5-9 and hear on Track 32.

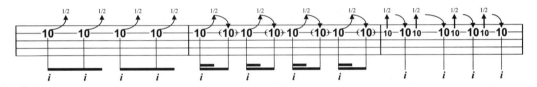

Tab 5-9: Playing chokes on the banjo: Foggy Mountain choke, choke and release, and pre-choke (Track 32).

Putting Your Hands Together

The slide, hammer-on, pull-off, and choke are key ingredients to great banjo playing, but it's not until you add these left-hand techniques to right-hand picking that you can really begin to cook. After you've coordinated the movements of the right and left hands together, you've taken a giant leap forward as a banjo player.

In the following sections, I go over a few of the right-hand basics I cover in Chapter 4 to make sure you're ready to move on. Then you begin to put the hands together to play short phrases that are some of the most important building blocks of clawhammer and bluegrass banjo music.

You want to be totally comfortable with the right-hand patterns before adding the left-hand techniques I discuss in this section. This means you should be able to play the right-hand patterns consecutively without stopping *and* without looking at the music. If you're a bluegrass player, you should be able to move from one roll to the next without interruption. If you're playing clawhammer, you want to have enough right-hand control so that your finger can go to whatever first note or melody note you want to play — and actually hit that note a great majority of the time. If you're uncertain about your right-hand skills, you may want to take a moment to go over the info on right-hand patterns for clawhammer and bluegrass banjo, which I cover in Chapter 4. (You can do it now, if you want. I can wait here.)

Make sure that you keep a constant rhythm with your right hand as you add the left-hand techniques. Begin by playing the following exercises slowly, building up speed as you gain confidence. Note that you play all the left-hand techniques relatively quickly, finishing the technique before you play the next note with the right hand. These slides, hammer-ons, pull-offs, and chokes are indicated with either eighth or sixteenth notes in the tab examples. And be sure to listen to the corresponding examples on the CD to internalize the sounds of these rhythms.

Making sure your clawhammer right-hand is ready

Try the basic clawhammer right-hand technique (see Tab 5-10), playing strings 4 through 1 for the *melody note* (which is what I call the first note played in the basic pattern). You can hear an example on Track 33.

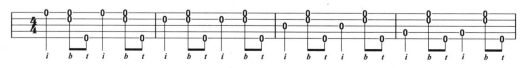

Tab 5-10: Playing basic clawhammer technique (Track 33).

Even though the tab indicates that the index finger plays the melody note and the brush, don't forget that you can use either the index or middle finger for these techniques. You can also choose to brush across one, two, or three strings, depending on how you want your playing to sound at that moment.

If you feel like you don't quite have your clawhammer right-hand ready, head back to Chapter 4 for a more detailed explanation of clawhammer right-hand positioning and technique.

Double-checking your bluegrass right-hand skills

Get those fingerpicks on your right-hand thumb, index, and middle fingers and warm up by playing the bluegrass right-hand patterns I introduce in Chapter 4 (and if you didn't know that bluegrass players use picks on their fingers, *definitely* check out Chapter 4 right now before proceeding!).

Following Tab 5-11 and Track 34, mix it up by playing alternating thumb, forward-backward, and forward rolls — bluegrass style.

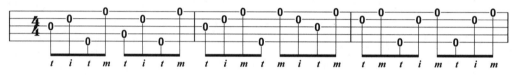

Tab 5-11: Playing the alternating thumb, forward-backward, and forward rolls in bluegrass style (Track 34).

Joining forces: Using both hands in clawhammer banjo

Banjo players use slides, hammer-ons, pull-offs, and chokes most often to add flavor or draw attention to melody notes. The first note you pick with basic clawhammer right-hand technique usually corresponds to a melody note in the song that you're playing. That's the note that's going to get the royal left-hand treatment.

In the following sections, you get to use all the left-hand embellishments I cover earlier in this chapter together with the basic right-hand clawhammer technique (from Chapter 4), adding up to some remarkable banjo sounds!

Clawhammer slides

You've probably mastered 4th-, 3rd-, and 1st-string slides (see the section "Slipping into the Slide" earlier in this chapter). All of these slides work in clawhammer banjo.

For each of the following examples, you want to execute the left-hand technique just after striking the string with the right hand, finishing the technique before the brush. Practice each individual measure over and over again until it feels comfortable and sounds smooth before moving on to the next measure.

You start by working on integrating the 3rd-string slide into clawhammer technique, because you play this slide most often, and then you move on to playing slides on the 1st and 4th strings.

3rd-string slides

Play the three 3rd-string slides from the section "Trying 3rd-string slides" earlier in this chapter: the second- to the fourth-fret slide, the second- to the third-fret slide, and the third- to the second-fret slide. Follow each slide with an index or middle finger brush and a 5th string played by the thumb.

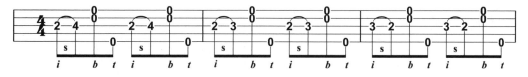

Tab 5-12: Playing 3rd-string slides in clawhammer banjo (Track 35).

1st-string slides

Play the two 1st-string slides I introduce earlier in this chapter: the fourth- to the fifth-fret slide and the second- to the fifth-fret slide, following each slide with a right-hand brush and 5th string to get the full clawhammer effect. See Tab 5-13 and listen to Track 36.

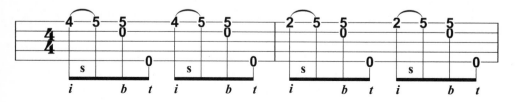

Tab 5-13: Playing 1st-string slides in clawhammer banjo (Track 36).

4th-string slides

The two 4th-string slides use the same fretted positions as the 1st-string slides (see preceding section), but don't be surprised if you have to fret the 4th string a bit harder to make the notes really ring. See Tab 5-14 and listen to Track 37.

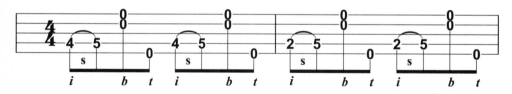

Tab 5-14: Playing 4th-string slides in clawhammer banjo (Track 37).

Clawhammer hammer-ons

If you know how to play a hammer-on, you're now ready to put the hammer-ons to work by integrating this technique into basic right-hand clawhammer playing (flip to the section "Nailing the hammer-on" earlier in this chapter for a refresher on hammer-ons).

One key to quickly integrating the action of the hands together is to first gain mastery over the skills required from each separate hand. Also, keep the rhythm of what you play with the right hand steady no matter what happens when you add the left hand. You can coordinate the activity of both hands much more quickly if you let the right hand lead the way.

The following exercises group the open hammer-ons together, followed by the fretted hammer-ons:

Open-string hammer-ons

As you play the open-string hammer-ons from Tab 5-15 in the clawhammer style, remember to repeat each individual measure over and over until it sounds good to you, and then move on to the following measure. Your ultimate goal is to play all three measures in succession without catastrophe, much like what you can hear on Track 38.

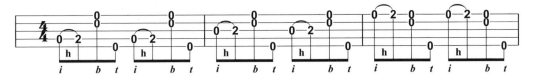

Tab 5-15: Playing open-string hammer-ons in clawhammer banjo (Track 38).

Fretted hammer-ons

Fretted hammer-ons are always a bit tougher to play than open-string hammer-ons, but you can master them with some dedicated practice. Try your hand at the exercise in Tab 5-16, which you can hear on Track 39. With this exercise, you're at least moving from the second to the third fret on each string to ease you in nice and slow.

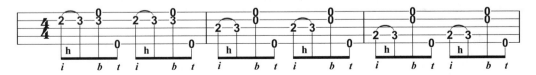

Tab 5-16: Playing fretted hammer-ons in clawhammer banjo (Track 39).

Clawhammer pull-offs

You're probably no stranger to 4th-, 3rd-, and 1st-string pull-offs by now (especially if you went through the section "Pulling Off the Pull-Off" earlier in this chapter). And — you guessed it — the pull-off works perfectly in clawhammer banjo.

Don't forget to make the pull-offs in the following sections really pop by putting some energy behind your left-hand motion. You want to play the pull-off so that it's rhythmically placed exactly between the first melody note and the right-hand brush, as you can see in the accompanying tab.

4th-string pull-offs

In the clawhammer 4th-string pull-off exercise in Tab 5-17, you play an open-string pull-off followed immediately by a fretted-string pull-off, both on the 4th string. Most players use their left-hand middle finger for both pull-offs. Note that you move the middle finger from the second to the third fret for the second measure of this exercise. Listen to the example on Track 40.

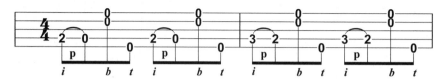

Tab 5-17: Playing 4th-string pull-offs in clawhammer banjo (Track 40).

3rd-string pull-offs

The left-hand fingering for these pull-offs in Tab 5-18 is the same as for the 4th-string variety (from the preceding section). Begin with an open-string pull-off from the second fret to an open string and follow it up with a fretted pull-off that begins at the third fret and ends on the second fret, as you can hear on Track 41.

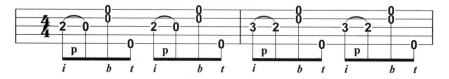

Tab 5-18: Playing 3rd-string pull-offs in clawhammer banjo (Track 41).

1st-string pull-offs

Clawhammer pull-offs work well on the 1st string too. However, don't pull so hard with your left hand as you execute the pull-off that you pull the string off of the fingerboard! Give the exercise in Tab 5-19 a try, and listen to the example on Track 42.

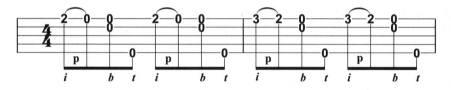

Tab 5-19: Playing 1st-string pull-offs in clawhammer banjo (Track 42).

Special clawhammer pull-off

What's so special about this pull-off? This technique is clawhammer-only — where you pull-off on the 1st string without hitting the string with the right hand first (and that's pretty special). The timing is the same as for all the other pull-offs in this section.

Most players use their left-hand middle finger for this pull-off, positioning it behind the second fret. You can play this pull-off after any initial melody note in clawhammer banjo. In the exercise in Tab 5-20, you use the pull-off while playing melody notes on the 2nd and 3rd strings. Give Track 43 a listen.

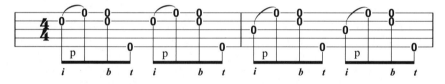

Tab 5-20: Playing the special clawhammer pull-off in clawhammer banjo (Track 43).

Clawhammer choke

Although the Foggy Mountain choke is usually the domain of bluegrass pickers, it is also a very hip thing to play in clawhammer banjo, as you can see as you play along with Tab 5-21. The secret to successfully integrating the choke into right-hand clawhammer technique is to concentrate on keeping the right-hand rhythm steady. Play very slowly at first to maximize the sound of the bending pitch in each stroke and to work into your motor memory the coordination required of the two hands. And it wouldn't hurt to listen to the example on Track 44.

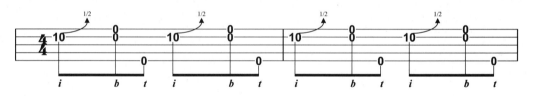

Tab 5-21: Playing the Foggy Mountain choke in clawhammer banjo (Track 44).

Keeping both hands busy in bluegrass banjo

Slides, hammer-ons, pull-offs, and chokes add tremendous excitement to bluegrass banjo music. In the following sections, you can take a look at how some of the left-hand techniques I introduce earlier in this chapter work with the alternating thumb, forward-backward, and forward rolls from Chapter 4.

You're taking a big step in your bluegrass education when you combine both hands in these ways. Don't forget to use the examples provided by the tablature and the accompanying CD as you work to gain mastery of these skills.

Bluegrass slides

Remember to keep the rhythm of your right-hand roll notes evenly spaced as you add slides to the bluegrass roll patterns. Play the slide quickly, letting it occupy the rhythmic space of one roll note. If you arrive at your destination fret with the slide just about the time you strike the next string in the roll pattern, you're playing it like the pros!

In the following sections, try playing slides in combination with the various right-hand roll patterns (for a refresher on how to play a slide, you can refer to the section "Slipping into Slides" earlier in this chapter).

As with clawhammer banjo (see previous section), having good command over the left- and right-hand techniques separately before you combine them is important. (For a bit more practice, you can turn to Chapter 4 for the right-hand instructions and to the sections on the specific left-hand techniques earlier in this chapter.) When you're ready to add the left hand, keep your rhythm steady with your right-hand picking, and it should sound great!

Alternating thumb–roll slides

Try a second- to fourth-fret slide on the 3rd string, followed by a second- to fifth-fret slide on the 4th string with the alternating thumb roll, using Tab 5-22 and Track 45 as a guide.

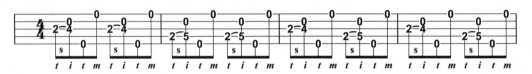

Tab 5-22: Playing slides with the alternating-thumb roll (Track 45).

Forward-backward roll slides

Try the 3rd-string slide from the preceding section, but at the beginning of a forward-backward roll. You then follow this with a 4th-string slide that starts at the second fret and ends at the fifth fret. You can use Tab 5-23 as a reference and listen to Track 46 as well.

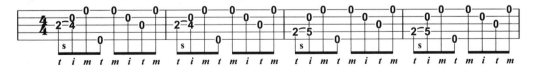

Tab 5-23: Playing slides with the forward-backward roll (Track 46).

Forward-roll slides

Using left-hand techniques with the forward roll is one of the trickiest bluegrass banjo moves, but it's well worth the effort, giving your playing an authentic and hard-driving sound.

Try playing the forward-roll slides pictured in Tab 5-24. In this exercise, you begin on the 3rd string in measures one and two, playing a second to fourth fret slide. For measures three and four, play a 4th-string slide that starts on the second fret and ends on the fifth fret. Note that after playing the 4th-string slide for these last two measures, you finish the roll by playing two 3rd strings with the right-hand index finger. Hear what I mean on Track 47.

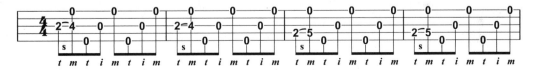

Tab 5-24: Playing slides with the forward roll (Track 47).

Bluegrass hammer-ons

Many bluegrass banjo players place the hammer-on *between* the notes of the roll pattern, especially on slower tempo songs. As the speed of a song increases, you don't have enough time in between your right-hand roll notes to worry about this, and your hammer-on may occur at the same time as you pick the next note in the roll. Both ways of playing the hammer-on are good — as long as you maintain a consistent rhythm in your right hand, that is! You can try out this technique in the following sections.

Repeat each measure over and over until you've mastered each technique, and then move on to conquer the next measure. Take things one step at a time, and you'll rule your own banjo kingdom in no time!

Alternating thumb–roll hammer-ons

Try mixing open-string hammer-ons and fretted hammer-ons in this exercise. Begin with open to second-fret hammer-ons on the 3rd and 4th strings before moving to second- to third-fret fretted hammer-ons, using the alternating-thumb roll as shown in Tab 5-25 and demonstrated on Track 48.

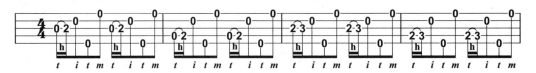

Tab 5-25: Playing hammer-ons with the alternating thumb roll (Track 48).

Forward-backward roll hammer-ons

Whatever works in the way of hammer-ons for an alternating thumb roll (see preceding section) also works for a forward-backward roll. In this exercise, you play four different hammer-ons: open to second-fret hammer-ons on the 3rd and 4th strings and second- to third-fret fretted hammer-ons on these same strings. Note how the reverse roll changes in measures two and four to accommodate these 4th-string slides. Jump in and get your feet wet following Tab 5-26 and listening to Track 49.

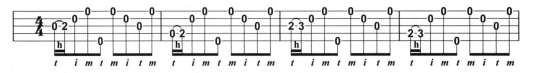

Tab 5-26: Playing hammer-ons with the forward-backward roll (Track 49).

Forward-roll hammer-ons

Try open and fretted hammer-ons on the 4th, 3rd, and 2nd strings with the forward roll by giving the exercise in Tab 5-27 a go. Note that the strings you play with the right hand change according to which hammer-on you choose to play. In measure one, you begin the forward roll on the 4th string, but in measure two, you start on the 3rd string. In the last two measures, you start the forward roll on the 2nd string. It's all on Track 50 of the CD.

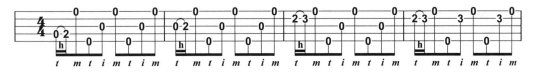

Tab 5-27: Playing hammer-ons with the forward roll (Track 50).

Bluegrass pull-offs

Aggressive, gritty-sounding pull-offs, like you hear master players such as J. D. Crowe and Ron Block play, are a hallmark of traditional bluegrass style. Professional players try to place pull-offs in between the notes of the roll pattern, which requires some quick and precise communication to the left hand. Start slowly with the exercises in the following sections and work up speed as you gain confidence.

Alternating thumb–roll pull-offs

Try open-string and fretted pull-offs in the bluegrass style by using the alternating-thumb roll (see Tab 5-28), taking note to how the notes you play with the right hand change according to the pull-off that you choose to play with the left hand. Listen to the example on Track 51.

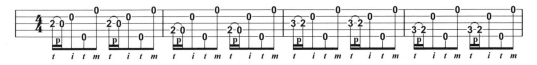

Tab 5-28: Playing pull-offs with the alternating thumb roll (Track 51).

Reverse-roll pull-offs

You can mix things up a bit and start this roll with a second- to third-fret slide on the 3rd string, followed by a third- to second-fret pull-off. (You can use Tab 5-29 and Track 52 as a guide.) Bluegrass players use this phrase frequently. Note that at measures two and four, you can relax by playing the reverse-roll pattern without these left-hand techniques.

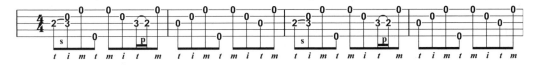

Tab 5-29: Playing slides and pull-offs with the reverse roll (Track 52).

Forward-roll pull-offs

You can take that third- to second-string pull-off on the 3rd string and use it in a forward roll, starting the measure with a fretted hammer-on on the second to third fret, as you can see in Tab 5-30 and hear on Track 53.

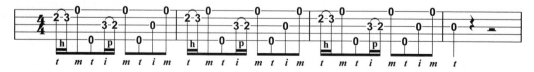

Tab 5-30: Playing hammer-ons and pull-offs with the forward roll (Track 53).

Bluegrass chokes

When combined with the right-hand forward roll, that Foggy Mountain choke can send listeners into paroxysms of wonder and joy (at least I *think* it's wonder and joy . . . I'm never quite sure, really!). This phrase, which you can see in Tab 5-31 and hear on Track 54, is an intensely idiomatic bluegrass banjo lick. Be sure to apply the left-hand choke each time you strike the 2nd string.

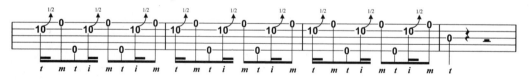

Tab 5-31: Playing chokes with the forward roll (Track 54).

Chapter 6

Working Up Your First Tunes: Clawhammer and Bluegrass

In This Chapter

▶ Unearthing the melody notes

▶ Arranging melodies for clawhammer and bluegrass banjo

▶ Using slides, hammer-ons, and pull-offs to enhance solos

▶ Playing four clawhammer and bluegrass tunes

*Y*ou've no doubt been waiting for this moment: You're ready to step into the spotlight and play your first melodies on the banjo! If you've worked through the previous few chapters, you're taking a big leap forward as you move from just playing along with a tune to being able to actually play the tune itself. In time, you'll not only be someone who can accompany others, but you'll also be a soloist (or, in banjo speak, a *picker*).

The beauty and challenge of working up a good solo is integrating the melody with the playing techniques that are unique to clawhammer and bluegrass banjo, which is what I help you tackle in this chapter. I break down the process of working up solos into a series of steps that can get you started down the road to creating your own music. You discover the relationship between scales and melodies and use this knowledge to more easily map out a song on the banjo fingerboard. You then apply right-hand clawhammer and bluegrass techniques to make this melody come alive. Next, you throw in left-hand slides, hammer-ons, and pull-offs to turn your tune into great-sounding banjo music.

I close the chapter by having you play clawhammer and bluegrass versions of four well-known tunes that all banjo players like to play: "Boil Them Cabbage Down," "Cripple Creek," "Goodbye Liza Jane," and "Ground Hog." You can follow along by listening to tracks on the CD that accompanies this book and by reading the banjo music (called *tablature*) that's in this chapter. You've got a lot of ground to cover, so get out your banjo, get in tune, and get started!

Finding the Melody

As unbelievable as it may sound, you can find folks out there who think that all banjo music sounds alike. They even assert that you can tell one tune apart from another only by its title (yes, a banjo joke is in here somewhere). I believe that our mission as banjo players should be to dispel this cultural misunderstanding by trying to play as much of the melody as possible in each song we play while still trying to make it sound like good banjo music. Because the melody of each tune is unique, each banjo version of a song also has the potential of being different.

A well-played banjo solo consists of a melody, but a lot more is usually going on as well. You may also hear the cascade of rolling notes that accompanies a bluegrass banjo solo or the percussive and syncopated brush and 5th-string techniques clawhammer players use. The real wonder of banjo music is how the melody can be expressed *inside* and *through* these techniques.

When you figure out a tab arrangement from a book (like, for instance, *Banjo For Dummies*), the melody is already provided for you, but bringing out that melody as you play the song so a listener can recognize it is still up to you. With more playing experience, you can work up your own arrangements from scratch. In this case, you have to locate the melody notes on your banjo on your own and combine the melody with the left- and right-hand techniques that you know can make your arrangement sound like good banjo music. Either way, knowing how to bring out the melody of a song is a must.

Because melodies are made up of a series of notes that can be organized into a scale, understanding just a little bit about scales can be a big help in finding the melody notes to any song on your banjo (yes, this is a bit of formal music theory, but I promise that you'll be a better banjo player for it). Armed with your scalar knowledge, you also have the opportunity to play a few tunes in the following sections.

Starting with the scale

The first step in working up a banjo solo is to locate the melody notes of the tune on your fingerboard. Unless you're moving straight to avant-garde modern classical music (in which case, this may not be the right *For Dummies* book for you), the majority of the melodies you encounter are made up of just a few notes. If these notes are grouped from low to high, they almost always form a scale.

You can begin a scale on any string or on any fret of the banjo. *Scales* are made up of a select group of notes on the banjo fingerboard, and different types of scales group notes in different ways. Melodies can start at the beginning, in the middle, or at the end of a scale.

Many advanced players, especially those interested in jazz on the banjo, take the time to locate the notes of a particular scale in every position and on each string of the banjo and learn all kinds of scales appropriate to this style of music. So if you're interested in playing jazz on the banjo, you better get to know your scales.

The *major scale* is the most commonly used scale in much of the music of the Western world as well as a great deal of banjo music (banjo music *is* part of country and western music, after all). Most people have the sound of the major scale thoroughly ingrained into their musical subconscious from years of hearing and singing this scale in all kinds of songs. Do you remember Julie Andrews singing "Do Re Mi" from *The Sound of Music* soundtrack? Okay, maybe you *don't* want to remember this, but at any rate, that song is all about the major scale.

To get started with playing melodies on the banjo, all you really need to know for now is how to construct a major scale. In the following sections, I show you how to do just that.

Scaling one string: Discovering the G-major and D-major scales

You can create a major scale on any note on the fretboard by following the formula in this section. The first note of the major scale indicates what kind of major scale you're playing.

For example, because many of the melodies you'll be playing use the notes found on the G-major scale, you can discover how to build a major scale by starting on the open 3rd string, which just happens to be a G note. You then travel up the 3rd string, finding all the notes of the G major scale (do - re - mi - fa - so - la - ti - do!) as you climb up the neck of the banjo.

To uncover a G-major scale, begin by picking up your banjo and following these steps:

1. **Play the 3rd string open, and as you hear the sound of this note on the banjo, try singing the same note.**

   Think of this note as the first note, or the "do" of a major scale. You can also think of this note as the first note in the melody "Frère Jacques."

2. **Sing what you think the second note of the major scale should be, using the syllable "re."**

You can also think of this note as the second note in the melody "Frère Jacques."

3. **Find this second note on your 3rd string.**

Because it's a higher note than the first note of the scale, you need to fret this string. Compare what you're singing (and hearing in your head) to the sound of the fretted string. You can find a match for the second note of the G-major scale, the "re" note, at the second fret.

4. **Sing "do" and "re" again, but now also continue up the scale by singing "mi," the third note of the G-major scale.**

This note is also the third note in the melody of your ol' buddy "Frère Jacques."

5. **Find this "mi" note on the 3rd string.**

The match is at the fourth fret of the 3rd string.

6. **Try singing the next note in the scale, the "fa" note, and try finding this note on the 3rd string.**

This *isn't* the next note in "Frère Jacques," by the way! You can find this note at the fifth fret, only one fret up from the "mi" note.

If you continue singing the rest of the notes of the major scale (so - la - ti - do) in this way and match the corresponding notes on the banjo's 3rd string to your singing, you end up with the scale in Figure 6-1 as it ascends up the banjo's 3rd string. And if you can't sing, Figure 6-1 shows you the notes, which you can hear on Track 55.

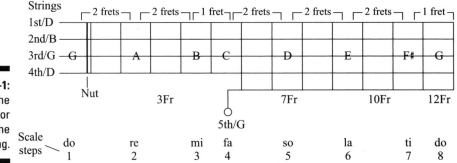

Figure 6-1:
Finding the
G-major
scale on the
3rd string.

As you can see in Figure 6-1, the names of the musical notes in a G-major scale are G / A / B / C / D / E / F♯ / G. However, when you're playing the banjo, you rarely think about the actual names of the notes — you don't have enough time to worry about this! Banjo players more often think about the distances between the notes in a scale, as measured by the number of frets between one note and the next and the sounds that they hear as they move from one note to another. When you think of the G-major scale in this way, the pattern shown in Figure 6-1 emerges.

Banjo players just love to play songs that use the G-major scale, but sooner or later you also have to find your way around other scales. D major is also a popular key for music played on the banjo (and you can play "Arkansas Traveler" in Chapter 9 with this scale). Using the same formula for finding a G-major scale, you can also discover the D-major scale if you start on your open 4th string D and choose the ascending notes. If you do it correctly, you end up playing a D-major scale, shown in Figure 6-2. You can also listen to Track 56 on the CD.

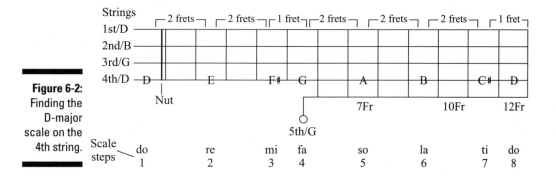

Figure 6-2:
Finding the D-major scale on the 4th string.

Bringing more than one string into play: The G-major scale

As you can probably guess, when you play melodies on the banjo, you don't usually run up and down just one string. It's more economical to play the higher notes of the scale on the 2nd and 1st strings and the lower scale notes on the 3rd string. This limits the movement of the left hand to the lower frets of the banjo and makes it a lot easier to quickly find the correct melody note.

Figure 6-3 provides a road map to the G-major scale as you can find it on the 3rd, 2nd, and 1st strings of your banjo.

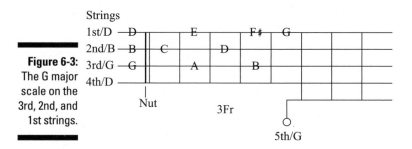

Figure 6-3:
The G major scale on the 3rd, 2nd, and 1st strings.

However, melodies often go below the starting point of the G-major scale, using notes found on the 4th string. You can now add these 4th-string notes to get the full picture of where you can find the notes of the G-major scale, using all four strings on the lower frets of your banjo. Be sure to note that by starting on the open 4th-string D, you're still playing a G-major scale, but you're now catching some of the lower scale notes that you use when playing melodies. Check out Figure 6-4 and listen to Track 57 on the CD.

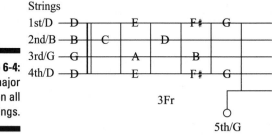

Figure 6-4:
The G-major scale on all four strings.

Although knowing the names of all the notes on the fingerboard of your banjo is an impressive feat (the kind of information that can certainly win you new friends at the next banjo players' cocktail party), this same info can be found in Appendix A in the back of this book! Remembering this kind of information isn't crucial right now. Focus instead on knowing where the notes of the G-major scale are located on the lower frets of your banjo and learn the *sounds* of these notes.

Trying out a tune (or two)

After you've found the notes of the G-major scale on the lower frets of the banjo (see preceding section), it's now time to work out some melodies by using this scale. Keep in mind that all the open, unfretted strings on your banjo in this tuning are also notes in the G-major scale.

With your banjo at the ready, try playing the melody of "Frère Jacques," which you can find in Tab 6-1 and on Track 58 on the CD. "Frère Jacques" shows the relationship between a melody and its scale: all of this song's melody notes are in the G-major scale. After playing this song, you can probably see how becoming familiar with this scale can make figuring out a melody on the banjo much easier.

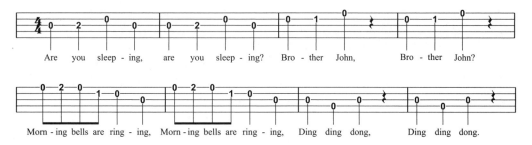

Tab 6-1: Playing the melody to "Frère Jacques" (Track 58).

Because you don't have much of a chance of hearing "Frère Jacques" at a jam session, you can try something a little closer to home with "Red River Valley." (If you don't know this song, listen to Track 8 on the CD, where I sing the song with a pinch-pattern accompaniment, which is covered in Chapter 3.)

I'd like for you to challenge yourself and make an attempt to figure out the melody first by using your ears in a trial-by-error approach before you look at the tab for "Red River Valley." This exercise trains your ears and brain to locate the melody by using your familiarity with the G-major scale on the banjo neck. Here's a hint to help you get started: Play the open 4th string, and then the open 3rd, followed by the open 2nd. These are the first three notes of the tune. Now try to find the rest of "Red River Valley" on your fretboard, using your memory of the melody or my sensitively beautiful vocal rendition on Track 8 of the CD to guide you.

Don't expect to get all the melody notes perfectly the first time around. As you experiment, you can learn from your mistakes, so don't be afraid to make them!

Try playing your version of the melody to a loved one and see whether she can guess what song you're playing. Did she hear "Red River Valley"? I hope so, but if not, that's okay too. You're just getting started with this process, and coordinating your brain, hands, and ears to figure out a melody and play it without stopping could take a while. Now, compare your version with the arrangement in Tab 6-2 and Track 59 on the CD.

Finding the melody by ear is the first step towards working up a great banjo solo. Remember to let your ear be your guide and keep in mind that not all songs use the G-major scale. After you've figured out the basic melody, you can then use it as your foundation to work up a more "banjoistic" version of the tune.

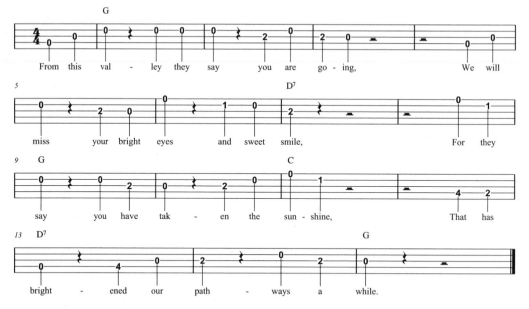

Tab 6-2: Playing the melody to "Red River Valley" (Track 59).

Making Melody with Style

After you feel like you've got a handle on a basic melody (see preceding section), it's then time to add right-hand clawhammer and bluegrass techniques and make the melody really come alive. As you begin to play honest-to-goodness, authentic-sounding banjo music, the excitement can really begin to kick in (let me hear a resounding "Well, alright!"). So as you make melodies in both the clawhammer and bluegrass styles in the following sections, hold on tight!

If you need a quick right-hand techniques refresher before moving forward, check out Chapter 4. And if your basic left-hand fretting techniques are giving you any trouble, you may want to look over Chapters 2 and 5.

Starting with the right hand

As you work up a solo, using either clawhammer or bluegrass right-hand technique, you want to preserve as much of the melody as possible so that your listeners (and you) can keep track of what you're playing. However, you also want to keep the right hand flowing by incorporating the basic clawhammer technique or bluegrass roll patterns with as little interruption in the music as possible. All players experience conflicts between these two goals at times. Listening and learning from other players and experimentation is the key to coming up with your own solutions.

Here are a few more tips to keep in mind as you start to work out melodies for clawhammer and bluegrass banjo:

- ✔ **Be flexible with the basic clawhammer technique and the bluegrass rolls and adjust these patterns to play those strings where the melody notes are located.** For example, if the melody is on an open 2nd string, make sure you play that note as part of your bluegrass roll pattern or basic clawhammer technique. Also, use the right-hand techniques to make the solo flow continuously, but don't be afraid to stop and play a few melody notes all by themselves if that's what seems to work the best at a given moment.

- ✔ **Although playing those melody notes that occur on the first beat of a chord change is a good idea, don't worry about trying to hit _every_ melody note.** Decide which notes are the most important and see how you can adjust the right-hand patterns to play as many of these notes as possible.

- ✔ **Relate the chord progression to the melody.** For instance, if the song's chord progression moves to a C chord, some of the melody notes will very likely be the same as the fretted notes that are part of the chord you're playing. Fret the full chord first and then go hunting for those melody notes.

- ✔ **Jump at the chance to enhance the melody.** Most melodies have some notes that are held for a relatively long time, alternating with notes that are shorter in duration. Long notes provide a great opportunity to continue playing either the basic clawhammer technique or a bluegrass roll that accentuates that same melody note.

- ✔ **Adjust your playing to the duration of the note.** Maintaining a flowing right-hand technique is more difficult in those passages with shorter melody notes. In these cases, you may have to interrupt your basic right-hand technique to play those notes, and then resume when the melody notes are once again of longer duration.

- ✔ **When playing with others, always try to hold up your end of the rhythm.** Playing in time and changing chords at the proper time is much more important than playing a solo that expresses every melody note but doesn't maintain the correct rhythm or follow the chord progression.

Ready to use these tips in action? In the following sections, you get the chance to add clawhammer and bluegrass right-hand techniques to the melody of "Red River Valley" and play two different arrangements of this song. Don't hesitate to use the tab and the CD together to help speed up the picking process.

Getting a feel for the clawhammer way

Try playing the arrangement of "Red River Valley" in Tab 6-3 and Track 60, using basic clawhammer right-hand technique to capture as many melody notes as possible. You can refer back to the bare bones melody of "Red River Valley" in the section "Trying out a tune (or two)," earlier in this chapter, to compare and see how the clawhammer version differs.

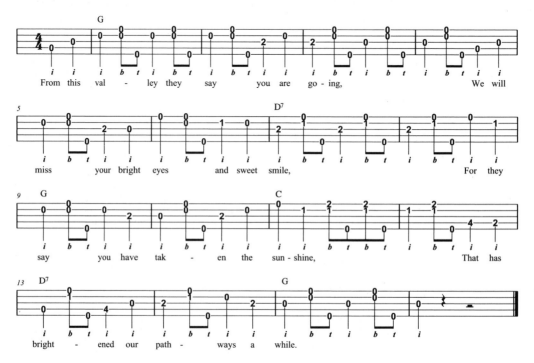

Tab 6-3: Playing "Red River Valley" the clawhammer way (Track 60).

Taking on the melody bluegrass style

For some serious melody-making, try "Red River Valley" in bluegrass style, using the alternating thumb, forward-backward, and forward rolls I indicate in Tab 6-4. You can always find more than one way to capture a melody with bluegrass rolls. The more you experiment with different solutions, the more skilled you become in working out your own arrangements of tunes. But for now, get the feel for a bluegrass melody by following along with my arrangement and listening to Track 61.

Note in Tab 6-4 how the melody note often determines which roll works best in each measure. For instance, in the first full measure (at the syllable "val-" of the word *valley*), I selected a forward roll that features the open 2nd string prominently, because at this point in the song, that's the melody note. The next measure has three melody notes (matching the lyrics "say you are"). These melody notes are the open 2nd string (a B note), a 3rd string fretted at the second fret (an A note), followed by an open-string B note once again. As you can see, the forward roll changes to accommodate each of these melody notes.

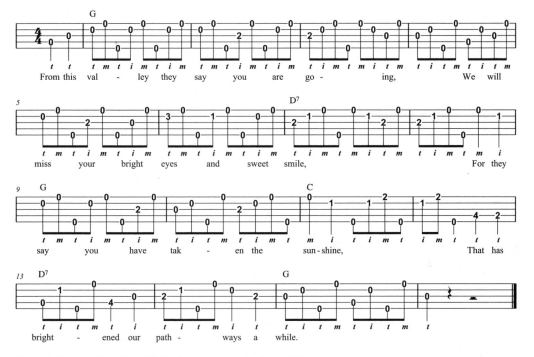

Tab 6-4: Playing "Red River Valley" bluegrass style (Track 61).

Adding the left hand

After you're comfortable incorporating melody notes into clawhammer and bluegrass right-hand technique (see preceding section), you can enhance your solos by adding left-hand slides, hammer-ons, pull-offs, and chokes. Because you use these left-hand techniques to draw attention to melody notes, banjo players naturally use them when they need to make a melody note really stand out in a solo.

Here are a few additional guidelines on how to use these left-hand techniques to make the melody really pop:

✔ **If a melody note falls on an open 3rd, 2nd, 1st, or 5th string, that's a good time to play a slide or a hammer-on on a lower string that moves up to the same pitch as the open string.** For example, if the melody note is on an open 3rd string, you can emphasize this same pitch by sliding from the second to the fifth fret on the 4th string.

✔ **If the melody moves down from one open string to the next, try a pull-off or a backward slide on the lower string to facilitate this movement.** For instance, if the melody moves from an open 2nd string to an open 3rd string, try a third- to second-fret pull-off on the 3rd string.

✔ **If a melody needs a bluesy or bent note, call on your left-hand choke.** You can use chokes in much the same way as a slide to make a transition from a lower to a higher note.

I'm still amazed how adding a bit of left-hand flash can enhance any arrangement. In the following section, you can play two versions of "Red River Valley" that both add slides, hammer-ons, and pull-offs to the basic right-hand techniques of clawhammer and bluegrass banjo.

Creating clawhammer melodies

Try the arrangement of "Red River Valley" shown in Tab 6-5 and on Track 62 of the CD. In this version, you play slides, hammer-ons, and pull-offs to create an even more authentic and exciting clawhammer banjo sound. In banjo tablature, these techniques are indicated by letters below the tab staff: *s* stands for slide, *h* for hammer-on, and *p* for pull-off.

Note that at measures 11 through 14 you're first fretting a C chord and then a D7 chord for two measures each. Sometimes you have to lift one of your fretting fingers up to play an open string (as in the first note of measure 11) or move a fretted note from one string to another to get ready for a slide (as in the fourth note of measure 13, where you move your middle finger from the 3rd string, second fret to the 4th string, second fret).

Compare this arrangement with the version presented earlier in this chapter as Tab 6-3 in the section "Playing Melody with Style" to explore how these left-hand techniques can add more stylistic impact to an arrangement.

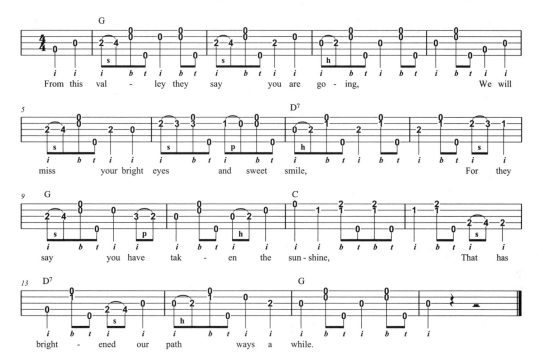

Tab 6-5: Playing "Red River Valley" the clawhammer way with slides, hammer-ons, and pull-offs (Track 62).

Playing the bluegrass way

Just as you can add slides, hammer-ons, and pull-offs to clawhammer banjo arrangements, you can also add these same techniques to right-hand roll patterns to create a more genuine bluegrass banjo sound. Give it a try by listening to Track 63 and playing the arrangement of "Red River Valley" in Tab 6-6.

Before tackling this bluegrass rendition of "Red River Valley," you may want to take a moment and look at the exercises in "Keeping both hands busy in bluegrass banjo" in Chapter 5 to make sure you're comfortable adding left-hand embellishments to bluegrass roll patterns.

You may notice how incorporating these techniques in bluegrass style makes your playing sound much closer to that of such greats as Earl Scruggs, Sonny Osborne, and J. D. Crowe.

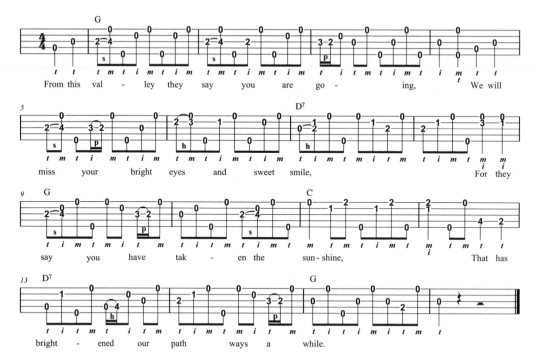

Tab 6-6: Playing "Red River Valley" bluegrass style with slides, hammer-ons, and pull-offs (Track 63).

Tackling a Few More Tunes

I close this chapter with a special bonus song section that includes arrangements of four banjo favorites in matching clawhammer and bluegrass versions that bring together all the important new skills you have covered in this chapter.

Review the following tab, listen to the corresponding tracks on the CD, and try to play along:

- ✔ Tab 6-7, Track 64: Clawhammer arrangement of "Boil Them Cabbage Down."

- ✔ Tab 6-8, Track 65: Bluegrass arrangement of "Boil Them Cabbage Down."

- ✔ Tab 6-9, Track 66: Clawhammer arrangement of "Cripple Creek."

- ✔ Tab 6-10, Track 67: Bluegrass arrangement of "Cripple Creek."

- ✔ Tab 6-11, Track 68: Clawhammer arrangement of "Goodbye Liza Jane."

✔ Tab 6-12, Track 69: Bluegrass arrangement of "Goodbye Liza Jane."

✔ Tab 6-13, Track 70: Clawhammer arrangement of "Ground Hog."

✔ Tab 6-14, Track 71: Bluegrass arrangement of "Ground Hog."

Don't forget to consult the CD as a primary resource as you work on these tunes, using the tablature sparingly.

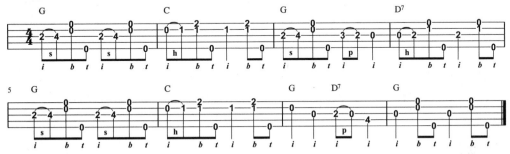

Tab 6-7: Clawhammer arrangement of "Boil Them Cabbage Down" (Track 64).

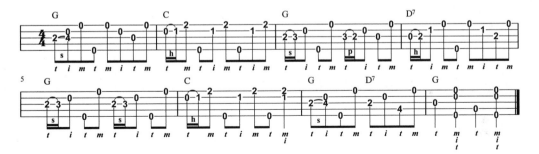

Tab 6-8: Bluegrass arrangement of "Boil Them Cabbage Down" (Track 65).

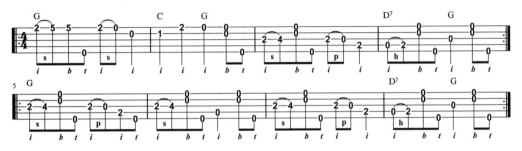

Tab 6-9: Clawhammer arrangement of "Cripple Creek" (Track 66).

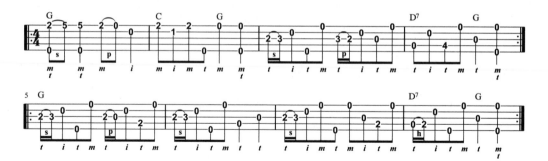

Tab 6-10: Bluegrass arrangement of "Cripple Creek" (Track 67).

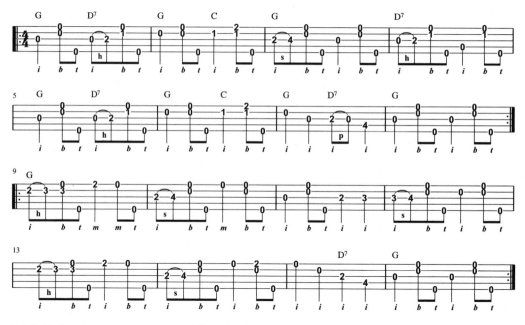

Tab 6-11: Clawhammer arrangement of "Goodbye Liza Jane" (Track 68).

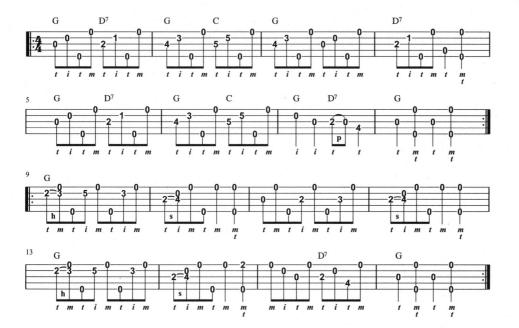

Tab 6-12: Bluegrass arrangement of "Goodbye Liza Jane" (Track 69).

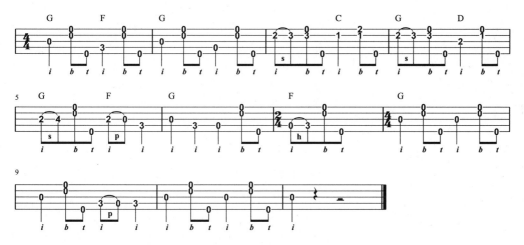

Tab 6-13: Clawhammer arrangement of "Ground Hog" (Track 70).

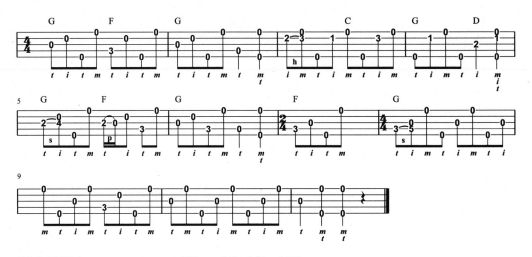

Tab 6-14: Bluegrass arrangement of "Ground Hog" (Track 71).

Part III
Playing Styles Past, Present, and Future

EXTREMELY DIFFICULT BANJO STYLE: GANGSTER BANJO

©RICHTENNANT

"Next, I'd like to do a tribute to 'Tupac."

In this part . . .

I take you beyond the beginners' material and present the historical roots of the banjo. I also explore the most recent stylistic and technical innovations. I take you back to the late-19th and early-20th centuries as you play two minstrel-style tunes and two classic-era pieces. You also get a more in-depth look at bluegrass style, exploring Scruggs, melodic, and single-string techniques and licks. And you can find a handful of great tunes scattered throughout this part, just ready for the playing.

Chapter 7

Playing Historical Styles: African, Minstrel, and Classic Banjo

In This Chapter

▶ Discovering the banjo's African heritage

▶ Getting acquainted with minstrel banjo style

▶ Playing in the classic banjo style

*B*anjo players have a thing about history. They play old songs and sing a lot about the "old days"; they like old instruments and playing things the old-time way. When you pick up your banjo to play "Cripple Creek" or "Soldier's Joy" or sing the old ballad "Pretty Polly," you become part of a deep and enduring current of music history. Clawhammer and bluegrass banjo, the two most popular ways of playing banjo today, have historical roots that go back over 150 years to late 19th and early 20th century classic banjo styles, mid-19th century minstrel banjo styles and to even earlier African musical influences. These historical banjo styles are the subject of this chapter.

Get ready to travel back in time to trace the African ancestry of the banjo and explore the fascinating world of 19th and early-20th century banjo music. I show you an African piece from the late 1700s along with some tunes in minstrel style from the pre-Civil War years that are historical predecessors to clawhammer banjo music. I also help you to test your skills with some pre-bluegrass classic banjo ragtime from the early 20th century. Whatever style of banjo you like to play, you can discover a whole new world of musical possibilities in these *really* old, historical sounds.

African-American Banjo Roots

The idea of stretching a skin tightly across a resonating chamber, attaching a neck, adding one or more drone strings, and playing the resulting instrument in a rhythmical and percussive manner originated with the West Africans who were forcibly imported as slaves to the New World. The first banjo-type instruments were documented in the Caribbean as early as 1689, and the first mention of the banjo in the American colonies occurs in 1754 (where it is called a "banjer" in a Maryland newspaper).

What music historians know about early African and African-American banjo music comes from what observers at the time had to say about banjo playing and from artists' drawings and illustrations of banjos and banjo players (check out *Sinful Tunes and Spirituals: Black Folk Music to the Civil War* by Dena Epstein [University of Illinois Press] for an excellent overview of this documentation). Researchers also look to how Africans play banjo-type instruments today for clues about historical African-American playing styles.

African and early African-American banjos consist of a gourd or a carved wood body with a stretched skin head and usually little more than a stick for a neck.

From early on, observers have commented on the complex and percussive playing style Africans and African-Americans used to play the banjo, and you can easily hear elements of this approach in modern clawhammer banjo playing. Clawhammer players strike the strings by moving their right-hand index or middle fingers down across the strings, in a very similar way to how many West Africans make music on their own native banjo-type instruments today. Most historians agree that this aspect of the American clawhammer approach is the result of African influence.

Although you can't know exactly what early African and African-American music sounded like 200 or more years ago, you can play my arrangement of an African tune that ended up in a 1782 collection of British Isles fiddle tunes! Called "Pompey Ran Away," this tune makes for a wonderful clawhammer banjo piece (see Tab 7-1 and listen to Track 72).

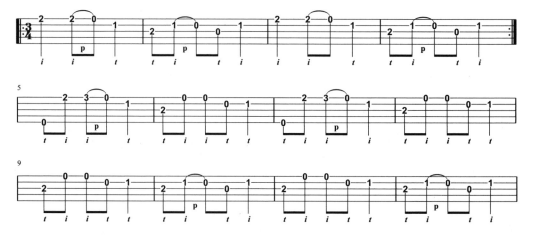

Tab 7-1: Playing "Pompey Ran Away," a clawhammer version of an 18th-century African tune (Track 72).

This piece has many of the characteristics commonly heard in traditional West African music. Each musical idea (or *phrase*) is made up of just a few notes (each phrase occupies one measure of tab in this particular tune). The second phrases of each line (which are the second and fourth measures of each line) answer the first phrases (which are the first and third measures of each line) in a call-and-response (or question-and-answer) relationship. Each phrase also offers a slight variation on the phrase heard just before it as this simple tune organically unfolds.

To play this tune using traditional clawhammer techniques, use the right-hand index finger to strike the first and second strings with a downward motion and let the right-hand thumb strike the 2nd 3rd, and 5th strings in a downward direction. (For more on the world of clawhammer banjo, check out Chapters 4 and 6.)

Converging Cultures: The World of Minstrel Banjo

When Africans and Europeans came together in North America, they had enough similarity in their ideas and attitudes about music for a new musical synthesis to occur despite the dramatically unequal status of black and white populations. In large part, the history of American music, from minstrelsy to jazz, rock 'n' roll to rap music, is the story of this continuing convergence of musical sensibilties.

Uncovering the historical background

The mid-19th-century minstrel banjo is one of the first manifestations of the meeting of these musical worlds. Along with the fiddle, the banjo was the most popular instrument in African-American music in the United States through the 18th and into the 19th century. A 19th-century banjo is shown in Figure 7-1. In the early 1800s, white musicians began to take up the banjo in imitation of southern African-American players. By the mid-1800s, white professional stage performers had popularized the banjo all across the United States and in England and had begun their own banjo traditions as they popularized new songs. Because these musicians usually performed with blackened faces, they came to be known as *blackface minstrels*.

In 19th century minstrel banjo, African elements — the instrument itself, the right-hand playing technique, and the use of varied and complex rhythms — combined with the musical influence of the British Isles as exhibited in song form, repertoire, and the use of harmony to create a uniquely American musical phenomenon.

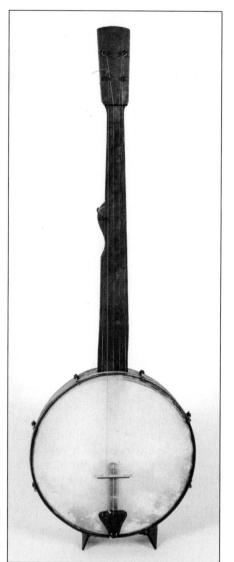

Figure 7-1:
A mid-19th century minstrel five-string banjo.

Because the minstrel stage depicted slaves and southern life in inaccurate and degrading ways, there are many negative aspects to the legacy of blackface minstrelsy. Nevertheless, as part of America's first nationally popular music, minstrelsy served to popularize the banjo and make it an instrument shared by both white and black populations. With this popularity came the publication of the first instruction manuals for the instrument and the first factory-made banjos in the 1840s. Soon after, five strings became the accepted norm for banjos.

Getting into minstrel banjo

As you play tunes using techniques that date from the 1840s, the sound of minstrel banjo opens a door to the instrument's past where you can hear and feel the echoes of the banjo's shared African and European heritage. If you're a clawhammer player, it should be an easy transition to minstrel style, as most of the playing techniques are similar for both approaches.

Although you can purchase a replica of a fretless 19th-century banjo, you can play the minstrel repertoire on any five-string instrument, fretted or not. Minstrel banjos are also usually strung with gut or nylon strings and are tuned several steps lower than the conventional tunings used by banjo players today. However, you can play these pieces with any kind of strings on your banjo, and in this section, I show you how to play in the minstrel style by staying as close to conventional G tuning as possible.

Discovering drop-C tuning

Minstrel banjo uses a tuning that's close to the familiar G tuning, but the 4th string is lowered in pitch the equivalent of two frets from a D to a C (see Chapter 2 if you need help with getting your banjo into G tuning). Usually called *drop-C tuning,* this technique is used in other popular banjo tunes like "Home Sweet Home" and "Farewell Blues." You also use drop-C tuning in classic banjo, so it's good to know this tuning even if your plans aren't to become a great minstrel player!

If your banjo is already in G tuning, lowering the 4th string from a D to a C is easy. Simply loosen the tension on the 4th string so that the pitch is lowered from a D to a C♯, and then keep going until your electronic tuner indicates that you've reached a C note. If you're trying this by ear, congratulations! That's *definitely* the old-time way, and in this case, you want to lower the 4th string so that it matches the 3rd string in pitch when you fret the 4th string at the seventh fret.

Unfortunately, after you've lowered that 4th string to C, there's a real good chance that the rest of your banjo will be out of tune. If that's the case, touch up the other strings by making sure that your 3rd string is tuned to G, the 2nd string to B, the 1st string to D and the 5th string to G.

Mastering minstrel technique

Minstrel banjo uses many of the same techniques used by clawhammer banjo players and it's a good idea to know basic clawhammer technique well before venturing into minstrel-banjo territory. As with clawhammer, in minstrel banjo, you move downward across the strings with your index or middle fingers to strike most melody notes, and you use your thumb for the fifth string.

Minstrel banjo also frequently uses *double-thumbing* patterns, a right-hand technique that is also used in advanced clawhammer banjo. In double-thumbing, the thumb not only plays the fifth string but also catches melody notes on the inside strings (for a review of basic clawhammer technique, visit Chapter 4).

You also encounter these new challenges with minstrel banjo:

✔ **Triplets:** Minstrel banjo frequently juxtaposes different kinds of rhythms — sometimes in the same measure. A *triplet* is a rhythm where you play three notes within a musical space normally occupied by two notes. Say "trip-o-let" while tapping your foot on the syllable "trip" and you've got the idea of a triplet.

✔ **Dotted notes:** A dot after a note indicates that the note's durational value is to be increased by half. If you increase the value of one note, you usually have to make the next note shorter by an equal amount. Dotted notes result in a more abrupt and syncopated rhythm, as heard in ragtime music.

For example, if you're playing two eighth notes, these notes would be counted as "1 +" (or "1 and") with each note having the same duration. However, if you increase the rhythmic value of the first note by one half (and give that note a dot in the tab notation), this new note would be *three* times as long as the second note (which would then be given another flag in tab notation, changing its value from an eighth note to a sixteenth note). These two notes are now counted as "1 e + uh" with the first note played on the "1" and the second note played on the "uh."

Trying some minstrel tunes

Are you ready for some banjo time travel by attempting a few tunes in the minstrel style? Both tunes in this section utilize the double-thumbing techniques discussed in the preceding section in addition to employing more conventional right-hand clawhammer patterns and left-hand pull-offs (for more info on pull-offs, see Chapter 5).

"Juba"

"Juba" is from *Frank B. Converse's New and Complete Method for the Banjo,* an instruction manual first published in 1865. *Juba* was also the name given to a popular minstrel dance as well as to this tune. This piece, a simple theme and variation, was often used in the instructional manuals to teach the basic minstrel technique, and it's a great way to practice your double-thumbing (see Tab 7-2 and listen to Track 73).

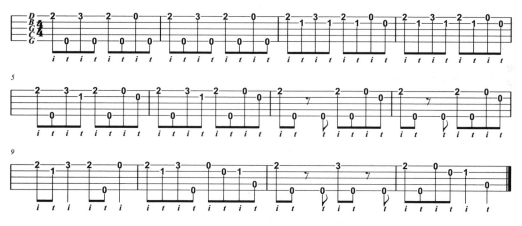

Tab 7-2: Playing "Juba," a minstrel banjo piece from 1865 (Track 73).

Note the use of the right-hand thumb on the second string throughout "Juba." Measures 5 and 6 alternate fifth string and second string notes, all played by the thumb, providing a real 19th-century workout!

"Hard Times"

"Hard Times" is a piece from *Briggs' Banjo Instructor* published in 1855 (see Tab 7-3). Note that the time signature to this piece is 6/8, which means there are six main beats per measure in this tune with an eighth note equaling one beat (or one count). Use a bit more right-hand punch to play the notes that fall on the "one" and "four" (as in ONE-two-three-FOUR-five-six) and you'll really make this tune come alive. Don't forget to listen to Track 74 on the CD to get the right feel for this tune.

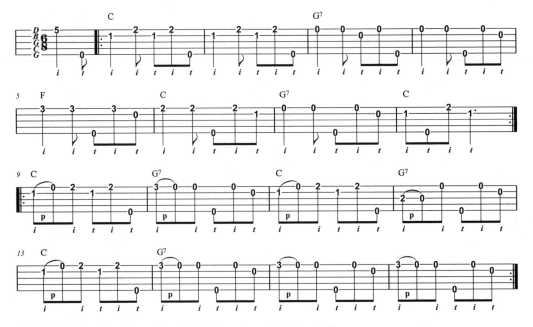

Tab 7-3: Playing "Hard Times," a minstrel piece from 1855 (Track 74).

Branching Out With Classic Banjo

In 1865, Frank B. Converse introduced the *guitar style* to the minstrel banjo world, adapting the right-hand finger-picking techniques used by 19th-century guitarists to the banjo and presenting a new way to play music on the banjo. In the guitar style, the right-hand fingers pick up on the strings as in bluegrass banjo (see Chapter 4 for an introduction to right-hand technique in bluegrass), rather than downward on the strings as in minstrel and clawhammer banjo (see the section "Mastering minstrel technique" earlier in this chapter).

The guitar style soon eclipsed the minstrel banjo in popularity with those mid- to late-19th century players who preferred to learn their banjo music from sheet music. By the early 1900s, a vast repertoire of banjo pieces were written and arranged in what is now called *classic banjo* style.

Classic banjo offers everything from Sousa marches to arrangements of classical works to ragtime pieces. Of special interest to banjo players are compositions written specifically for the instrument by American and English banjo composers such as Joe Morley, Alfred Cammeyer, and Parke Hunter in the late-19th and early-20th centuries. A great deal of technical expertise is required to play many of these pieces, which were often performed with piano accompaniment or perhaps played by a banjo duo or trio. In these days, there were even entire banjo orchestras made up of — you guessed it — many, many different-sized banjos playing orchestral scores. Amazing, isn't it?

Classic banjo refers not only to a specific repertoire (those pieces written or arranged between approximately 1880 and 1920) but also to a specific way of playing these pieces on the banjo. In the following sections, you're introduced to the ways of classic banjo and get the chance to try your hand at a few beginners classic pieces.

Understanding classic banjo technique

Bona fide classic players use their bare fingers to play (no fingerpicks!) and employ open-back instruments strung with nylon or gut strings. However, it's fine to use whatever kind of banjo you have handy to get started. Most classic pieces (including the two examples to follow) are in drop-C tuning, as in minstrel banjo (see the section "Discovering drop-C tuning" earlier in this chapter).

Although all five fingers of the right hand are sometimes required to play some passages in classic banjo music, the thumb, index finger, and middle fingers are the ones you most often use to play this style (similar to bluegrass banjo). Like the ragtime piano compositions of Scott Joplin (like "Maple Leaf Rag" or "The Entertainer"), classic banjo pieces often consist of several contrasting sections in different keys and use many up-the-neck chords. For these reasons, the best classic banjo players are very familiar with the location and left-hand fingering of notes and chords on the banjo neck. The best way for you to follow in these footsteps is to play as many pieces as possible, internalizing new fretted positions as you tackle new pieces.

If you're really going to get into classic-style playing, you should become comfortable with reading conventional music notation, because the great majority of pieces use regular music rather than banjo tablature. Check out *Music Theory For Dummies* by Michael Pilhofer and Holly Day (Wiley) for more information on reading conventional music notation as well as a lot of other useful information that comes in handy for whatever banjo style you choose to play.

The American Banjo Fraternity

If you're serious about playing classic banjo, you should consider joining the American Banjo Fraternity, the group that's dedicated to the preservation of this banjo style. I guarantee that there are no hazing rituals or beer runs with this fraternity; however, you get access to boatloads of sheet music, and you'll be welcomed by other classic players who are glad to share their expertise. The ABF hosts two get-togethers each year, usually in either New York state or Pennsylvania, and these gatherings bring together the best classic style players in the United States. The organization also publishes two newsletters annually (containing music!) to its members (you can find this organization on the Web at www.abfbanjo.org).

Introducing yourself to the classics

If you're a bluegrass player, you can be right at home with many of the right-hand finger-picking techniques used in classic banjo. However don't be surprised if you find that these pieces are challenging. Classic banjo pieces are typically longer than bluegrass pieces, with a lot of material to memorize (you don't usually improvise on classic pieces — you play them as they appear on the printed page, adding your own expression and feeling).

Also, prepare your left hand for a good workout as you travel up and down the neck in the following pieces. Listen to the CD as you carefully work through the tabs, but above all, have fun with these sounds from a century ago!

Don't forget to tune your fourth string down to C for both of the following classic pieces. Your playing will sound a lot better that way!

"Colorado Buck Dance"

A. H. Nassau-Kennedy's "Colorado Buck Dance" is taken from *Turner's Banjo Budget* series from around 1898. This piece is a great introduction to classic banjo, as you can hear on Track 75. In Tab 7-4, I give you the tune's first two sections. You may find some of the right-hand work a challenge, especially as you use your right-hand index and middle fingers to play consecutive notes on the first string in the second section (as in measures 10, 12, and 16).

"Banjoisticus"

Tab 7-5 presents two sections of a piece from 1909, "Banjoisticus," written by Philadelphia banjo orchestra leader and composer Paul Eno, one of the best composers of classic banjo music. This tune has strong ragtime leanings and is typical of the kinds of banjo pieces enjoyed in the United States at the turn of the *last* century by listening to cylinder recordings (these were the first "records" and were played on a phonograph with a needle, but were cylindrically shaped rather than flat as their latter-day predecessors, the 45 rpm and LP record — remember *those?*). Anyway, give it a listen on Track 76 of the CD.

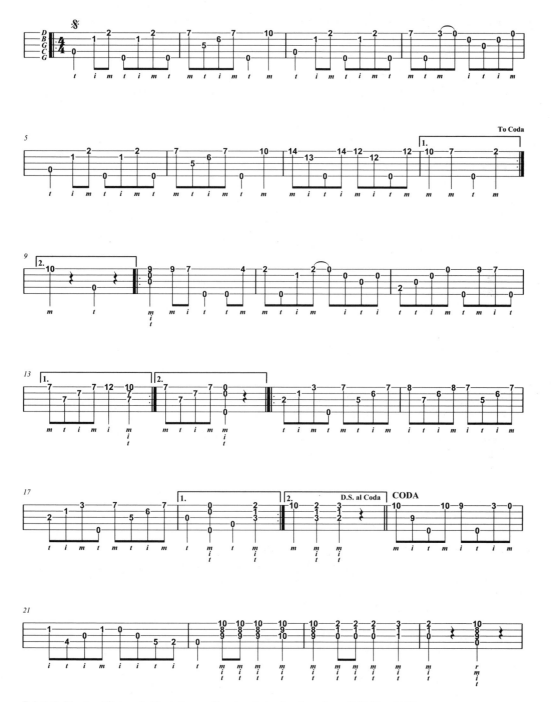

Tab 7-4: Playing "Colorado Buck Dance," a classic banjo piece from 1898 (Track 75).

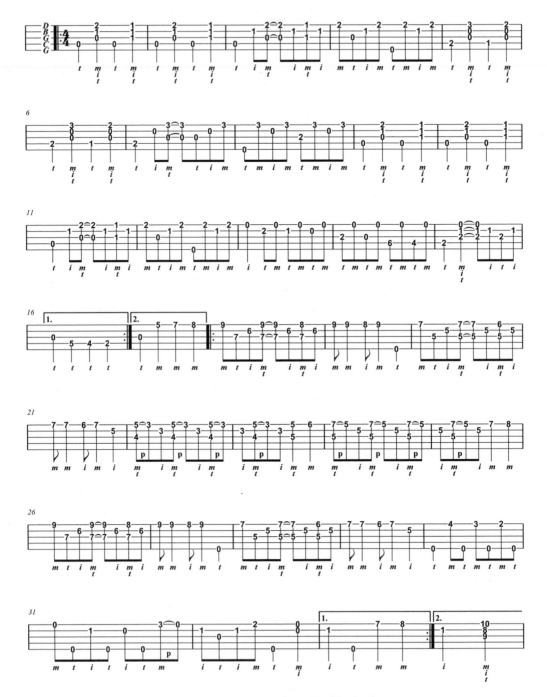

Tab 7-5: Playing "Banjoisticus," a classic banjo piece from 1909 (Track 76).

Chapter 8

Playing Three-Finger Styles: Scruggs, Melodic, and Single String

. . . .

In This Chapter

▶ Getting deeper into Scruggs-style banjo

▶ Branching out with melodic style

▶ Discovering single-string-style banjo

▶ Using three-finger techniques together

. . . .

*F*rom bluegrass to jazz, country, classical, folk, and rock, the banjo is right at home in all kinds of music today (okay, maybe not Wagnerian opera . . . not yet, anyway!). *Three-finger* style (where you use the thumb, index, and middle fingers of the right hand to strike the strings) is the playing technique that's being used to blaze most of these new trails for the banjo these days.

Three-finger banjo is usually associated with the bluegrass banjo style that was first developed by North Carolina banjo player Earl Scruggs. Earl Scruggs's banjo style is based around capturing the melody using right-hand roll patterns that create a bold, fast flurry of notes. Scruggs ushered in a banjo revolution in the mid-1940s when he introduced this technique to bluegrass and country music. Scruggs style is one of the most emulated playing styles in the world — on any instrument — and has truly become a universal way of playing music on the banjo (yes, if aliens were to play the banjo, it would probably be in Scruggs style — it's that good!).

Succeeding generations of players have built on Earl's contributions to come up with new three-finger possibilities that continue to expand the musical potential of the banjo. Melodic and single-string styles are the most important of these innovations. Both approaches enable you to more easily use scales in your playing (*scales* are the collections of notes you use to play melodies). In *melodic style,* you play scales and melodies by using roll patterns that are similar to those used in Scruggs style. With *single-string* playing, you use a technique that enables you to play notes on the same string consecutively when needed, much like guitar and mandolin players do when playing with their flatpicks.

To play the Scruggs, melodic, and single-string styles I describe in this chapter, you use a thumb pick and two finger picks on your fingers as well as the right-hand position favored by bluegrass players. If you're new to the banjo, you may want to visit Chapter 4 to get a feel for these topics before jumping into the great music that awaits you here.

Playing Scruggs-Style Banjo

Overestimating the contribution of Earl Scruggs to the world of the banjo is impossible. Although other players used three-finger techniques before him, Scruggs took this way of playing the banjo and perfected it, literally creating a entirely new musical vocabulary for the banjo that enabled him both to play blazing-fast solos and to accompany others in a bluegrass band. (To read more about Earl Scruggs's life and music, check out Chapter 14.)

Scruggs style is practically synonymous with bluegrass-banjo style. If your goal is to someday play banjo in a bluegrass band, you need to soak in as much of Earl's playing as you can. Scruggs-style banjo is also an essential foundation for playing melodic and single-string styles, and Earl's techniques are also great to use when accompanying others. If you want to play any three-finger style that uses fingerpicks, you just about have to get into Earl!

Some great fun lies ahead! In the following sections, you discover the right-hand patterns used in Scruggs-style banjo and use these patterns to play short interchangeable phrases called *licks* by using left-hand slides, hammer-ons, and pull-offs. You then combine these phrases to play full-length banjo solos and songs in Scruggs style.

Flowing with the rolls

Much of Scruggs-style playing is based around *roll patterns* — right-hand sequences of notes that crop up again and again when playing in this style. Roll patterns are made up of eight notes played by the right-hand thumb, index, and middle fingers. As a general rule, you use a different right-hand finger to strike a different string for each consecutive note when playing a roll pattern (in other words, you don't want to use the same right-hand finger or hit the same string twice in a row). This way of playing creates a smooth and constant flow of notes and is a big part of what make Scruggs-style banjo sound so great.

I include the most important roll patterns used in Scruggs-style playing in the following list, which you can see in Tab 8-1. Players often categorize rolls by the sequence of right-hand notes played (using *T* for thumb, *I* for index, and *M* for middle), along with the string sequence used (with numbers standing for each of the five strings on your banjo), which is what I do here:

- **Alternating thumb roll:** The right-hand sequence of this roll is T - I - T - M - T - I - T - M. Use this sequence with the following string order: 3 - 2 - 5 - 1 - 4 - 2 - 5 - 1.

- **Forward-backward roll:** This roll's right-hand sequence is T - I - M - T - M - I - T - M and uses a string order of 3 - 2 - 1 - 5 - 1 - 2 - 3 - 1. Note that this roll begins like the alternating-thumb roll but moves in a new direction with the third note you play.

- **Forward roll:** This roll is very exciting to play in bluegrass banjo. You can play with more power if you kick off the roll by using your right-hand thumb, as indicated in the tab's right-hand sequence: T - M - T - I - M - T - I - M. This example uses the following order of strings: 2 - 1 - 5 - 2 - 1 - 5 - 2 - 1.

- **Forward-reverse roll:** This roll starts with the same sequence of right-hand notes that you use in the forward roll but then shifts to the sequence used in the last four notes of the forward-backward roll: T - M - T - I - M - I - T - M. The string order for this example is 3 - 1 - 5 - 3 - 1 - 3 - 5 - 1.

- **Foggy Mountain roll:** Yes, this is the roll used to play the first measures of "Foggy Mountain Breakdown"! Be careful to play the first four notes of this roll correctly: begin with the right-hand index finger striking the second string and the middle finger playing the first string but then be sure to use the thumb to strike the next second string. This approach will provide you with more speed and power as you get comfortable playing this roll. The right-hand sequence is I - M - T - M - T - I - M - T, playing these strings: 2 - 1 - 2 - 1 - 5 - 2 - 1- 5.

- **Backward roll:** This roll begins with the middle finger and moves backwards towards the fifth string. Note the right-hand sequence for this roll: M - I - T - M - I - T - M - I. The strings indicated in the tab example are 1 - 2 - 5 - 1 - 2 - 5 - 2 -1.

- **Middle-leading roll:** As you might have guessed, there are a lot of middle fingers used in this roll pattern as revealed in the right-hand sequence: M - I - M - T - M - I - M - T. The strings you'll play in this example are 1 - 2 - 1 - 5 - 1 - 2 - 1- 5.

- **Index-leading roll:** This roll begins with the right-hand index finger playing the second string. The right-hand sequence for this roll is: I - T - I - M - I - T - I - M. The strings played in this example are 2 - 3 - 2 - 1 - 2 - 3 - 2 - 1.

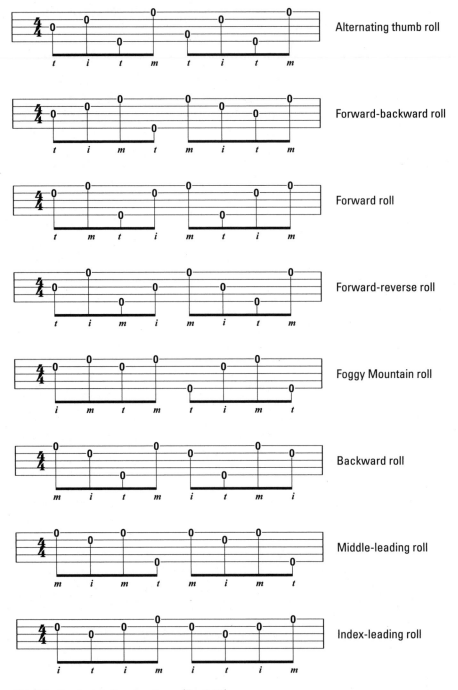

Tab 8-1: Scruggs-style roll patterns (Track 77).

Listen to Track 77 to hear the sound of each roll and to double-check your playing against these tab examples.

Practice these rolls until they become second nature. You can then cover ground much faster when you encounter these roll patterns in actual tunes. If any of these patterns are new to you, try using them as an accompaniment to "Red River Valley" by playing along with CD Track 24. (For more on how to play along with songs, visit Chapter 4.)

Making your music hot with some licks

In Chapter 5, I show you how to add left-hand slides, hammer-ons, and pull-offs to the right-hand roll patterns to begin making some real banjo music. Scruggs-style playing is based around creating music that uniquely combines these elements. As you listen and play pieces in this style, you may begin to notice short phrases that appear in more than one tune. These phrases, called *licks,* are the building blocks of Scruggs-style banjo. In the following sections, you can figure out what licks are and how to play them Scruggs style.

Figuring out the basics about licks

A short phrase that can be lifted out of one tune and played in another is called a *lick* (a *hot lick* is a particularly great-sounding phrase that is perfectly acceptable to play in public or even in front of your parents). Licks are used in melodic and single-string playing as well, but are especially at home in Scruggs style. Licks make your playing sound more interesting and varied and are essential elements to improvising on the banjo.

You can sometimes use licks as part of a melody, but often licks stand by themselves as good things to play on the banjo even when they aren't necessarily related to the melody of the song that's being played. Becoming comfortable integrating licks into melodies and knowing which licks can be used at what points in a song takes a lot of playing experience and a lot of listening to other good banjo players.

Using licks in your playing

Licks are almost always associated with chords. For example, you play G licks at that part of the song where the accompaniment is a G chord; you use C licks when everyone else is playing a C chord, and so on.

Each lick is a bit different, depending on which chord goes along with it and the specific roll patterns and left-hand techniques you use. When you encounter a new lick in tablature, do the following:

1. **Figure out the right-hand pattern indicated in the tab and practice this by itself until it sounds steady and solid (if you can memorize the right-hand sequence as you play, all the better!).**

2. **Add whatever left-hand techniques the tab shows (slides, hammer-ons, or pull-offs) while maintaining a solid rhythm in your right hand.**

The best way to figure out whether a lick works in a particular place in a song is to try it and see what happens. You usually know pretty quickly whether you've played something that works by the expressions on the faces of the other musicians around you! And for the songs in this book, don't forget to listen to the corresponding CD track and aim to match your sound to what you hear me play on the recording.

By listening to Tracks 78, 79, and 80 on the CD (and using Tabs 8-2, 8-3, and 8-4), play a group of essential licks for the G, C, and D chords — the three most frequently played chords in bluegrass banjo music. These phrases pop up time and again in the playing of Earl Scruggs, Sonny Osborne, and other bluegrass masters.

The process of adding licks to your musical vocabulary is a lot like adding new words and phrases when mastering a foreign language. In both cases, you expand the range of your expression as you internalize new things to say and new ways of saying them. After a lot of practice, you can combine licks into original phrases and come up with your own unique musical thoughts.

Incorporating fill-in licks

A special kind of lick that's frequently played at the end of a banjo solo or used in accompaniment when a singer takes a breath or pauses between the lines of a song is called a *fill-in lick*. This lick is especially useful to have in your grab bag of banjo tricks.

To play fill-in licks, you utilize the same techniques and roll patterns that you use for regular licks (see previous sections). However, fill-in licks tend to pack more left-hand techniques into the same amount of musical space as a regular lick and for this reason can be more challenging to play.

Tab 8-2: G licks (Track 78).

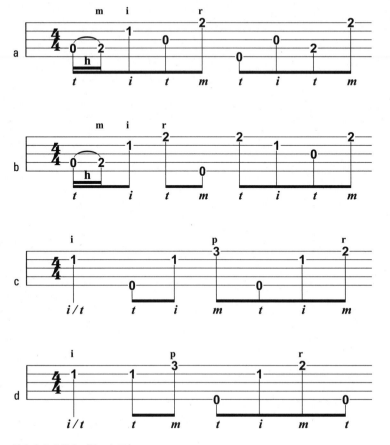

Tab 8-3: C licks (Track 79).

Tab 8-4: D licks (Track 80).

By playing Tab 8-5 (and listening to CD Track 81), you can get a feel for the four common fill-in licks that you use when you return to the G chord at the end of a tune's chord progression. You use at least one of these fill-in licks just about every time you play a song in the key of G.

Tab 8-5: Four common G fill-in licks (Track 81).

Combining licks to play a solo

You can build entire solos by stringing licks together. Although you probably won't be able to capture much of the melody of a song this way, following one lick with another is great survival strategy to use in a jam session as you fake your way through a song that you don't really know. Don't forget to make sure that your lick matches the chord that everyone else is playing!

You can see how this strategy works by creating a solo from the licks I present in the previous two sections. You can see (and play) it for yourself in Tab 8-6 (Track 82). The chord progression is an eight-measure cycle made up of two measures of G, followed by two measures of C, and then two measures of D, ending with two measures of G.

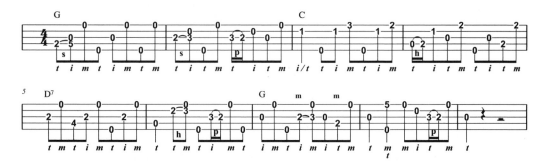

Tab 8-6: Creating a solo by combining licks (Track 82).

Progressing to Scruggs-style songs

As you gain confidence playing licks and combining them to create longer phrases, you eventually want to use the licks you know to create and enhance the melodies of songs. The following two tunes show you just how this can be done.

"Everyday Breakdown"

Because this song is made up of a number of essential two-measure phrases commonly used for the G, C, and D chords, "Everyday Breakdown" can get you started in your quest to create longer phrases and play entire songs by combining licks.

Many bluegrass banjo solos begin with a short, characteristic phrase that propels you into the main melody. These phrases are called *kick offs*. "Everyday Breakdown," which you can see in Tab 8-7 (Track 83), uses a three-note kick off that also works with "Foggy Mountain Breakdown."

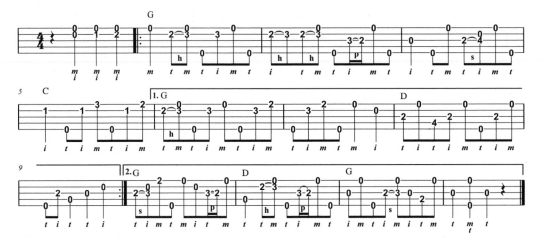

Tab 8-7: Playing "Everyday Breakdown," composed by me (Track 83).

"Shortening Bread"

To conclude this section on Scruggs style, you can take a look at my arrangement of a melody that Earl played often on radio and television broadcasts in the 1950s and '60s. "Shortening Bread" is the familiar melody you may have first heard as a child ("Mama's little baby loves shortening, shortening/Mama's little baby loves shortening bread").

Sometimes trying to capture the melody of a song in the simplest and most elegant way possible is best — something that Earl Scruggs seemed to do with ease just about all the time. I've tried to continue in Scruggs's footsteps with my arrangement of "Shortening Bread" in Tab 8-8 (Track 84).

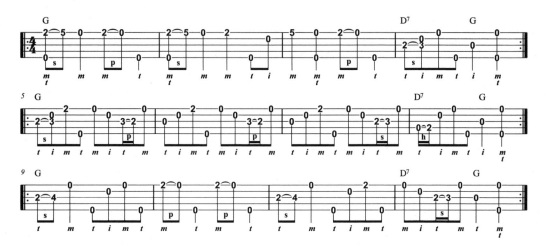

Tab 8-8: Playing "Shortening Bread" (Track 84).

Making Music with Melodic Banjo

Although Scruggs style (see preceding section) is just about the most logical and ingenious technique ever created to play music on the banjo, you unfortunately can't play *everything* in this way. Because you strike a different string with each roll note in Scruggs style, playing note-for-note versions of a melody that happens to contain lots of consecutive notes adjacent to one another in a scale can sometimes be difficult.

In the early 1960s, bluegrass banjo players Bill Keith and Bobby Thompson were independently working on solving this problem as they tried to find a way to play fiddle tunes more easily in a three-finger style on the banjo. These musicians came up with a new way of playing scales on the banjo called *melodic banjo,* where a different string is picked with each successive note, as in roll pattern–based styles of playing.

Melodic banjo is great to use as an addition to Scruggs style within bluegrass. This way of playing, which I describe in the following sections, gives you a new set of three-finger tools that you can apply to all kinds of music and also use in improvising. In addition to playing complex melodies with this approach, you can also create virtuosic improvisations that rival the best work of any jazz improviser!

Melodic style banjo is a real attention getter and is great for playing melodies that can't easily be played by using Scruggs style and for improvising. However, when it comes time to playing with others, you should rely on the roll patterns and techniques used in Scruggs style to provide the most appropriate accompaniment (see Chapters 4 and 12 for Scruggs-style accompaniment ideas).

Discovering how to play melodic scales

Although Scruggs style uses right-hand roll patterns as the basic building blocks of banjo technique, *melodic banjo* is based on finding and playing scales up and down the neck.

In Chapter 6, I locate all the notes for the G-major scale on the first five frets of the banjo (so if you want some additional scale info, you may want to turn to that chapter). In this section, instead of labeling the notes with the syllables "do - re - mi" as the Von Trapp Family Singers might do, I'm going to be more scientific and assign numbers to each step of the scale, with the number 1 indicating your starting point on the G note, as shown in Tab 8-9.

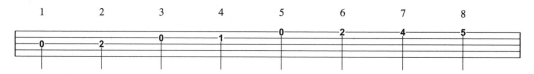

Tab 8-9: Assigning numbers to the notes in the G-major scale.

Note in Tab 8-9 how many consecutive scale notes are located on the same string (for instance, scale notes three and four are both on the 2nd string while scale notes five, six, seven, and eight are all on the 1st string). With the melodic banjo approach, you play the same pitches, but you locate each consecutive note on a different string, using a different right-hand picking finger to play each string, as you can see in the following sections.

Beginning with the melodic banjo G-major scale

The secret to playing a melodic banjo G-major scale is to relocate the fretted notes in Tab 8-9 to a lower string on your banjo (these are notes two, four, six, and seven of the G-major scale). You can then play different strings consecutively as you climb up the scale, using right-hand roll patterns that are related to Scruggs' rolls.

For example, the second note of the G scale (called an A note) is not only found on the second fret of the 3rd string, but is also at the seventh fret of the 4th string. The fourth note of the G scale, the C note, is at the first fret of the 2nd string, but you can also find it at the fifth fret of the 3rd string. Playing these fretted notes on a lower string allows you to play a different string and can make your playing sound smoother and more flowing.

To play a G-major scale by using melodic banjo technique, do the following:

1. **Pick the 3rd string open with the right-hand index finger.**

   You're playing the G note: the first note of the G-major scale.

2. **Fret the 4th string at the seventh fret with the left-hand ring finger and pick this string with your right-hand thumb.**

   This note is an A note, the second note of the G-major scale.

3. **Pick the 2nd string open with the right-hand index finger.**

   In this step, you play the third note of the G-major scale, the B note.

4. **Fret the 3rd string at the fifth fret with the left-hand index finger and pick this string with the right-hand thumb.**

   You're playing the fourth note of the G-major scale, which is the C note.

5. **Pick the 1st string open with the right-hand middle finger.**

   You play the D note, the fifth note of the G-major scale, in this step.

6. **Fret the 2nd string at the fifth fret with the left-hand middle finger and pick this string with the right-hand index finger.**

   Here you play an E note, and if you've been counting, you know that this is the sixth note of the G-major scale.

7. **Fret the 1st string at the fourth fret with the left-hand index finger and pick this string with the right-hand middle finger.**

   This note is an F♯ note — the seventh note of the G-major scale.

8. **Play the 5th string open with the right-hand thumb.**

   You're playing a G note that is one octave higher than the G note found on your open 3rd string.

The right-hand index finger does a lot of work in melodic banjo, so make sure you're playing these notes with good volume and power. In the left hand, you can add speed to your fingering if you release each fretting finger soon after striking the note with the right hand. This allows the left hand to get ready for the next fretted position.

Tab 8-10 shows you how you can play the G-major scale using melodic-banjo technique. You can follow the left-hand fingering indications by looking at the lower case letters above the tab staff (*i* stands for index, *m* for middle, *r* for ring, and *p* for the pinky finger).

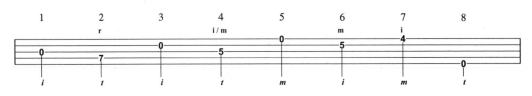

Tab 8-10: Playing the G-major scale by using melodic-banjo techniques.

The trickiest aspect of melodic technique on this part of the banjo finger-board is getting used to the idea of playing a higher-sounding fretted note on a lower-pitched string. Practicing a good bit to work melodic scales into your motor memory can really come in handy. After you've internalized the finger-board "route," you won't think about how unusual playing a scale this way really is!

Getting acquainted with more scales

Although getting comfortable with the G-major scale first is best (see preceding section), sooner or later you need to play scales that start on other notes. If you keep in mind that the principle behind melodic banjo is to find an adjacent scale note on a different string, you can figure out and play many different scales using the melodic approach.

For example, to play a melodic banjo C-major scale, you start on the fifth fret, 3rd string. The next note (D) is the open 1st string. Although you can play the following scale note (E) on the second fret of the 1st string, playing this note on the fifth fret of the 2nd string is better in melodic banjo. The next note of the C-major scale is an F note, and you can find it on the third fret, 1st string. The open 5th string is the next note (G) in the C-major scale.

The last three notes of the C-major scale are A, B, and C and require you to fret notes above the fifth fret. Because you just played the open 5th string, the best choice for the A note is the 2nd string, tenth fret; followed by a ninth fret, 1st string for the B note; and a tenth fret, 5th string for the G, as shown in Tab 8-11.

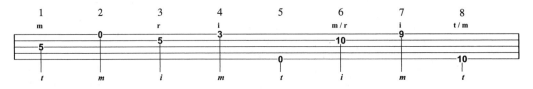

Tab 8-11: Playing the C-major scale by using melodic-banjo techniques.

Melodic-banjo playing up the neck often uses left-hand positions where you're not only fretting the 5th string, but also fretting two or three other strings with the left hand at the same time — not easy! Some players prefer to use their thumb to fret the 5th string in these situations, but others rely on their index finger. The finger (or thumb) you use then determines which left-hand fingers you use to fret the other strings in a melodic position. In the example in Tab 8-11, I've indicated both options above the tab staff. See which way works best for you!

Getting a feel for melodic-banjo songs

Practicing scales familiarizes you with the basic moves you use in melodic style, but this isn't nearly as much fun as playing tunes that utilize this approach. As you branch out and apply melodic-banjo techniques to your own arrangements, the following tips can help guide your choices of what to play:

- **Melodic style works best when you play melodies that have a lot of quick notes that are adjacent to one another in a scale.** Many fiddle tunes fit this description exactly, making this a great time to go melodic. Most vocal songs have melodies with longer notes and usually sound better with Scruggs-based playing.

- **The key of the song is directly related to the scales and licks you use.** For songs in the key of G, you can use the G-major scale to create melodic licks that also work for C and D chords. However, songs with more complex chord progressions sound better by using other scales that match the chords being played. Check out Tony Trischka's *Hot Licks for Bluegrass Banjo* (Oak Publications) to find melodic scales and licks for other chords and keys.

- **You can expand the possibilities of melodic banjo beyond just playing scales by applying roll-pattern ideas to the left-hand fretted melodic positions to create impressive-sounding descending and ascending runs.** If you simply race up and down a major scale for any extended length of time, your music could become boring pretty quickly (for your listeners at least — I can personally do this all day and be as happy as a clam!). For more info on roll patterns, check out the section "Flowing with the rolls" earlier in this chapter. You can use roll patterns with melodic banjo in the song "Banjo Cascade" later in this section.

- **Melodic style is great for improvising too!** You have different melodic licks for different chords, just as in Scruggs style. Don't be afraid to play your favorite C melodic lick (or G or D lick) each time that chord comes around in whatever song you're playing (it may not always work, but you'll never know until you actually try it).

- **Try different left-hand fingerings, especially when using melodic techniques up the neck.** You usually have more than one way to play the same note sequence in melodic style. You can determine how to play a note largely by what your left hand needs to be fretting at that moment.

In this section, you can try two tunes, using the melodic approach. The first, "Banjo Cascade," is really more of an exercise to get you used to playing descending and ascending scale patterns. The second is the perennial favorite "Turkey in the Straw." Don't forget that the tabs indicate left-hand fingering above the staff, using lower-case letters, and right-hand fingering below the staff, using italics.

Enhancing melodic techniques with roll patterns: "Banjo Cascade"

Try your hand (or fingers) at "Banjo Cascade," a short song that explores some of these possibilities with a chord progression that moves from G to C to D by using forward and backward rolls (see Tab 8-12, which is Track 85 on the CD). These kinds of sounds are what three-finger players draw on when improvising over chord progressions in the melodic style. Note how the left hand shifts from one fretted position to another as you move down and then up the scale.

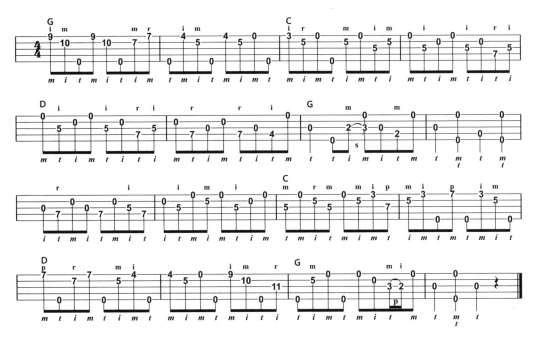

Tab 8-12: "Banjo Cascade" by yours truly (Track 85).

Getting fancy with fiddle tunes: "Turkey in the Straw"

Fiddle tunes are a staple of any bluegrass jam session (especially if a fiddle is present!). Bluegrass and old-time musicians use the label *fiddle tune* to refer to a large body of instrumental pieces which may or may not have their actual origin as fiddle music. Regardless of the instrument you play, everyone loves to play fiddle tunes and encountering many of them in jam sessions isn't unusual (you don't even have to have a fiddle in your jam session to play a fiddle tune either, by the way).

Most fiddle tunes are made up of two sections with different melodies. Musicians usually repeat each section once before moving on to the next section (players sometimes describe this tune structure as an *AABB form*). Using melodic banjo technique for the first section and a more Scruggs-oriented approach for the tune's second half (see the section "Playing Scruggs-Style Banjo" for more info), try to work out the familiar fiddle tune "Turkey in the Straw."

In this version of "Turkey in the Straw," you use a lot of the fretted positions you use in "Banjo Cascade," and you also put in some laps running up and down the G-major scale (see Tab 8-13, which is Track 86). When in doubt about the left-hand fingering, don't forget to look up for answers (not to the heavens, but above the tab staff).

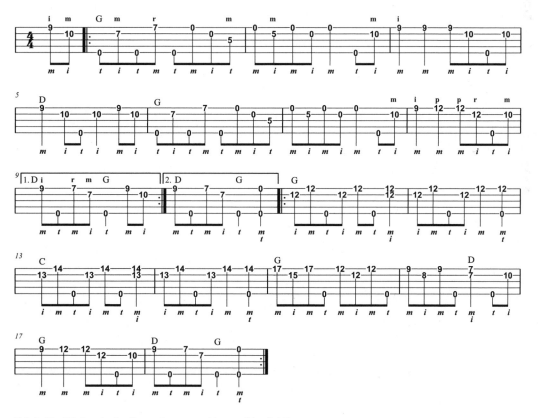

Tab 8-13: "Turkey in the Straw," arranged by me (Track 86).

Playing Single-String Banjo

In the hands of such skilled innovators as Béla Fleck, Alison Brown, Tony Trischka, and Noam Pikelny, the musical possibilities of three-finger banjo are expanding ever outward from bluegrass to jazz, classical, and other musical styles. Incredibly virtuosic and complex music is being made on the banjo today in significant measure because of new developments in single-string banjo technique.

Single-string banjo provides another solution to the dilemma of finding a way to play scales and scale-based melodies on the banjo. Instead of playing consecutive scale notes on different strings as in melodic banjo (see preceding section), *single-string* banjo utilizes a right-hand technique that's based around finding ways to play notes on the same string. The left-hand fretting moves are also different with single-string banjo because you're finding the notes in different places on the fingerboard with this way of playing.

Short single-string passages abound in the classic banjo music of the late-19th and early-20th centuries (for more on classic banjo, take a short trip to Chapter 7). Bluegrass pioneers Don Reno and Eddie Adcock introduced this way of playing to bluegrass banjo style in the late 1950s and early 1960s. Over the next several decades, younger players incorporated ideas from rock and jazz guitar technique to expand the range of single-string technique.

In the following sections, you become familiar with the right-hand picking patterns used in single-string banjo before moving on to experiment with different ways to play a single-string G scale. After playing the following exercises, you'll have a much better picture of what single-string banjo is all about and grasp the many exciting musical possibilities that are possible with this approach.

Using the right hand

Single-string banjo technique is similar in many ways to playing lead guitar with a flatpick. In lieu of the flatpick moving up and down to play notes on the same string, in single-string banjo you use your thumb and index fingers in alternation or use roll-pattern combinations of your thumb, index, and middle fingers to play melodies on individual (or *single*) strings.

Your choice of which right-hand pattern to use is determined by the specific song or lick you're playing, so feel free to experiment to see what works best for your playing and that particular song!

And keep in mind that creating a smooth and flowing sound using single-string techniques can be a real challenge. So as you play the following right-hand exercises, keep as steady and even rhythm as possible and play each note with the same volume.

Single string with thumb and index finger

Currently, banjo players are in moment of transition in how they choose to play single-string techniques with the right hand. The more established way is to use a steady alternation of right-hand thumb and index fingers, as in the following exercise (you can follow along with Tab 8-14, which is Track 87, part a):

1. **Pick the 1st string with the right-hand thumb and then strike it again, using the right-hand index finger.**

2. **Repeat Step 1, alternating the thumb and index to play the 1st string a total of four times in a row.**

   Each of these notes should be equal in length and in volume.

3. **Play the same pattern from Steps 1 and 2 on the 2nd, 3rd, and 4th strings, keeping a steady rhythm throughout and striking each string four times.**

4. **Move up from the 4th string, playing the four-note pattern on the 3rd, 2nd, and 1st strings before ending on the 3rd string.**

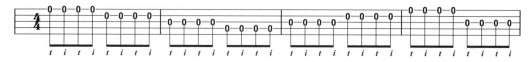

Tab 8-14: Single-string exercise, using the right-hand thumb and index finger (Track 87, part a).

Single string with thumb, index, and middle fingers

Another way of playing single-string patterns is to bring the middle finger into the picture to play roll patterns on individual strings. For example, try playing the same string sequence as in Tab 8-14, but this time use an alternating-thumb roll on just *one* string, as shown in Tab 8-15, which is Track 87, part b. (For more info on roll patterns and the alternating thumb roll, check out the section "Flowing with the rolls" earlier in this chapter.)

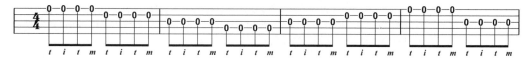
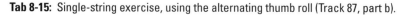

Tab 8-15: Single-string exercise, using the alternating thumb roll (Track 87, part b).

If you have six notes per measure (as you do in an Irish-inspired jig in 6/8 time later in this chapter), you can try a three-note forward roll on each string. To do this, you strike each string first with the right-hand thumb, followed by the index and middle fingers, as you move from the 1st string to the 2nd, 3rd, and 4th strings, as shown in Tab 8-16, which is Track 87, part c.

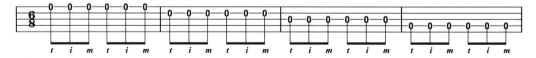

Tab 8-16: Single-string exercise in 6/8 time, using the forward roll (Track 87, part c).

Taking a crack at single-string scales

Much of the left-hand work in single-string banjo is in mapping out the fretted positions that provide an easy reach to the notes you use to play a particular lick or melody fragment. You almost always have more than one way to play just about anything in single-string style. But don't let this discourage you — when you begin to play licks and songs by using these techniques, you'll appreciate having choices!

When you play scales using single-string techniques down the neck (on the first five frets of the banjo), you play a combination of both open (or unfretted) and fretted strings, using what banjo players call *open* positions for your left-hand fretting. However, when you begin to play single-string patterns up the neck (above the fifth fret), you use left-hand fingerings in which most, if not all, of the notes are fretted. These left-hand positions are called *closed* positions.

And borrowing a bit of terminology from guitar players, you may notice that in this section I refer to the various positions you use to play a scale across strings as *boxes*. Where you're coming from and where you're going to on the banjo fingerboard in a particular passage of a song determines which box you use for a particular phrase. As you gain more experience playing single-string banjo, you gain more confidence shifting from one box to another.

To get a taste of the technique that is at the heart of great single-string playing, it's time to take a look at four different ways to play the G-major scale as well as D-major single-string scales. In the tablature examples, I ask you to alternate the thumb and index finger in the right hand. However, if you feel like using your right-hand middle finger to catch a note here and there, go for it and see whether it works for you.

Unfortunately, this section doesn't have enough room to cover every scale you'll ever need. However, after you can handle the closed-position G-scale formations (later in this section), you can play other major scales by playing the same exercise but starting on a different fret (musicians call this process of playing licks and songs in different keys *transposing;* check out Appendix A to locate all the notes on the banjo neck). To find out more about scales of all kinds, check out *Music Theory For Dummies* by Michael Pilhofer and Holly Day (Wiley).

Single-string open G-major scale

Get out your banjo and try a G-major scale in an open position, playing as many unfretted strings as possible:

1. **Begin by striking the open 3rd string with your right-hand thumb.**

2. **Pick the 3rd string, second fret with your right-hand index finger.**

   Playing the same string twice in a row using different right-hand fingers is the heart of the single-string technique.

3. **Play the open 2nd string, followed by the 2nd string fretted at the first fret, using your thumb and index fingers to play these strings.**

4. **Play the last four notes of this G-major scale on the 1st string, once again alternating between the thumb and index in the right hand.**

   Take a moment to check out the left-hand fingering, which is indicated above the tab staff with lower-case letters in Tab 8-17, which corresponds to Track 88, part a.

5. **After playing the open 1st string, climb up this string, using your left-hand index, ring, and pinky fingers, to play the 1st string at the second, fourth, and fifth frets.**

6. **Finish up the exercise by moving back down the G-major scale to the open 3rd-string G where you originally started.**

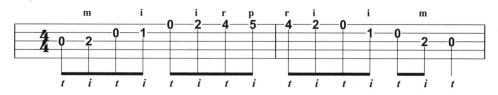

Tab 8-17: Playing an open-position single-string G-major scale (Track 88, part a).

Single-string closed G-major scales

You can also play the same notes from Tab 8-17 by using a fifth-fret closed box. This way of playing takes a little more left-hand firepower, but a big advantage is that you can move closed box patterns anywhere on the neck to match other chords and scales.

Here's one way to play a closed G-major scale (you can also check out Tab 8-18, which is Track 88, part b); remember that this particular exercise travels up the G-major scale all the way to an A note located on the 1st string, seventh fret:

1. **Begin by playing the open 4th string.**

2. **Climb up to the G note at the fifth fret of the 4th string by playing the 4th string at the second fret (an E note) and the 4th string at the fourth fret (an F♯ note).**

3. **Use the fretted positions from Step 2 to play all the subsequent notes of the G-major scale out of this box.**

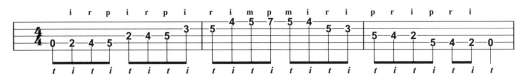

Tab 8-18: Playing a second- to fifth-fret box-position single-string G-major scale (Track 88, part b).

Box positions help you to remember left-hand fingering patterns. Many players take advantage of what I call the *one-finger-per-fret rule* when using box positions. After you're in a box position, your left hand covers a fretting range of four (and sometimes five) frets — with one left-hand finger responsible for each fret in the box. Your first choice in left-hand fingering on any string is to use the finger in the box that's designated for this fret.

For example, in this exercise (and in Tab 8-18), the pinky finger is used to fret the fifth fret on any string, the ring on the fourth fret, the middle on the third fret, and the index on the second fret. You don't want to remain in just one region of the fretboard for very long however, so players often shift the box up or down one or more frets as needed to reach the notes that they want to play. This is exactly what happens in Tab 8-18 at the last note of measure one as the left-hand index finger shifts from a second- to a third-fret position, moving the entire box up one fret. This movement allows the left hand to catch the A note on the 1st string by extending the box (and the reach of the pinky finger) up to the 1st string, seventh fret, as shown in Tab 8-18.

After you have these basic steps down pat, try the same G-major scale, but this time, use the middle finger to play the G note on the fifth fret of the 4th string instead of the pinky finger. Note that four fingers of your left-hand have now created a box that is two frets higher than the box you used for Tab 8-18. Another left-hand finger shift occurs in this scale exercise at the beginning of measure two as the index finger moves up one fret to fret the 1st string, fifth fret.

As you shift either up or down the fretboard, you can play higher or lower notes as needed. Check out Tab 8-19 for all the details and listen to Track 88, part c.

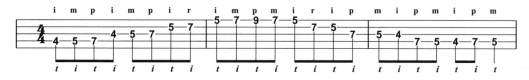

Tab 8-19: Using a fourth- to seventh- and fifth- to ninth-fret-box positions (Track 88, part c).

Now try moving the box up one more fret and play a G scale in which the left-hand index finger frets the G note located at the fifth fret of the 4th string (see Tab 8-20 and listen to Track 88, part d). Note that your box now covers five frets, enabling you to play three scale notes on each string. Also, you have a left-hand shift at the next to last note of the first measure (where the left-hand index moves up two frets to the seventh fret) and again at the second note of the second measure (where the index moves up two frets again to play the ninth fret, 1st string). These shifts are common in single-string playing, allowing greater fretting range in the left hand.

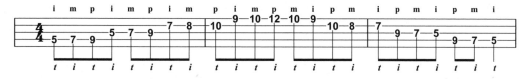

Tab: 8-20: Using fifth- to ninth-, seventh- to tenth-, and ninth- to twelfth-fret box positions (Track 88, part d).

Single-string D-major scale

After you're comfortable using single-string ideas in the key of G (see preceding sections), branching out to new keys, using single-string techniques, is fairly easy.

Try an open-position D-major scale beginning on the open 4th string (you can follow along in Tab 8-21, which is Track 89). You can find the second and third notes of the D-major scale (E and F♯) on the second and fourth frets of the 4th string. Next, play an open 3rd-string G followed by a 3rd-string, second-fret A note. You can find the B note by playing an open 2nd string. Follow this with a C♯ on the 2nd string, second fret and an open 1st-string D.

You can extend the D-major scale a few more notes by playing the 1st-string, second-fret E; the 1st-string, fourth-fret F♯; and the 1st-string, fifth-fret G.

Tab 8-21: Playing an open-position single-string D-major scale (Track 89).

Exercising single-string techniques in songs

Single-string banjo provides another way to broaden your range of musical expression. Depending on what each musical situation needs, you can use single-string techniques to play an entire solo or song, or you can just play a few fancy single-string licks to add variety to a tune played in Scruggs or melodic style. However you decide to incorporate these ideas into your playing, the following tips can help you master using single-string techniques in a tune faster and make them more fun to play:

- ✔ **Make your single-string playing sound as smooth and as flowing as you possibly can.** You can do this by keeping a very steady rhythm in your right-hand picking as well as holding one fretted note down for as long as possible before moving to the next fretted note with your left hand.

- ✔ **Know your scales and your box positions.** You'll quickly appreciate how much easier it is to figure out a new tune if you've already spent time working on scales and the different box positions you can use to play single-string passages (see previous sections on these topics). Do your homework (jazz musicians call this *woodshedding*)!

- ✔ **Work up speed slowly.** Playing single string fast isn't easy! Don't be discouraged if it takes months, or even years, to sound like your progressive banjo heroes. Begin by playing as slowly as you need to in order to sound good and increase speed very gradually over time.

Now you're ready to tackle a few tunes in single-string style!

"Arkansas Traveler"

This first tune is the fiddle-tune favorite "Arkansas Traveler." Most people play this song in the key of D major, so you need to first map out a D-major scale before jumping into the tune (see section "Single-string D-major scale earlier in this chapter). For this song, the version of the D-major scale you need begins on the open 4th string and climbs all the way up to the G note on the fifth fret of the 1st string.

Now you're ready to play "Arkansas Traveler," using single-string techniques. It's Tab 8-22 and Track 90 on the CD. Note that the second half of the tune shifts to a higher box as it climbs up to the A note found at the seventh fret of the 1st string. You play a lot of consecutive 1st-string notes in the right hand in this section, so be sure to pay close attention to the left-hand fingering indicated above the tab staff. If you do that, you'll be just fine!

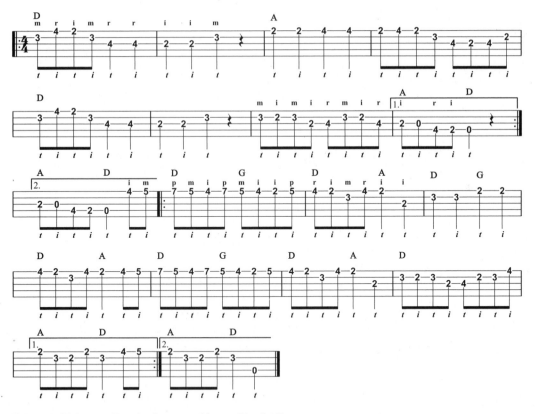

Tab 8-22: "Arkansas Traveler," arranged by me (Track 90).

"Reno's Rag"

One of the advantages of single-string banjo is that you have easy access to many different notes within a single box position. You can figure out much of the left-hand fingering for the chord-based licks in "Reno's Rag" by using the one-finger-per-fret rule (which I describe in the section "Single-string closed G-major scales," earlier in this chapter). This tune is shown in Tab 8-23 and is Track 91 on the CD.

With the G chord that begins this piece, you want to use your left-hand index finger to fret across the seventh fret on all strings. You then use your middle finger to fret any note that falls on the eighth fret and your ring finger to fret all ninth-fret notes. You then shift this box down two frets for the A chord, using one finger per fret once again.

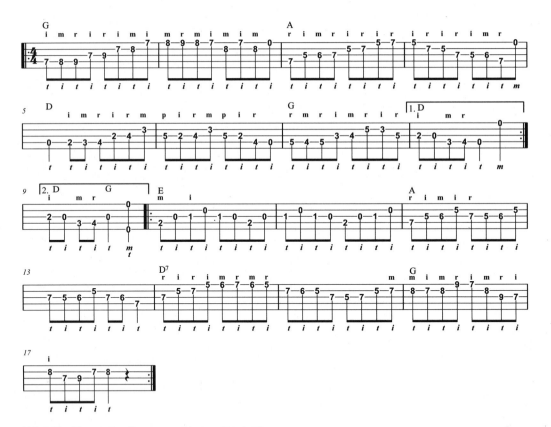

Tab 8-23: "Reno's Rag," composed by me (Track 91).

Single-string innovator Don Reno created some great-sounding single-string licks based around the F and D chord positions way back in the 1950s, and these rock 'n' roll–influenced licks still sound great on the banjo today. Several of these licks are incorporated into the melody of my tune "Reno's Rag."

"Winston's Jig"

You can try a bit of Irish-inspired music by using single-string techniques on the song "Winston's Jig" (Tab 8-24). Jigs have a different rhythm than other kinds of fiddle tunes, with six beats in each cycle and six right-hand notes per measure. When playing jigs, you have a prime opportunity to bring the right-hand middle finger into your playing technique to use forward rolls that match this rhythm (you can read more about using the forward roll in single-string playing in the section "Playing Single-String Banjo: Using the right hand" earlier in this chapter). Be sure to pay attention to this unique feature of jigs as you work your way through this tune — and don't forget to listen to the Track 92 on the CD to hear my version.

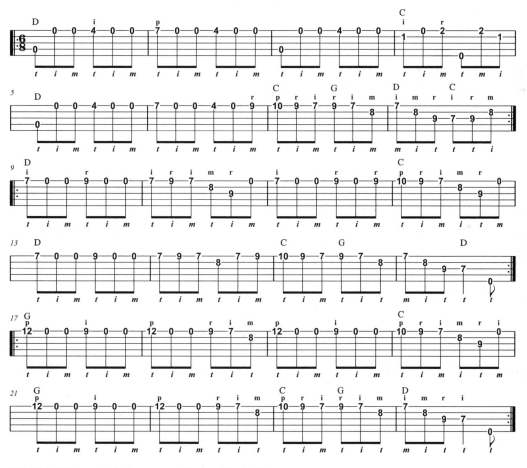

Tab 8-24: "Winston's Jig," composed by me (Track 92).

Combining Three-Finger Techniques

Modern banjo players combine Scruggs, melodic, and single-string techniques to create a wide variety of three-finger soundscapes. Although you can't find any rules written in stone, Scruggs style is generally used for hard-driving bluegrass songs and for accompanying other musicians, while melodic and single-string banjo techniques launch the instrument into musical fusions blending bluegrass with jazz, classical, and international music styles.

You shift from one technique to another in order to best capture what you want to play at any particular moment. The greater your technical facility on the instrument — something that comes with years of hard work — the more you can express on the banjo. This lifelong journey provides great personal rewards when you reach the point where you can instantly connect mind and fingers to play the music you hear in your head and feel in your heart.

Until you've gained a lot of experience in each style on its own, you can't really put them all together. So if you need a refresher or some more experience on these three-finger techniques before tackling this section, I suggest you take a look at the previous sections of this chapter.

To close out this chapter's survey of modern three-finger styles, I'd like to present my tune "Meadows of Dan" from the CD *Bill Evans Plays Banjo,* which is shown in Tab 8-25. (You can hear more about this recording by visiting my homepage at `www.nativeandfine.com`.)

This advanced-level tune demonstrates how many of the techniques I discuss in this chapter can be blended together and used as inspiration in original tunes. You can find a bit of everything in "Meadows of Dan" — from shifts in time signature to a change of key in the tune's second half. Although Scruggs rolls predominate in the tune's first half, the second half uses single-string techniques in the key of E♭ major.

The accompanying CD has a track of me playing the tune slowly (Track 93), followed by the full band track (Track 94) from the *Bill Evans Plays Banjo* CD. Playing along with me are some of the best musicians in bluegrass music today: John Reischman, mandolin; Missy Raines, bass; Rob Ickes, dobro; Jim Nunally, guitar; and Greg Spatz, fiddle. I hope you enjoy this tune!

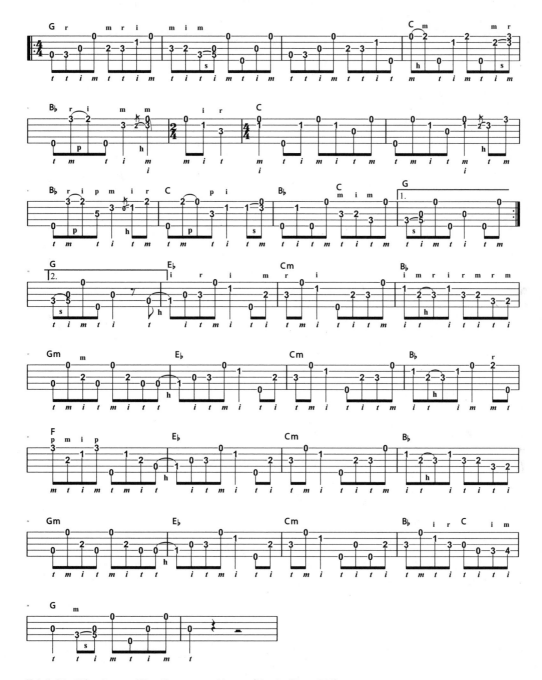

Tab 8-25: "Meadows of Dan," composed by me (Tracks 93 and 94).

Part IV

Buyer's Guide, Care and Feeding, and More

...and on banjo is Vic Strange who learned his instrument sitting in his dad's recliner.

In this part . . .

1 include a complete (and completely honest) buyer's guide and maintenance advice in this part. The buyer's guide can help you spend your money wisely on anything from a beginners' instrument to a professional-model banjo. I also cover those accessories you *really* need as well as those extras that are just fun to have around the house. I also provide useful tips on banjo maintenance and string changing. Finally, I help you find a good teacher, survive your first jam session, and expand your musical horizons through workshops, camps, and music festivals.

Chapter 9

Finding Your Banjo Bliss: A Buyer's Guide

I'm going to let you in on a secret: Buying a banjo can be really fun *if* you know how to do it. You can find more choices and more ways to buy a banjo today than ever before — and an instrument is out there for just about every budget. Your banjo *is* waiting for you, and this chapter helps you to find it.

Whether you have your eye on a beginner's model or a professional instrument, you need to know some fundamental differences in banjos before you lay down your hard-earned cash. If (or when) you've been playing for a few years, the time comes to step up to a better instrument, or you may someday want to make the ultimate investment and buy a collectable vintage banjo. This chapter guides you through each step of the process and helps you avoid some of the common pitfalls that you may encounter on your banjo acquisition quest.

Establishing Your Banjo Boundaries

Before you step into a music store or venture onto the Internet to begin your banjo search, you need to set some guidelines to make your search more fun and effective:

✔ **Setting your expectations:** Do you have a track record of getting excited about various hobbies but then moving on quickly to something else that strikes your fancy? Or do you have a gut feeling that the banjo is just the thing that you've been waiting for all your life? Your answers to these questions help you determine how much to invest or whether to invest at all (and if you want to be sure you're being honest with yourself, consider asking for your significant other's opinion).

✔ **Deciding what's important:** Do you want an instrument with flash or something simple? Do you want something just to play around the house, or do you ever expect to travel with your banjo? Do you see yourself playing by yourself or with others? Are you also budgeting for banjo lessons or instructional materials? The answers to these kinds of questions help you sharpen your focus.

Here's another important thing to consider: As a rule, banjos tend to be heavier than guitars or mandolins. If you have back problems, you want to find an instrument that's on the lighter side.

✔ **Determining your budget:** I realize that thinking about the financial part is a drag, but you've got to do it. After you've had some time to think about what will make you happy (and what you can live with!), you then need to determine both how much you can afford and the quality of banjo you're seeking. The minimum amount you need to spend for a playable new beginner's banjo and a few essential accessories is about $350 to $400. A banjo with "all the right stuff" sets you back anywhere from $600 to $4,500 or more, depending on just how much of the extra goodies you really need! My advice is to get the kind of banjo that's best for the style you think you want to play, even if it costs more.

If you're discovering a fretted instrument for the first time and have a busy life full of work and family commitments, count on 9 to 18 months of dedicated practice before you can move past the beginners' level. If you purchase the right beginners' banjo, two years may go by before you want or need to buy up. However, if you already play, a better-sounding instrument can jump-start your enthusiasm and push you onward and upward. In this case, I suggest you head to the section "Stepping Up to a Better Banjo" later in this chapter.

Making the Leap: Resonator or Open-back?

You have a choice of two different kinds of five-string banjos:

✔ A **resonator** banjo has a wooden back that is attached to the back of the instrument (see Figure 9-1).

✔ An **open-back** banjo doesn't have anything attached to the back. You can easily look into the inside of the banjo's sound-producing chamber (also see Figure 9-1).

You can identify a resonator or an open-back banjo by simply looking at the back of the instrument: If it doesn't have a resonator, the banjo is an open-back.

Your decision as to which kind of banjo is best for you should be based primarily on the style of music that you think you want to play. The differences between these two types of banjos can be hard to understand at first, but they're mainly about the sounds that skilled players prefer from each kind of instrument. After you try out both kinds of banjos at a music store by holding them in your hands, strumming a few chords, or playing a song or two, you can immediately begin to understand some of these differences, even if you've never played banjo before. The following sections discuss the advantages of each type of banjo.

Pumping up the volume: Resonator banjos

Over the last 150 years, banjo builders have continually tried to make banjos louder. I know what you're asking yourself: Aren't banjos loud enough *already?* Well, maybe they are now, but it wasn't always that way. Around 1860, someone came up with the idea of attaching a wooden chamber, or *resonator,* to the back of the banjo body in order to increase the volume of the instrument. The resonator reflects the sound off of its inside surface and projects the sound out of the front of the instrument and away from the player. The result is more volume and a brighter banjo sound. The resonator is usually attached to the banjo with thumbscrews.

In bluegrass music, you need to be able to play with enough volume so that the other band members and your audience can hear your virtuosic solos (for more on bluegrass banjo, see Chapters 4, 6, and 8). Therefore, practically all bluegrass-based banjo players prefer a resonator banjo strung with metal strings. Musicians also use resonator banjos whenever they desire additional volume and a brighter tone for other styles, from folk and old-time to progressive three-finger approaches that are elaborations of bluegrass technique.

Entry-level resonator banjos are more expensive than comparable open-back instruments. You can expect to pay from $50 to $150 more for a beginner's resonator banjo than for the same instrument in an open-back configuration. However, if you're interested in playing bluegrass, you should spend the extra money and get a resonator banjo.

If you ever need less volume or the tone of an open-back banjo, you can always loosen the thumbscrews and remove the resonator to create an instant open-back instrument. (For an overview of the parts of the banjo, see Chapter 1.)

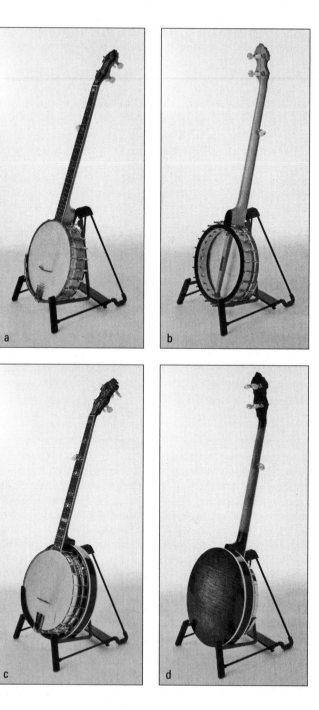

Figure 9-1:
An open-
back banjo
(a & b) and
a resonator
banjo
(c & d).

Going the old-time way: Open-back banjos

Open-back banjos generally have a mellower tone, are lighter in weight, and can be less expensive than resonator banjos. They also usually have a different setup than a resonator banjo, often with a higher string action that is the preference of clawhammer players (*string action* refers to how high the strings are positioned above the fingerboard of the instrument). Open-back players use metal, nylon, or gut strings, depending upon the specific style of music they're playing, how their instrument is set up, and the sound they want to get from their banjo.

Beginners can find new entry-level open-back banjos starting at around $300. You can find differences in price, look, and construction between open-back models depending upon whether they are made for old-time (including clawhammer) playing, or for classic or minstrel styles.

The power of tradition

The sound and style of a particular piece of music, how instruments are played, and the way that musicians interact with each other all have to do with agreed-upon ideas about music-making traditions. Musical traditions take shape as musicians think about music over many years, passing down what works and what sounds good from one generation to the next. These traditions relate to people's deepest-held beliefs about what good music should sound like and what role music plays in their lives. However, these traditions aren't written in stone: They change and evolve as musicians contribute new ideas and innovative ways of playing.

Traditions also involve aspects of music that aren't strictly connected to the sound of the music itself. For instance, if you went to a bluegrass festival expecting to hear Ralph Stanley and the Clinch Mountain Boys but the heavy metal band Kiss suddenly took the stage, plugged in their electric instruments and started wailing at top volume, you would at least be, well, *surprised.* When you attend a bluegrass concert

(or a heavy metal show for that matter), you have certain expectations about what the musicians will look like, what kind of instruments they play, and even the content of their stage patter. I'd never expect Ralph Stanley to yell at the top of his lungs, "Hello, Poughkeepsie! Let's rock and roll!" at a bluegrass show. This display would certainly be *interesting,* but it would be totally out of place.

For the most part, banjo players take comfort and even pleasure in following the traditions already in place for the music that they play. One of the most powerful of these traditions is using the right kind of banjo for the style that you're playing. For better or worse, almost all bluegrass players choose resonator instruments, and most folk and old-time banjo players prefer open-back banjos. If you're thinking of getting anything above the least expensive beginners instrument, you should strongly consider buying either an open-back or a resonator banjo based on the style that you think you will be playing most of the time.

Several manufacturers have entry-level open-back banjos with the same sound chamber (or *pot*) and overall design and construction as a matching resonator model available. However, more expensive open-back banjos likely have a different configuration of metal and wood than you find on a resonator banjo.

Banjos were around for 100 years or more before someone thought it would be a good idea to put resonators on them. The minstrel style of the mid-19th century, the classic style of the late 19th and early 20th century and many of the old-time styles of the early years of country music in the 1920s and '30s were all played at the time on open-back banjos. Folk music patriarch Pete Seeger prefers an open-back instrument, and most clawhammer players find the sound of an open-back banjo just right for playing old-time string band music. (For more on clawhammer banjo, see Chapters 4, 5, and 6; for minstrel and classic banjo, visit Chapter 7.)

Finding a Great Beginner's Banjo

When I was learning to play banjo in the 1970s, I had virtually *no* good choices in a beginner's instrument. Luckily, that's not the story today. You can purchase a good startup banjo for a little more than $300 (or even less if you can find a used model). However, you can also purchase an instrument that's perfectly awful. The following sections help you separate the good from the bad.

Although the appearance of an instrument may provide an initial attraction, the banjo that sounds the best to you is the one that you will be most happy owning in the long run. You need to determine which instrument within your price range speaks to you most powerfully. If your gut choice matches your stylistic aspirations, you're definitely on the right track to making a good decision.

When you're in a music store that has several different kinds of banjos in stock, don't be afraid to ask a salesperson to demonstrate each type. Better yet, if the store has a banjo teacher, introduce yourself and arrange a time where you can meet and be treated to a mini-concert. Another option would be to take a banjo-playing friend with you to play each instrument and offer advice. Sit directly across so that you can absorb the sound of each instrument as deeply as possible.

Knowing what's in the pot

The body of the banjo — the round part plus the resonator if it has one — is called the banjo *pot*. Good banjo pots are built around laminated pieces of wood called a *rim,* usually made of maple, that is pressed into a circular ring shape (see Figure 9-2). More expensive instruments also have a circular piece of metal or an unseen metal hoop called the *tone ring* resting on top of the wooden rim. The *banjo head* is stretched across either the top surface of the wooden rim or of the tone ring.

The pots on some inexpensive banjos are made of a single piece of aluminum. These banjos not only don't sound as good as a banjo pot built from a wooden rim, but may also distort out of their round shape over time. Regardless of your budget, go for wood in your pot!

Getting good string action

How high the strings are from the fingerboard of the banjo refers to the *string action.* You want a string action that is high enough so that you don't hear buzzing against the frets when you play, but low enough so that the banjo is easy to fret and stays in tune. Remember, players generally prefer higher action for some styles (like clawhammer) than for others (like bluegrass). One exactly correct string action doesn't exist. You must develop your own preferences as you play.

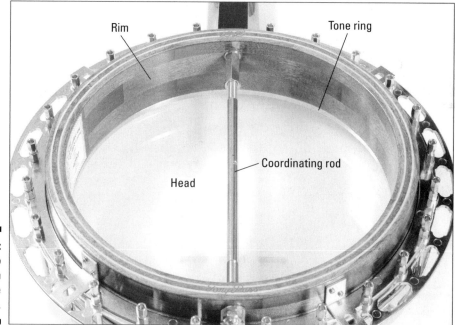

Figure 9-2:
The banjo pot (as seen from the back).

Rim

Tone ring

Coordinating rod

Head

For now, make sure that the string action is around ⅛" above the 12th fret for a bluegrass banjo by measuring the distance from the top of the fret to the 1st string. For clawhammer playing, it's fine for the action to be ¹⁄₁₆" or more higher than this (see Figure 9-3). The 5th string sits closer to the neck than the other four banjo strings, so you don't want to use this string as your reference. You may have to turn the banjo around to make the measurement. If the string action is ¹⁄₁₆" more or less than ⅛", that's okay. You have several ways to precisely adjust the string action, and at this point, you just want to make sure that it's in the ballpark. If the string action is wildly higher or lower, move on to another banjo — or to another music store!

The string action over the banjo fingerboard should be the lowest where the strings meet the nut and highest where the banjo neck meets the body (the *nut* is the notched white bar at the end of the fretboard at the opposite end of the banjo from the bridge and guides the strings to the tuners). The banjo should have a gradual and consistent increase in the string action as you look from the lowest to the highest fret. If you see a big jump in the string action occurring at one point on the neck, avoid this banjo because the neck of the instrument could have problems.

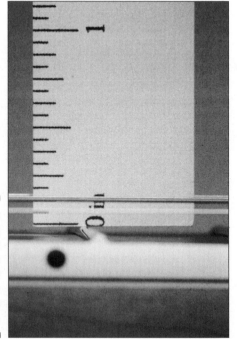

Figure 9-3:
Measuring string action: ⅛" above the 12th fret is good for a bluegrass banjo.

You don't need to carry a toolbox in with you to each music store as you go banjo shopping. However, have a ruler close by for measuring banjo bridges and string heights and whatever else strikes your fancy. You can download free, small printable rulers that you can cut out, fold up, stick in a wallet, and take with you everywhere. I know this sounds tremendously geeky, but these darned things have really come in handy for me. Visit `www.vendian.org/mncharity/dir3/paper_rulers` for more choices in rulers than any normal human may ever need.

Finding bridge height

A proper bridge height is essential if you want to enjoy playing your banjo. Some inexpensive imported banjos come with bridges that are so short that getting a good right-hand position for any playing style is difficult. You want a banjo bridge that measures around ⅝" or more from bottom to top. You can take this measurement on either the 1st- or 5th-string side of the bridge (see Figure 9-4).

Stay away from any instrument with a bridge that's less than ⅝" tall *and* has string action above ³⁄₁₆". This combination of ingredients will result in a banjo that is difficult to play and keep in tune.

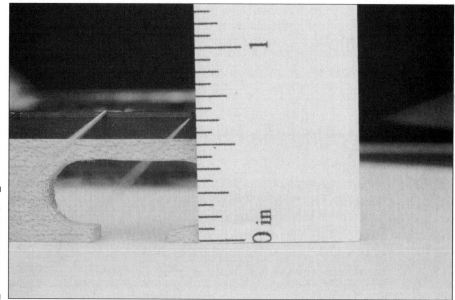

Figure 9-4: Measuring bridge height: ⅝" or more is best.

Unlike a guitar or mandolin, banjo bridges are easily removable from the instrument (after you know how to do it, that is). Professional players often try many different kinds of bridges on their banjos to find one that makes the banjo sound great and is just the right height (for more on this, see Chapter 10).

If the bridge on your banjo is just a bit too short or tall, but the other aspects of your prospective banjo purchase look good, you can always replace the bridge later. If your string action is too high and the bridge is over ⅝", you can replace the bridge with a shorter one and also adjust your string action at the same time.

Measuring string spacing

The distance between the strings is called the *string spacing* and is usually measured at the nut. If the strings are too close together, you will have trouble fretting cleanly, or you may find yourself muting adjacent open strings. You need more space between the strings if your hands are large or if your fingers are stubby. On the other hand, if the strings are too far apart for the size of your hand, reaching across the fingerboard to accurately fret chords will be a chore, and your left hand will tire quickly.

To measure the string spacing, measure across the top of the nut from the 4th string notch across to the 1st string (see Figure 9-5). For most folks, the string spacing at the nut should be around 1", give or take ¹⁄₁₆". These days, encountering a banjo that doesn't have adequate string spacing is unusual. However, you can still find a few new imported banjos that don't have enough room between the strings to ever allow the left hand to feel comfortable. Avoid these banjos unless your hands are really small!

Checking the tuners

It probably goes without saying that the job of the tuners on a banjo is to keep the instrument in tune (although knowing *when* the banjo's in tune is up to you — check out Chapter 2 to find out how). These days, most banjos have geared tuners, with gears attached to the tuning shaft that make tuning easier and more precise. The tuners on an entry-level instrument likely have external gears that you can easily locate by looking at the back of the peghead. More expensive banjos have tuners with gears that are housed inside the tuner's body itself. Although internal tuners tend to work better, tuners with external gears are fine on a beginner's banjo if they're in good working order. Both kinds are shown in Figure 9-6.

In either case, you want to check to make sure that the tuners move smoothly by tuning the strings up and down a bit and feeling the string movement through the peg. If necessary, have someone in the music store put the banjo back in tune for you after you've experimented in this way!

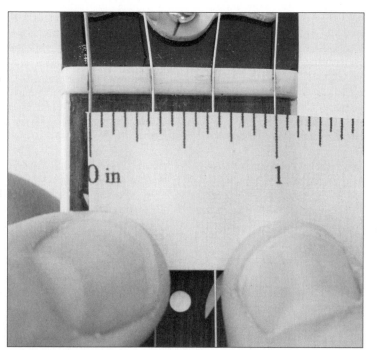

Figure 9-5:
Measuring
string
spacing:
around 1"
between 1st
and 4th
strings is
good.

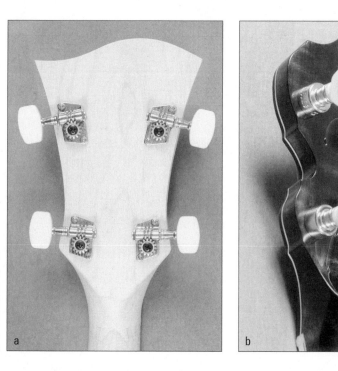

Figure 9-6:
External (a)
and internal
(b) geared
tuners.

a

b

I'm sure that you've already noticed that the banjo has a tuning peg that sits on the top part of the neck, almost right in the middle of the fingerboard. That's the 5th string's tuner. In order to cut corners, some builders make inexpensive banjos that have a 5th-string tuner with no gears at all (see Figure 9-7). With this type of tuning peg (called a *friction peg*), the string fluctuates wildly up and down in pitch with just the slightest movement, making your attempt to get the string precisely in tune very difficult. These kinds of tuners are common on banjos that are over 100 years old, but on a new instrument, let your warning flags go up and avoid this banjo.

If you already own a banjo with this kind of tuner on the 5th string, don't toss the entire instrument! Have a knowledgeable music store replace it with a geared 5th-string tuning peg (shown in Figure 9-7). The cost of this kind of tuner plus the installation charge shouldn't run more than about $30. This amount of money is a small price to pay to save yourself hours of tuning frustration. Your loved ones will also be more appreciative of your practice sessions if you're playing in tune.

Figure 9-7:
Friction (a)
and
geared (b)
5th-string
tuning pegs.

Help! I'm left handed. Can I find a banjo for me?

Eight to 15 percent of the world population is left handed. A left-handed banjo player may naturally want to pick the strings with the left hand and fret with the right. On a guitar, this matter is simple because you can reset the strings so that they're in the proper low to high pitch relationship to your hands. (This is how Paul McCartney, who is perhaps the world's most well-known left-handed musician, plays both guitar and bass.) However, because the banjo has the shorter 5th string that sits on the top side of the neck, you simply can't flip the banjo around and immediately begin playing the banjo left handed (well, you *could,* but it may not sound very good because the 5th string would be in the wrong place in relation to your picking hand).

Playing the banjo takes both hands. For adult learners, the issue isn't so much what the left hand is doing versus what the right hand is doing as much as coordinating the different actions of both hands at the same time. I'm left handed, but I first learned to play the guitar right handed. Then I learned to play the banjo. If I can do it, anyone can!

However, to play left handed, you have to have a banjo with a special neck that's a mirror image of a normal banjo neck so that the 5th string is on the top side of the instrument when you turn the banjo the opposite way. If you buy an entry level banjo with a left-handed neck, you have a choice of just a few instruments and have to spend an additional $100 for this option. As you buy up to more professional-sounding banjos, your choices still remain limited, and you may have to have your necks custom built, which usually adds to the instrument's price.

Unless you already play another stringed instrument left handed, I suggest that you try a regular right-handed banjo first. Try to make an arrangement with a music store to return your banjo in trade for a left-handed model if your experiment doesn't work out. If you feel extreme frustration after trying a right-handed banjo for a few weeks, consult with a local teacher or player to check your technique and ask his advice. If you both agree to try a left-handed instrument, then go for it.

Taking the plunge

If you've read the previous sections, you're now ready to make an informed decision on purchasing a beginner's banjo. The good news is that several banjos that combine all the necessary elements are available for under $400, giving you an instrument that plays well, sounds good, and is built to last until the time that you want to step up to something better. Check out banjos from the Deering, Gold Tone, and Epiphone companies, among others.

Don't worry too much about how these entry-level banjos look. These instruments don't have elaborate inlay patterns on the fingerboard or even a glossy finish, because the manufacturers are stressing good playability over fancy looks. These banjos also aren't going to sound as loud or as clear as more expensive instruments. However, they should *feel* like a higher-priced banjo and, at this point, that's the most important thing you need as a beginning player.

As a banjo teacher, every now and then I've witnessed new students who get so excited about their new hobby that they rush out and buy a professional-quality instrument that costs $2,000 or more before they're able to play a single song. For some reason, this kind of behavior seems to run rampant among middle-aged men like me! Although this impulse often works out in the long run to everyone's satisfaction, owning a professional instrument right off the bat can create too high of expectations of what you think you should be able to accomplish on the banjo. Remember, spending money doesn't make you a good banjo player — only practice can do that. Don't mistake the commitment of your financial resources with the commitment of the time that it takes to become a good banjo player.

The music store should offer to set up your banjo for free before handing it over to you and in addition may offer semiannual checkups. Take advantage of these services to keep your banjo in optimal playing condition (and for more on maintaining your banjo, see Chapter 11).

Stepping Up to a Better Banjo

A good deal of complex psychology is involved in knowing when you're ready for a better (and higher-priced) banjo. Here's the most honest way of knowing that it's time: When you've reached the point in your playing where you honestly feel that your current instrument is holding you back from becoming a better player, consider it time to start looking for a better banjo.

If you hear greater clarity and volume as you play another instrument, then you're in the company of a potential new soul mate. A new banjo that's better than what you already have should also be easier to play and should sound good when you play up and down the neck. The high notes should sound bright and brilliant, and the low notes should be deep and penetrating. If the banjo is considerably more expensive than what you already own, it should look better than your current instrument and may have elaborate and beautiful inlays in the fingerboard and on the headstock. Also, a better banjo is likely heavier than your typical entry-level banjo.

In the following sections, you match your musical goals to your budget and personality. You then train your eye to identify good components on a quality instrument and get acquainted with the differences between upper end resonator and open-back banjos to help narrow your future purchase choices.

Budgeting for a quality banjo

You have a number of different ways to think about an additional banjo purchase (your significant other may call these *rationalizations,* but you can pretend that this word is too big for you to understand). All of these various strategies have worked for me at different times as I've considered a new banjo purchase. See which of the approaches in the following sections is the best match for you.

I can't tell you how much to spend on your next banjo or which instrument you should buy. You have to figure this out on your own. However, keep in mind that banjos typically cost more than guitars for the same level of quality. Banjo players often spend $2,000 to $5,000 for a new professional-quality, American-made instrument with a case. The more money you plan to spend, the more time you should spend researching your options. Don't forget to spend time talking with family and loved ones about your purchase plans. In this way, you may end up with a banjo that provides pleasure for the rest of your playing days and could also become a valuable family heirloom.

The gradual-upgrade approach

You're the sensible type. You never like to get into anything over your head, and you're slow and steady in regard to your long-range commitments. You started by playing on one of those entry-level banjos that costs around $300, but now you've got your eye set on the next most expensive banjo, which costs about $200 more than your current instrument.

In the long run, you'll be satisfied with this strategy only if you're really getting more instrument for your money. The potential downside is that you may feel compelled to make a new purchase every couple of years. However, when I was learning to play as a teenager, this buying strategy was the only one that I could afford, and it worked out fine for me! If you follow this path, you want to spend from $200 to $500 or more for each step up to a better-sounding banjo.

The leap-frog approach

You're a bit more compulsive than the person described in the preceding section, but you've reached a sure conclusion that playing the banjo makes you happier than just about anything else in the world. You aren't getting any younger and because you only go around once in life, you've decided not to wait on an instrument that's close to the banjo of your dreams.

If you're interested in an open-back banjo, be ready to spend from $750 to $2,000 or more for a professional-grade banjo ready for old-time playing. A vintage open-back banjo from the first decades of the 20th century can top out at $7,000 or more. Prices for professional-quality bluegrass banjos start at around $1,000 and quickly escalate up to $4,500 and above. Vintage collector's bluegrass banjos from the 1920s, '30s, and '40s have skyrocketed in value in recent years, costing from $3,000 to as much as $40,000 to $100,000 or more for the most coveted models.

What have you got to lose with this approach? New banjos generally don't appreciate in value until they're several decades old, and vintage instruments are just downright expensive. Make sure with the leap-frog approach that you're buying an instrument from a respected and well-known builder or company so you can get back something close to your original investment if you and your banjo have to part ways.

The buy-something-different approach

You're a person who craves variety in life, and you don't limit yourself to enjoying and playing just one style of music. You love how various styles call for different banjo sounds and setups, and you may even be interested in starting a collection.

In this case, you want to purchase something that contrasts with what you already own by buying a banjo with a different sound or appearance or perhaps buying a bluegrass banjo if you already own an open back (or vice versa). With this approach, you can set a budget more flexibly based on your interest in the styles that you'll play on a different kind of banjo.

This approach is usually the domain of experienced players or collectors who are buying (or trading) professional caliber instruments. In this case, the sky's the limit. But even new players can add variety to their lives by buying a different kind of entry-level instrument, like an electric banjo (which I discuss later in this chapter), to complement an acoustic resonator or open-back model. You can get away with spending as little as $400 to $500 with this approach if you're a beginner who craves variety out of their banjos.

Knowing a quality banjo when you see it

Unlike a guitar, a banjo can be taken apart and put back together again with little more than an adjustable wrench. Many parts like necks, rims, tone rings, tuners, and even resonators, are interchangeable with other similar kinds of banjos. This case is especially true with professional-grade bluegrass banjos. Therefore, knowing your components is crucial in selecting a quality instrument. The following sections discuss what to look for in terms of the internal parts when choosing a quality banjo.

A good banjo is the result of using well-made components that are matched and fit together with care. A *great* banjo comes from using the best components and fitting them together with the utmost skill and precision.

If you're in the market for a quality bluegrass banjo, be sure to check out the following builders: Huber, Gibson, Deering, Stelling, Nechville, Tennessee, Sullivan, Kel Kroyden, Osborne, Louzee, Gold Star, Recording King, and Williams, among others. For a quality open-back banjo, don't forget to take a look at these makers: Wildwood, Bart Reiter, Chanterelle, Chuck Lee, Kevin Enoch, Jason Romero, Vega, Ome, and Recording King.

It's all in the wood: Banjo rims

Like the engine of a car, the rim and tone ring (see the following section) are the heart and soul of a banjo. The *rim* (or *shell*) is the ring-shaped piece of wood that, along with the tone ring, gives shape and definition to the banjo's sound. Banjo rims are made of maple, but beech, mahogany, and other woods are sometimes used. Most rims are made from pieces of wood laminated together and pressed into a circular shape. However, some rims are assembled from blocks of glued-together wood and are called, appropriately enough, *block rims*. Both types of rims are shown in Figure 9-8.

Rims are fairly standardized on quality bluegrass banjos, measuring 11" in diameter and around ¾" in thickness. Most bluegrass players desire a dense, hard piece of maple for the rim because they feel that this type of wood conveys the banjo's sound more efficiently. If the rim is made from hard rock northern maple, then you've got a top-of-the-line rim most desired today by bluegrass players.

You find much more variety in the sizes of rims used for open-back instruments, because open-back banjos come in many different sizes. Open-back rims can measure up to 12" in diameter but are typically thinner in width than a standard bluegrass rim.

Just about everyone agrees that older is better when it comes to the wood that goes into a banjo rim, but good wood is getting increasingly hard to come by all over the world. Some of the best "new" rims made today are assembled from North American old-growth wood or wood that has been submerged underwater for many years. These rims are often glued together by using organic hide glue, as used in the first half of the 20th century. An "old wood" rim is often a valued component in a top-of-the-line banjo built by a small shop, but you can also add this option to a quality banjo later.

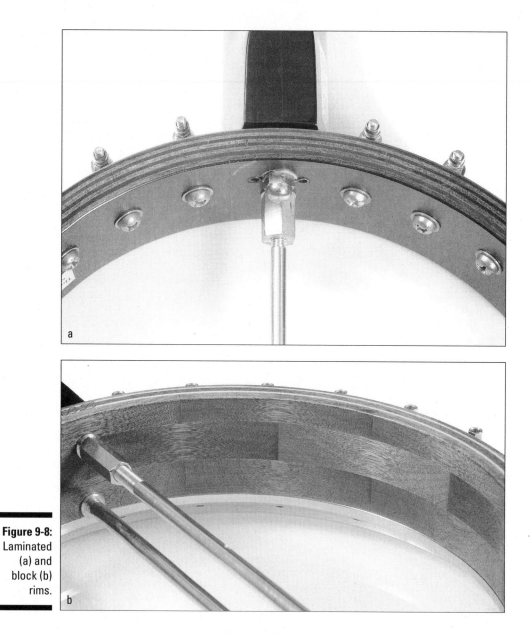

Figure 9-8:
Laminated
(a) and
block (b)
rims.

The fellowship of the tone ring

The other vital part of the banjo pot is the *tone ring*, which sits on top of the wooden rim, increases the banjo's volume, and brightens its tone. On a more expensive banjo, the tone ring should be made from high-quality brass (often called *bell brass*), not aluminum. Bluegrass banjo tone rings come in the following two types:

✓ **Flathead tone rings:** Most banjos made today have flathead rings. Most bluegrass banjo players, including the first-generation masters Earl Scruggs and Don Reno, use this kind of ring. The flathead ring causes more surface area of the banjo head to vibrate, thereby giving the banjo a deeper tone.

✓ **Arch-top tone rings:** An arch-top ring is most common among banjos from the 1920s and 1930s. This type of ring uses a different profile that causes less surface area of the banjo head to vibrate, usually resulting in a brighter tone. Bluegrass icon Ralph Stanley has long been associated with the sound of an arch-top bluegrass banjo.

As in the case of banjo rims, some builders have gone to great lengths to re-create the exact metal formulas found in banjo tone rings from the 1930s and 1940s, and these types of rings are found in the best (and most costly) new bluegrass banjos. Bluegrass tone ring sizes have become more or less standardized for new bluegrass banjos in the last 15 years, enabling players to experiment with their banjo's sound by swapping out one ring for another. A player may spend $2,000 to $3,000 on a new professional quality banjo, only to replace its tone ring somewhere down the line. These so-called pre-war formula tone rings range in price from $375 to $1,500, but can dramatically change the sound of an instrument.

You can find more variety in the kinds of tone rings used in quality open-back banjos, but also keep in mind that some old-time players prefer banjos with no tone ring at all (in this case, the head is simply stretched across the top of the wooden rim). Other old-time players prefer banjos that use a rolled brass hoop (called a *hoop ring*) for a tone ring. A hoop ring is a round, ring-shaped piece of brass that sits in a channel cut into the top of the rim with the head stretched across its top. The more muted tone of a hoop-ringed banjo is sometimes just right for the old-time sound, and, better yet, these instruments are usually less expensive than a banjo with a tone ring.

Some open-back banjos have tone rings that are virtually the same as those found on a matching model bluegrass banjo. However, new high-end open-back banjos are often fitted with specially made replicas, using tone-ring designs originally found on banjos dating back 100 years or more. The Tubaphone and Whyte Laydie styles of ring are two examples of replica tone rings found on many new professional grade open-back banjos today (see Figure 9-9 to see all the different kinds of tone rings mentioned in this section).

Figure 9-9:
Banjo tone
rings. From
left to right:
arch-top,
flathead,
Tubaphone,
hoop.

Necks and resonators

Necks are typically made from maple (in either straight-grained or curly varieties), mahogany, or walnut. If the banjo has a resonator, its wood is almost always of the same kind as the neck (although some high-end bluegrass banjos now offer maple necks with mahogany resonators). Most necks on high-end banjos are made from a single piece of wood and are called *one-piece necks.* Although these kinds of necks are preferred by most players, some builders prefer to outfit a quality banjo with a two-piece neck for additional stability and durability.

Builders and players alike agree that the type of wood used in the neck can have a significant impact on banjo sound, but actually describing these subjective differences can be very difficult! Generally speaking, walnut necks tend to impart the deepest tone of the three woods; maple necks add sweetness and clarity to the banjo's tone, while mahogany necks provide a more immediate response. However, the tone of any individual instrument is the result of many different factors acting together, including the mass of the neck itself. You can get a variety of banjo sounds from any of these kinds of wood.

Many players choose one type of wood over another based on appearance. You can make this factor the basis of your buying decision even on a professional-grade banjo as long as all the other component parts are of high quality. Elaborately figured maple or walnut and deep-grained mahogany are each beautiful in their own way. Go with what makes the best impression on your senses — both visual and aural!

Radiused fingerboards

The *fingerboard,* or *fretboard,* is the thin strip of wood glued to the neck that serves as a mounting surface for the frets. When you fret a note with your left hand, you're pushing against the fingerboard. Most banjo necks have a flat fingerboard, but some players prefer a fingerboard that is curved across its playing surface. This kind of fingerboard is called a *radiused fingerboard* and is an option on more expensive bluegrass instruments. You can expect to pay up to $200 or more for this option. However, if you're into more progressive bluegrass and jazz styles on the banjo, you may find that you can more easily strut your left-hand stuff on a neck with a radiused fingerboard.

Banjo bling: Inlays, plating, and engraving

Banjos are not only usually louder than guitars or mandolins, but they're traditionally adorned with more ornate decoration — yet another reason why banjos rule! Aesthetic enhancements come in the form of elaborate inlay patterns in the neck and fingerboard, intricately carved neck heels, and engraved metal parts (see Figure 9-10 for some stellar examples).

Banjos with gold-plated or chrome metal parts may also grab your attention. These features not only brighten up the look of a banjo but some players assert that gold plating also positively affects the banjo's overall tone by softening it.

For both open-back and bluegrass banjos, builders tend to decorate their banjos based on earlier tried-and-true designs. However, these days you can find planets, space ships, peace signs, Buddhas, the family dog, and just about anything else you can think of to adorn a banjo fingerboard on a custom-built instrument.

Figure 9-10:
Check out the engraved inlay on an 1890s Cole Eclipse (a); a custom headstock inlay made by California luthier Paul Hostetter (b); and an elaborately carved heel with engraved inlay on an early 1900s Vega Whyte Ladie banjo (c).

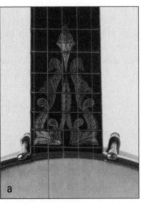

Banjo bling can add to the cost of an instrument, but these decorative aspects of a banjo don't enhance its sound or playability (outside of the gold plating). The overall worth of a banjo is determined by the quality of its component parts and how well these parts have been put together. For a more expensive banjo, the proof is always in the sound, not the bling. So don't get too carried away with appearance at the expense of good components, playability, and great sound.

Plugging in: Electric banjos

You can play just about any kind of music successfully on the banjo, and for those musicians who want to play in a rock, country, or jazz context or who just need the extra volume that comes with pickups and amplifiers, an electric banjo is just the ticket. These days, stylistic innovators such as Béla Fleck and Alison Brown are coaxing all kinds of exciting new sounds from electric banjos. Nothing is stopping you from forging your own bold musical horizons on an electric instrument, so check out some of your options in the sections that follow.

Adding a pickup to an acoustic banjo

If additional volume is the main concern, you can add an electric pickup to your regular acoustic banjo and be ready to take the stage at the next Banjo-palooza festival. Banjo pickups are attached to the coordinating rods inside the pot of the banjo and use a small piece of metal that is placed underneath one of the bridge feet as a pickup (see Figure 9-11). Installation is usually quick and easy. You can select from several different kinds of banjo pickups that range in price from $70 to $170 from the McIntyre, Jones, and Fishman companies, as well as others.

Don't expect the sound of your banjo with an electric pickup to exactly (or even closely) resemble the acoustic sound of your banjo. Because of the placement of the pickup inside the pot and the physics of electric sound technology, you may be frustrated if you're expecting *great* banjo sound from this kind of setup. Remember, players elect to reinforce their banjo sound in this way to get more volume, not to get better tone!

Boldly going electric

If you're interested in getting all kinds of different sounds from an electrified banjo and you have your sights on being the first banjo rock star, you want to purchase a fully electric instrument. You need to budget from $400 at the low end to $4,000 or more at the high end for a top-of-the-line custom-made banjo equipped with a *MIDI interface,* which essentially turns your electric instrument into a five-string synthesizer.

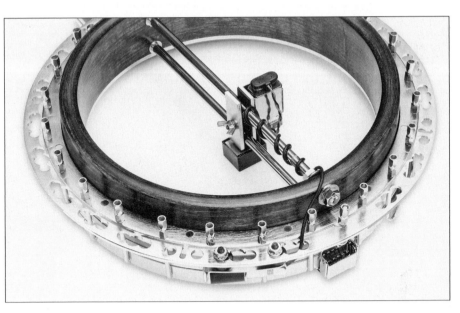

Figure 9-11:
A banjo
pickup
attaches to
the banjo's
coordinating
rods.

Electric banjos combine some of the structural features of banjos with the electronics and body shapes of electric guitars. Most electric banjos have a banjo head integrated into its body with two electric pickups positioned underneath the head. A toggle switch allows you to mix and match the different tones of the pickups to get a wider variety of sounds than you would find with an acoustic banjo outfitted with a pickup (and they also look really cool). Some instruments, like the Nechville Meteor, have small banjo heads and bodies that retain the circular banjo shape, but others, like the Deering Crossfire, have standard-sized heads and a larger body with the look of an electric guitar.

Because the sound is relayed from the bridge to the head just like on an acoustic banjo, these types of electric instruments retain the general sound quality of an acoustic banjo, but they aren't nearly as loud (until you plug them in, that is!). You can also get sounds out of these electric marvels that are very close to what you'd hear from an electric guitar, and the playability of these instruments is much closer to an electric guitar than a banjo as well. The strings feel light and fast underneath your fingers, and you can play with a lighter right-hand attack and still get a very big sound when you're amped up.

Some electric banjos dispense entirely with the banjo head and have only wood for their bodies. Called *solid body electrics,* this type of electric banjo comes even closer to the design and sound of an electric guitar (but won't sound like an acoustic banjo at all). Check out three options for electric banjos in Figure 9-12.

Figure 9-12:
Three electric banjo options: the Nechville Meteor (a), Deering Crossfire (b), and the solid-body Blue Star Banjoblaster (c).

Finding many different types of electric banjos in one place may be difficult except at the largest of national acoustic retail outlets or at a major banjo camp or bluegrass festival (check out "Finding the Right Music Store" section below for some tips on where to buy). If you make a purchase, find out whether you can return an instrument for an exchange or refund if you find that the banjo doesn't suit your needs after playing it for a day or two.

Electric banjos are way cool, big fun, and allow you to live out your rock-and-roll fantasies, but keep in mind that you can't be heard on an electric banjo in a jam session without plugging in to an amplifier. Even more important, electric instruments are usually not a welcome sight at your typical all-acoustic bluegrass, folk, or old-time jam session. The electric banjo is best viewed as an instrument that is designed for a different performance context than a regular banjo and should be used accordingly (or at least ask permission from the other musicians before plugging in and wailing away on "Tom Dooley").

Going vintage

If you explore the "used and vintage instruments" section of an acoustic specialty store's Internet inventory, your eyes may likely pop out at the high value of some older banjos. The most prized open-back banjos such as an 1890s Cole Eclipse (see Figure 9-13) can very easily change hands for $6,000 to $10,000 or more. A prized pre–World War II 1930s Gibson Mastertone flathead banjo (also shown in Figure 9-13) with an original five-string neck can go for more than $100,000.

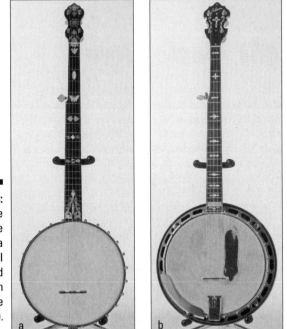

Figure 9-13:
A vintage Cole Eclipse (a) and a pre–WW II flathead Gibson Mastertone (b).

What's up with this? Well, you can't find anything like the beautiful craftsmanship of a 100-year-old ornate vintage open-back banjo or the rich, booming sound of an old flathead Gibson banjo — in the eyes and ears of the right beholder that is! Demand has fueled the market for vintage instruments of all kinds in recent years, which has caused resale prices to take a dramatic leap, not only for banjos but also for mandolins and acoustic and electric guitars.

One irony of this situation is that many of the best players, including those who make their living playing banjos, most likely can't afford these holy grails. These instruments tend to be purchased by amateur players or collectors with disposable income who often view vintage banjos as long-term investments.

Buying a very expensive vintage instrument without first thoroughly educating yourself about the history of banjo manufacturing, knowing which instruments players and collectors treasure, and getting a handle on the ever-changing state of the market is unwise. A good way to begin is to read up on banjo history and visit those Internet sites of stores carrying vintage inventories (see the following section for a list of these stores). Track resale prices on those instruments that interest you most and start saving for a *big* future purchase!

Finding the Right Music Store

The first store you think to visit on your banjo quest could be the local branch of one of those large national music outlets designed to serve customers more interested in rock music. As you enter through the front door, you're blasted by a shriek of heavy metal electric guitar. You gradually regain your hearing as Music Store Dude, a teenaged sales clerk dressed in black from head to toe with piercings in various parts of his anatomy, approaches you.

You meekly ask, "Do you have any banjos?" Music Store Dude sneers, shrugs, and raises his eyes to the ceiling, leaving you to explore the deep recesses of the cavernous store. If you're lucky, you may find a dust-covered beginner's instrument sitting forlornly in a corner, but you can't tell what it sounds like because the banjo's sorely out of tune. Even if the banjo was playable, you couldn't hear it anyway because of the young Jimi Hendrix wannabe wailing over in the next aisle. Consider it time to leave and find a music store better fitted for your needs (and your hearing).

In the following sections, I help you find a store that can provide you with quality service and banjos — either in person or online.

Buying from an acoustic specialty store

Banjo music is *real* music made by *real* musicians. You don't have synthesizers, lip-synching, or wardrobe malfunctions in the styles of music you play on the banjo (well, alright, there was that *Beverly Hillbillies* episode where Lester Flatt's city-raised wife shrunk his clothes by boiling them in Granny's iron kettle, but that doesn't count). When you go looking to buy a banjo, you should start with a retail outlet that specializes not only in acoustic music, but whose staff also knows something about banjos. If that store has a variety of different banjos and the sales staff can offer advice as to which banjo is going to be best suited to your musical aspirations, then you can feel confident that you've found a good place to shop. If the store hosts weekly jam sessions and has a banjo teacher on staff, even better!

Start your search by looking in your local yellow pages under "Music Instruments: Retail." Let your fingers do the walking until you find a listing that indicates a focus on acoustic, folk, and bluegrass music. Here's an example from my yellow pages in the San Francisco Bay Area: "Since 1969; New - Used - Vintage; Guitars - Mandolins - Banjos; Harps - Violins - Ukuleles; Repairs - Appraisals; We Buy Used Instruments," followed by a Web site address. A quick search on the Internet showed me that this particular store's inventory included banjos in a wide range of price categories. You should be looking for this kind of store.

If you can find a similar store in your area, the drive is worth it, even if it takes you several hours away from home. By taking the time to get to know the folks who work at this store, you can not only have access to their expertise, but you also get lots of good advice regarding local teachers, jam sessions, concerts, festivals, and workshops.

If you're considering a purchase of a professional quality instrument — a banjo that could easily cost $2,000 or more — your visit to an acoustic specialty store is practically mandatory. Whether you're buying a beginner's instrument or the best that they've got in stock, you want to actually see and play as many different banjos as possible. As you compare each banjo's sound, construction, craftsmanship, and playability, don't be afraid to ask a lot of questions of the banjo specialist at the store.

Buying online

The Internet is a great place to buy some things, but what about a banjo? If you're a new player and don't have a more experienced banjo-playing friend or a teacher to help you, I'd advise against it. Internet buying usually requires a knowledgeable buyer, and if you're new to banjos, you may not be able to make the best purchase on your own. Take the stress off yourself and make that personal connection with the acoustic specialty store to find just the right instrument for you and your budget. You support your regional acoustic music scene and aren't at the mercy of the dreaded Music Store Dude!

If you're already playing and looking to step up to a better-sounding instrument, shopping on the Internet can be a positive experience. The key is knowing what you're looking for and being an educated buyer in regard to the particular instrument you're looking for (check out "Stepping Up to a Better Banjo" earlier in this chapter for help in how to begin your banjo search).

Many of the best regional music stores maintain an active presence on the Internet and update their inventory daily on their homepages. Several of these retail outlets have a true international reach and are very dependable places to buy both new and used instruments and accessories.

Be sure to check an Internet store's return policy before you purchase. Don't buy from anyone who won't allow you to return a banjo that you don't like after you've had it for a couple of days. And for now, I'd totally avoid online purchases from individual buyers, unless you've been able to establish direct phone contact with a seller and come to total agreement on a return policy, method of payment, and how the instrument is to be shipped. Finally, never buy an instrument from someone claiming in an e-mail to be a member of a royal family or who wants to send $10 million dollars to you along with your banjo!

Getting you started: A banjo store directory

Here's a short list of some of the best regional and national stores that specialize in new and used resonator and open-back banjos, along with their Web-site addresses. Each store is a brick-and-mortar walk-in establishment as well as a retail outlet providing excellent Internet and telephone customer service. Inventory varies at each store depending upon what's in stock:

- **Banjo.Com:** Atlanta, GA; www.banjo.com

- **Denver Folklore Center:** Denver, CO; www.denverfolklore.com

- **Dusty Strings:** Seattle, WA; www.dustystrings.com

- **Elderly Instruments:** Lansing, MI; www.elderly.com

- **First Quality Music:** Louisville, KY; www.fqms.com

- **Greg Boyd's House of Fine Instruments:** Missoula, MT; www.gregboyd.com

- **Gruhn Guitars:** Nashville, TN; www.gruhn.com

- **Gryphon Stringed Instruments:** Palo Alto, CA; www.gryphonstrings.com

- **Jack Hatfield Music:** Pigeon Forge, TN; www.hatfieldmusic.com

- **Janet Davis Music Company:** Bella Vista, AR; www.janetdavismusic.com

- **Mandolin Brothers:** Staten Island, NY; www.mandoweb.com

- **Mass Street Music:** Lawrence, KS; www.massstreetmusic.com

- **McPeake's Unique Instruments:** Mt. Juliet, TN; www.cmcpeake.com

- **The Music Emporium:** Lexington, MA; www.themusicemporium.com

- **Picker's Supply:** Fredericksburg, VA; www.pickerssupply.com

- **Turtle Hill Banjo Company:** Bryantown, MD; www.turtlehillbanjo.com

Please Mr. Postman: Shipping your banjo

If you purchase a banjo that has to be mailed to you, I strongly suggest paying more and using an overnight or two-day service for shipping. Package companies do inflict damage on banjos every now and then. However, shipping by air, rather than by the cheaper ground service, dramatically decreases the risk of your new banjo arriving in multiple pieces.

If your banjo does meet unfortunate circumstances in transit, immediately contact the store or buyer from which you made the purchase. The store will arrange for the shipping company to come and inspect the banjo. Then, they either take the instrument with them or have you return it. Be sure to save all packing materials, because this is crucial evidence in the shipping company's determination of damages. A reputable music store either sends a replacement or arranges for a repair as soon as the damaged banjo is received.

Chapter 10

Getting the Right Stuff: Banjo Gear

. . . .

In This Chapter

▶ Picking up the essentials

▶ Choosing accessories that make practicing more fun

▶ Upgrading banjo parts to make your instrument sound better

. . . .

*B*anjo players are real "gear heads." They keep up on the latest products that help get banjos from one place to another with greater ease, make practicing and playing more fun, and make their instruments sound better. Join me for a voyage to the Island of Banjo Gear in this chapter, where you encounter items (like cases, strings, picks, straps, capos, and tuners) that are just about essential for happy picking and other things (like metronomes, computer software and banjo bridges, heads, tailpieces and "D" tuners) that just make playing a lot more fun or can improve the sound of your banjo. (Are you still in the market for a banjo? If so, sail on back to Chapter 9 for a complete banjo buyer's guide.)

If the significant others in your household start to complain about how long your banjo gear wish list has become after you complete this chapter, feel free to go ahead and put the blame on me!

Picking Up the Stuff You Really Need

Whether you're practicing at home or playing in a jam session at a festival, all banjo players need to have certain pieces of equipment — in addition to the actual banjo, of course. The following sections provide the vital info on the stuff you don't want to be without either at home or on the road.

At the top of this list is a banjo case (after all, you won't enhance the reputation of banjo players very much if you carry your banjo around town without something to put it in — and no brown paper bags, please!). Although most new instruments come with a case, you may want to grab a lightweight gig bag to make walking around the festival campground a breeze or consider a deluxe flight case so you can take your banjo with you on your next vacation (won't *that* make your family happy!). Check out the following sections for the total lowdown on banjo storage and transport.

Cases: Becoming King of the Road

Most banjos stand up pretty well to the rigors of changing temperatures and humidity in a house, but even so, you want a good case for keeping your baby safe when you aren't practicing and for providing secure transport to your next lesson, rehearsal, or gig (yes, banjo players occasionally *do* get work).

Cases come in four basic varieties: hard-shell, soft-shell, gig bag, and flight cases. Each of these cases have a time and a place, but keep in mind that the primary purpose of a case is to protect your instrument. Usually, the more you invest in a case, the better that protection is. If you plan on traveling a great deal with your banjo, including taking your banjo with you on an airplane, choosing the right case for a quality instrument is an important decision — a decision I help you make in the following sections.

Cases or bags usually aren't included in the purchase price with most entry-level banjos. Although you can go through life without proper storage for your instrument, it makes good sense to budget an extra $30 to $50 for a simple case or bag. In addition to providing some basic protection for your banjo, you have a pocket or two to store some of your other accessories, like picks, a tuner, and a capo.

Come fly with me: Banjos on a plane!

Whether you're headed to your next vacation spot or your destination is halfway across the country to attend a music camp or festival, sooner or later you'll want to take your banjo with you on an airplane. I fly with my most valuable instrument frequently and although I've never had an instrument damaged in transit (as I write with fingers crossed), I know many other musicians who have had pegheads snapped, necks broken, and flanges busted on their way to or from a show.

Even in the best of conditions, you can never be entirely sure how you'll be able to store your banjo on an airplane, and this unpredictability can be maddening. Despite this state of affairs, here are a few valuable strategies that I've picked up over the years in dealing with banjos at 30,000 feet. All of these tips are directed towards the primary goal of getting your banjo on board with you as carry-on luggage:

✔ **Travel with a flight case.** No matter what happens, you're still offering your instrument the best protection possible with a flight case. Taking your banjo in a gig bag is an alternative option that works for some musicians. But the idea of using gig bags on a plane has always made me nervous, because if you're one of the last on board a full plane and the overhead compartments are full, you still have to surrender your banjo to a flight attendant for storage down below. If this happens to you and your banjo is in a gig bag, your banjo won't have close to the same kind of protection a flight case offers. If I know that I'll be doing a lot of heavy lifting with the banjo after I get to my destination, I also bring along a gig bag, temporarily stuffed with clothing, and check that as baggage. I can then use the gig bag as my primary means of banjo transport after I've landed.

✔ **Know your airlines, figure out their boarding procedures, and choose routes with as few changes of planes as possible.** In my experience, Southwest Airlines is the most accommodating of all carriers for allowing banjos on board. United, Jet Blue, Virgin, Delta and West Jet are pretty good; American and Alaska Airlines are fair; America West is poor and is to be avoided (I include these airlines because they're the ones I've used most frequently in the last decade). Boarding procedures vary by airline, by plane, by airport, and seemingly by the mood of the airline workers on that day. Despite these obstacles, see what you can do to figure out how to be in one of the first boarding groups. For instance, if you know that passengers board a particular plane from the rear to the front, book a seat in the rear. Apart from the individual airline's policy, the key to getting your instrument on board is getting yourself on the plane while overhead and closet space is still available for storage.

✔ **Don't draw attention to your banjo while checking in and boarding.** Act like taking your banjo on board as a carry-on is a natural thing, and it will be! If you approach an airline representative saying "I have a banjo with me. What should I do with it?" you could be asking for trouble, especially if the representative hasn't had enough morning coffee.

✔ **Don't try to preboard with your banjo.** Unless you have an otherwise valid reason, carrying a banjo with you usually isn't deemed a good enough reason to earn membership in the preboarding group. For every time this strategy has succeeded, I've been stopped an equal number of times by an airline representative. In one case, I was put on the plane *last* because I had the nerve to request a preboard with a banjo!

✔ **Be friendly, cooperative, and creative in order to get your banjo onboard.** If you're courteous and exercise some creative thinking, you'll be treated with respect in return from the flight attendants and the other passengers whose help you're going to need to get your banjo on board. I was once the last person to board a Seattle to Oakland flight with seemingly no room left in the overhead bins. After politely explaining to the flight attendant that I was carrying my most valuable possession with me, she helped me rearrange quite a few overhead bags to make room for my banjo, after we asked passengers' permission to gently displace them. On another flight, the attendant removed her own bags and tucked the banjo behind the last seat. The bottom line: If you make a request with kindness, you receive the same in return.

✔ **Remove items from your case that won't get through the security checkpoint.** These items include strings, wire cutters, screwdrivers, banjo wrenches, and other tools you may use for banjo setup, but not fingerpicks or tuners.

Hard- and soft-shell cases

Hard-shell cases are the most common case option and usually accompany most intermediate to high-quality banjo purchases (see Figure 10-1). *Hard-shell cases* are made of wood and are covered with nylon or fabric (I especially like the vintage tweed look myself). This type of case is usually just fine for day-to-day use, as long as the banjo fits in it well. With proper care, a hard-shell case should last for many years. Expect to pay from $75 to $135 for one of these, if you're purchasing the case separately.

Soft-shell cases are usually made of cardboard. Although they prevent your banjo from getting wet if some over-enthusiastic audience member spills her beer while requesting "Rocky Top" for the umpteenth time, keeping your banjo dry is about all these cases are good for. At around $30, they're an inexpensive option and are lightweight, but they don't offer much protection for your instrument. If you paid more than $400 for your banjo, go for broke and invest in a hard-shell case or a well-padded gig bag.

A banjo is usually damaged while inside a case due to a loose fit that allows the banjo to move inside the case when it meets an impact. If you're purchasing a hard-shell case separately, look for the tightest fit possible between the inside of the case and the instrument. Padding on the inside top of the case and plenty of support for the neck are characteristics of a case that should provide good protection. If you can see or feel the banjo move within the case when you gently shake it, the case isn't doing its job. Keep looking for something that fits your banjo more snugly. Look to these brands, among others, for good quality in hard-shell cases: Ameritage, Golden Gate, American Vintage, Canadian/TKL, and Gold Tone.

Gig bags

Many musicians prefer the soft, padded *gig bag* either as their main case of choice or as an alternative way of getting around with the banjo when weight and portability are important considerations (check out the gig bag look in Figure 10-1). Gig bags range from $30 for a no-frills nylon model to $300 for a fine leather-padded bag that offers almost as much protection as a hard-shell case (short of driving a tour bus over it).

Gig bags are lighter than hard-shell cases and are great when you need to walk with your banjo over considerable distances at a banjo camp or bluegrass festival. Higher quality gig bags have more padding, thereby offering more protection for your banjo, and are often outfitted with shoulder straps that convert it into a backpack. Storage for accessories is also more generous on higher-priced models than what you find with hard-shell cases.

Check out the following brands, among others, when you're shopping for quality gig bags: Reunion Blues, Colorado Case, Superior Trailpak, and Boulder Alpine.

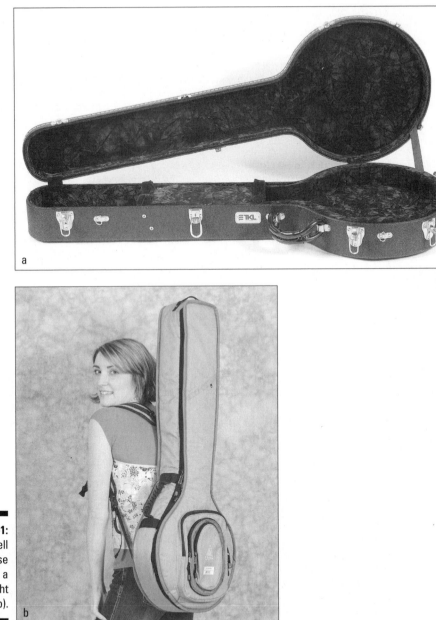

Figure 10-1:
A hard-shell banjo case (a) and a lightweight gig bag (b).

Flight cases

If you ever plan on flying with an expensive banjo or you just want to pile all of Aunt Myrna's heaviest luggage on top of your banjo case in the trunk of your car without fear, a flight case may be in your future. *Flight cases* are the Hummers of the banjo-case world; heavy and large, they offer the utmost in protection for your instrument (see Figure 10-2). Made from molded fiberglass, flight cases are watertight, offer extensive protection from movement inside the case, and have generous inside storage and functional external locks. One case should last a lifetime.

I bet you can already predict the negatives of this type of case. Yes, you guessed it: price and weight. You can expect to pay $575 or more for top-of-the-line cases, and you may have to be on a waiting list for a few months to get one in your favorite exterior and interior color combination. These cases are also *heavy,* as in *really* heavy — weighing in at 10 to 15 pounds. After you put a ten-pound bluegrass banjo in one of these, you're carrying around as much as 25 pounds of music. Believe me, you'll start to feel this somewhere between Concourse A and Concourse D!

However, flight cases are the way to go if you're looking for the best protection available for your instrument. Check out Price and Calton deluxe banjo cases if you're looking to buy the best.

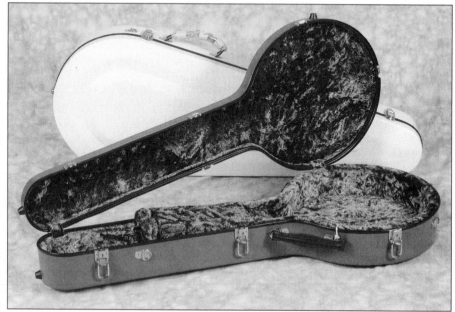

Figure 10-2: Flight cases offer the best protection for your banjo. A Price case (rear) and a Calton case (front).

Strings: You can't pick without 'em

You've probably figured out by now that you need all five strings on your banjo to make good music (if not, you may want to start at the first chapters of this book!). Although your banjo probably had all its strings when you got it, these strings aren't lifetime guaranteed; it isn't unusual for a string to break every now and then while you're tuning or playing. In this case, you need to have the right kind of replacement string on hand to continue playing.

The most economical way to buy strings is to purchase a set that contains all five strings. String sets aren't expensive; you should expect to pay from $3 to $8 for a good name-brand set, and it isn't uncommon to get a discount for purchasing multiple sets. You also can buy individual strings from most music stores. If you need to replace one string on your banjo more frequently than the others (for most players, it's the 1st string), you should purchase several extras of this particular string so that you don't have to constantly break up entire sets. *Note:* You need to ask a sales clerk for help with purchasing individual strings, because stores usually don't put them on display.

Most players keep one or more extra string sets on hand to replace broken strings on the spot. Many players replace an entire set of strings when they sound dull, build up a lot of grit and grime, or become difficult to tune (visit Chapter 11 for a step-by-step guide on to how to change strings). Be sure to throw one or two sets in your case, along with a small pair of wire cutters to slice off the unneeded string ends.

A dizzying array of different kinds of banjo strings is available today. Your choice should be determined by the kind of banjo you play, the sound you want to get, and how you want the strings to feel when you play them. The following sections share the secrets of making good string choices.

Loop-end and ball-end strings

Banjo strings come in *loop-end* and *ball-end* varieties, shown in Figure 10-3. You use one or the other depending on the design of your banjo's tailpiece (the *tailpiece* holds one end of the strings at the pot end of the banjo; different kinds of tailpieces require different kinds of strings, as explained in the following section):

✔ A tailpiece with finger-like attachments made for grabbing the loops that you can find at one end of the strings takes loop-end strings. The great majority of banjo tailpieces feature this design, and most of the strings you'll find available are loop-end strings. Nylon and gut strings (see the following section) require that you tie your own looped ends to the banjo's tailpiece.

✔ If your tailpiece has only small holes at its end, you need ball-end strings for your banjo. The round ball at the end of the string prevents it from feeding itself back through the small tailpiece hole.

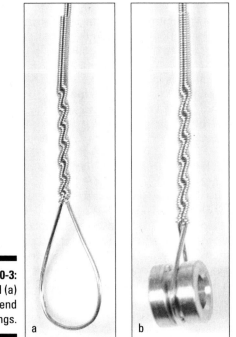

Figure 10-3:
Loop-end (a) and ball-end (b) strings.

a   b

Nickel-plated, stainless-steel, nylon, and gut strings

Practically all bluegrass players and most clawhammer players (see Chapters 4, 5, 6, and 8 to discover these ways of playing banjo) use nickel-plated or stainless-steel strings. These two kinds of *steel string sets* include a wound 4th string, which has additional wire wrapped around its core to add thickness and mass to the banjo's lowest-pitched string. Both kinds of metal strings produce the bright, ringing sound that is associated with the banjo and are appropriate for all kinds of playing at any ability level.

Steel string sets differ according to the kind of material used as a wrap around the 4th string. Fourth strings can be wound with bronze, stainless steel, nickel, or monel (a nickel alloy). Each type of winding provides a slightly different tonal quality:

✔ Bronze and stainless-steel 4th strings tend to produce a brighter sound.

✔ Monel produces a darker tone.

✔ Nickel falls somewhere in the middle.

Some open-back banjo players prefer to use nylon or gut strings on their banjos. These strings produce a more authentic sound for clawhammer, classic, and minstrel styles. (Yes, I do mean *gut* strings, as in a totally carbon-based, once-was-a-life-form product. Visit Chapter 7 to find out more about classic and minstrel styles).

A new type of string has recently caught the ear of many players: a synthetic string called *nylgut,* which combines the durability and affordability of a nylon string with the preferred "natural" tone of a gut string. It's a great alternative to both nylon and gut, and you should try it if you want that organic sound without having to actually harm any living thing in the process.

You need to search out an acoustic specialty store to find the relatively rare types of strings such as nylon, gut, and nylgut. If you want an alternative to steel strings, try them all and see which one suits your banjo and your way of playing the best.

String gauges: Light, medium, or heavy

String thickness is expressed in terms of *string gauge* and is measured in thousandths of an inch, believe it or not! A light gauge string set has slightly thinner strings (and smaller gauge numbers) than a medium or heavy gauge set. Your preference in strings should be determined by your playing style, your banjo, and the kind of sound you want to produce with your instrument.

You can find a wide variety of string sets available today (an example is shown in Figure 10-4), but the most important thing to remember is that designers put string sets together according to whether they are loop- or ball-end and also by the diameter of the strings and to the kind of wrap used around the low 4th string.

My own string preferences have evolved over the years. These days, I prefer lighter-gauge strings because they sound the best to me on my banjo, and they enable me to play *fast* as I creep into middle age! For bluegrass playing, I prefer to use a string set with the following string gauges: .010, .011, .013, .020w, and .010. Now let me translate! My first string is 10/1,000th of an inch thick; my second string is 11/1,000th of an inch thick; and so on. My fourth string measures 20/1,000th of an inch thick, and is a wound string (hence the *w*). You name the 5th string last; it will almost always be of the same gauge as the 1st string. This is how catalogs and store Web sites describe string sets (I bet you never associated the banjo with such precision!).

Many other players prefer medium gauge string sets because of their tone and playability. A typical medium gauge set may have the following gauges: .011, .012, .014, .022w, and .011. As you can see, these strings feature variations of only a couple of thousandths of an inch compared to a light set, but you can definitely feel and hear the difference as you play. The heavier the gauge of string, the stiffer it feels against your fingers and the darker its sound will be. Unless you're playing a banjo with a long neck or are experimenting with tuning the banjo below normal pitch, most players don't use heavy gauge strings. However, these are available as individual string options from acoustic specialty retailers.

Figure 10-4:
A typical
five-string
banjo
string set.

I can't identify a single best set of strings — this is something that you figure out over time. You should try different gauges and types of strings to see what works best for you. Don't be surprised if your choices change many times over the years as you continue to play banjo.

Here's a short list of some of the most popular strings brands: GHS, American Made Banjo Company, D'Addario, Elixir, Gibson, John Pearse, Black Diamond, LaBella, Martin/Vega, Chris Sands (for classic nylon strings), and Aquila (for gut and nylgut strings).

Picks: Giving your fingers playing power

A thumbpick and one or more fingerpicks give you the ability to play with more volume, greater dynamics, and a more forceful attack. Whether or not you need picks is dependent upon the style of music you're making and your personal taste in how you want your music to sound. Most (but not all) players feel that clawhammer and other old-time styles sound best when played with the bare fingers of your right hand and most all classic and minstrel style players go pick-less in their playing. However, the bluegrass style pretty much requires the use of a plastic or metal thumbpick along with two metal fingerpicks shaped to fit the player's index and middle fingers.

Although the feel of the picks on the ends of your digits can be uncomfortable at first, in the long run you'll play with more volume and power for the styles that need it.

Numerous choices of thumb and fingerpicks patiently await you at your local acoustic music store. They range in price from a couple bucks to $35 or more for a pair of hand-crafted, stainless-steel fingerpicks.

You should try as many different kinds of picks as you can to hear what makes your banjo playing sound the best. Check out Chapter 4 for detailed information on selecting picks that are right for you and for tips on how to fit them on your fingers.

Straps: Take a load off!

A quality banjo weighs up to ten pounds, so using a comfortable strap can save wear and tear on your back, shoulder, and neck. And banjo players don't use straps only to play while standing up. If the banjo neck is heavier than the banjo pot, which is the case on most entry-level instruments (see Chapter 1 for more info on banjo parts), you should use a properly fitted strap even while sitting down. This helps balance the weight of the banjo and frees up your left hand for gymnastic feats of fretting.

Banjo straps range in price from $8, for a simple nylon or woven-fabric strap, to $60 or more, for a fancy, handmade leather beauty. I prefer a simple and sturdy leather strap that has little to no decoration; these cost about $40. You also may want to explore dual shoulder strap models and straps with shoulder pads, because these types of straps help cushion the impact of the banjo on your body.

Don't try to fit a strap by attaching one end of it to the banjo peghead. Banjo straps attach to the tension hooks of your banjo pot by using metal or plastic clips or with the strap ends fastened to the banjo with Chicago screws (see Chapter 2 for detailed help with fitting a strap on your instrument).

If you have an extra guitar strap around your house, you can turn it into a serviceable temporary strap for a lighter banjo; just attach shoelaces to each end and securely tie the shoelaces around the banjo's tension hooks.

Capos: Playing easily in different keys

Capo is shorthand for the Italian word *capotasto,* which unfortunately doesn't refer to the latest variety of flavored cappuccino drink. It literally means "head of fretboard." A *capo* (pronounced KAY-po) is an adjustable tension clamp that shortens the effective length of the fingerboard of your banjo (the *fingerboard* is the flat surface of the neck that's used by the left hand to fret the strings). In so doing, the capo also shortens the length of your strings (which causes them to sound higher in pitch). A capo allows you to play in different keys by transferring the chords, licks, and songs you already play to a new place on the banjo neck. A capo is a required piece of musical gear to take along whenever you may be playing music with others.

Banjo capos are designed to fret the 4th to the 1st strings on your banjo, but not the short 5th string. Because the 5th string needs to be raised the same number of frets as the other strings when using a capo, it gets its own special equipment to raise its pitch when you also use a capo on the other strings. Raising the pitch of the banjo to play in a new key is a two-step process: First, you apply the capo to raise strings 1 through 4 and then you work with the 5th string to adjust its pitch.

The following sections explore capo options, how to properly use a capo, and the equipment you can use to raise the 5th string's pitch.

Choosing a capo

Banjo capos cost between $5 and $100. Your choices range from inexpensive elastic-band models to spring-loaded capos to fancy, professional, hand-tooled, stainless-steel capos in velvet cases (really, I'm not kidding!). Figure 10-5 shows a variety of capos that you can choose from.

Figure 10-5:
Different varieties of capos allow you to raise the pitch to play in new keys.

A banjo player uses a capo a lot, so it doesn't make sense to cut corners with this purchase. Fortunately, you can find perfectly good capos for under $20. Although some players prefer spring-loaded capos for quick installation and removal, I use a capo that wraps all the way around the banjo's neck and attaches to the banjo using a quick-release button lock. I control the amount of tension that the capo applies to the strings by loosening or tightening a thumbscrew in the back. One advantage of this kind of capo is that you can place it out of the way behind the nut when you aren't using it (the *nut* is the white strip below the first fret that guides the strings from the fingerboard to the headstock).

Using a capo

Here's a step-by-step guide to hassle-free capo use:

1. **Bring the edge of the capo just behind (but not on top of) the fret on the banjo neck where you want to place it.**

   As indicated in Figure 10-6a.

2. **Slowly tighten the adjustment screw a few turns while maintaining pressure on the top of the capo with your other hand.**

   Just as in Figure 10-6b.

3. **When you think that the capo is tight enough, try playing a few notes with the right hand.**

4. **Continue to tighten the adjustment screw just until all the fretted strings sound clear with no buzzing.**

   Don't apply any more pressure than is needed because this will cause the strings to sound sharp.

5. **Experiment with capo placement: some capos may apply just the right amount of pressure if they are a slight distance away from the fret instead of right up against it (as in Figure 10-6c); however, in most cases, you'll stay in tune more easily and your banjo will sound better with the capo positioned as close to the fret as possible.**

Figure 10-6: Placing the capo right up against the fret (a); tightening the capo (b); alternate placement for the capo (c).

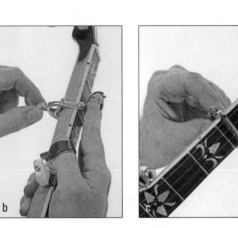

Tuning with a capo

It's not uncommon to find that the banjo has gone just a bit out of tune with the capo on, even if it was in very fine tune without it. When this happens to you, don't retune by using the tuning pegs, because this will result in an out-of-tune banjo when you take the capo off again. Here's what you should do:

- ✔ If the string is sharp (which it usually is when using the capo), try pushing down on the string on the bridge side of the capo (as in Figure 10-7a).

- ✔ If the string is flat, press down on the string at the peghead (see Figure 10-7b). You'll be equalizing the tension of the string on both sides of the capo with this slick maneuver and the string should still remain in tune when removing the capo.

REMEMBER

Some spring-loaded capos grip the strings with such force that they cause the strings to fret sharp, causing the banjo to go out of tune. Be sure to select a capo with adjustable tension to deal with this common problem.

Figure 10-7:
Pushing down on a string near the bridge to lower a string's pitch (a); pushing down at the headstock to raise its pitch (b).

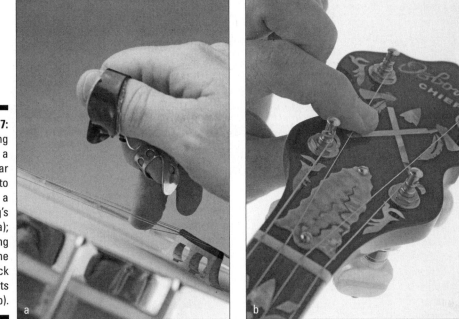

The 5th-string capo and spikes: Going along for the ride

If you place a capo at the second fret, you also need to raise the pitch of your 5th string the same number of frets so that all your banjo strings are in the same relationship as before you used the capo. How does that work? In this case, the 5th string is so special that it gets its *own* equipment to raise its pitch. Check out the following options to achieve this miraculous 5th string feat:

- ✔ **Slide-mounted 5th-string capos:** The distinguishing characteristic of this capo is the long, slim metal bar that is attached with two small screws to the banjo neck. You slide the capo along the bar to the fret you want to use, and then lower the capo against the string by tightening the thumbscrew. Because the hand screw controls the amount of tension against the string, the 5th string stays in better tune with this kind of capo. Disadvantages? The metal bar adds just a bit of width to the neck and your left hand may have to move around the capo screw when moving up and down the neck. However, this kind of capo works well for many players.

- ✔ **Fifth-string railroad spikes**: Another ingenious solution to the problem of raising the 5th string's pitch is to use the small railroad spikes from the train tracks of an HO gauge model train set. The spikes are gently nailed into the banjo fingerboard above the 5th string with the hook of the spike remaining just high enough off of the fingerboard to hook the 5th string behind the appropriate fret. Hey, I know this sounds strange, but I'm completely serious here!

  Luckily, you don't have to ruin your neighbor's model train display by hiring a bunch of miniature John Henrys to steal the spikes right off of the track. This operation is best left to a good repair person, but if you insist on doing this yourself, you can buy a package of spikes with instructions from most acoustic specialty stores. The spikes are installed at the frets where you want or need them. Most players have just two spikes installed for the 5th string at the seventh and ninth frets for playing in the keys of A and B, but some players prefer having additional spikes at other frets.

The more spikes you want on your banjo, the more you need to have a professional repair person do this installation work for you. Placing the spike in just the right place so that it doesn't get in the way of your left-hand fretting fingers or any other spikes when in use is important.

If you have 5th-string spikes already installed on your banjo, look to see which way the hook is pointed. Most spikes are installed so that the hook points down towards the 1st string. If this is the case, you can hook the 5th string underneath the spike by pushing the string down and underneath the hook (as I show in Figure 10-8). At first you may need both hands pushing down on the string on either side of the spike to do this, but after a few tries, you should get the hang of it.

Your 5th string will probably be sharp after it's underneath the spike, so take a moment to tune it to the rest of your banjo. Now you're ready to pick!

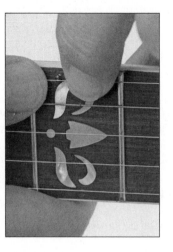

Figure 10-8:
Using a railroad spike to raise the 5th string's pitch.

Electronic tuners: Getting by with a little help

I'm not sure how banjo players survived in the era before portable tuners! Although these amazing little devices never replace a good ear, they have made getting the banjo in tune a lot easier by adding a visual reinforcement to what you hear. Tuners especially come in handy at a festival, a jam session, or even onstage — where you sometimes have so much noise around you that using your ear alone to tune the banjo is difficult. Just about everyone carries a portable tuner along with them, and you should too.

You want to choose a chromatic tuner. Unlike a guitar or bass tuner, a *chromatic tuner* gives you all the notes available in Western music (what more could you ask for?). Believe it or not, you'll eventually need most if not all of these reference points for tuning your banjo, especially if you're an old-time player.

Tuners give an astounding amount of information to help you get in tune. When you pick a string, the tuner responds by indicating which note you're closest to and a moving needle tells you just how sharp or flat you are from that note. As you tune the string up or down in pitch, the meter responds accordingly, letting you know when you've tuned your string exactly to the correct pitch. Tuners also work equally well whether or not you're using a capo (but don't forget, if you're tuning with a capo in position, you'll get different note readings than you would if the banjo were in an open position).

There are two main varieties of portable tuners:

✔ **Internal microphone tuners:** These tuners (one is shown in Figure 10-9) have a built-in microphone that picks up the sound of your banjo if the tuner is placed on a nearby music stand, table top, or even resting on your knee. These tuners are affordable at $20 or more and are durable (I have a Boss tuner of this type that's lasted over 20 years). On the downside, although these tuners can be accurate in a quiet room, they experience problems if another musician is playing nearby or if the room has too much ambient noise.

✔ **Clip-on tuners:** Portable clip-on tuners made a huge splash on the acoustic scene when they were introduced about a decade ago. These types of tuners attach directly to your banjo at the peghead or onto the pot and focus only on the sound of your instrument, excluding whatever noise is around you. This feature is a real lifesaver if you're trying to tune while other musicians are playing or if you're in a workshop with 15 other players, who are all using their clip-on tuners to tune at the same time! One disadvantage of these tuners is that they're sometimes not as accurate as the internal microphone variety of tuner. They also tend to be more delicate and a bit more expensive, with prices running from $30 to $60.

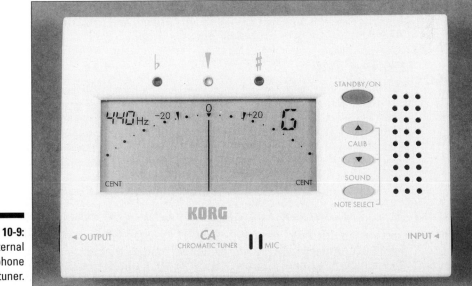

Figure 10-9: An internal microphone tuner.

Many tuners have a backlight that allows you to see the tuner's readout in a dim or dark environment. You pay more for this feature, but you may be surprised at how often this little light comes in handy around a festival campfire or waiting in the backstage wings for your *American Banjo Idol* audition.

Collecting More Cool Tools to Help Your Playing

From banjo mutes to string winders and finger exercisers to torque wrenches, there's no end to the available accessories promising to make you a better player. Although buying everything in sight is tempting, you want to know about a few items that can actually enhance your playing and make your banjo sound its best.

Metronomes and drum machines

Keeping a steady rhythm is essential to great banjo playing and figuring out how to play with a metronome or drum machine is a good way to develop this important musical skill.

A *metronome* maintains a steady beat at whatever tempo you choose while a *drum machine* goes to the next level by providing realistic drum sounds for different styles and rhythms at different speeds. In either case, it's difficult for most players to jump right in and start playing along. In the following sections, I show you different kinds of metronomes and provide a practical guide to using these tools in your daily practice routine.

How they work

The metronome has come a long way from the pyramid-shaped wooden box with the moving pendulum that used to sit on top of your grandmother's piano all those years ago (although there's no question that these retro models are still very cool). Today's metronomes use digital technology to combine a myriad of features in increasingly small packages (see Figure 10-10). Although they all share the primary function of allowing you to control the speed of a clicking beat, most electronic metronomes also provide a visual component, with small lights and arrows providing additional cues for playing in rhythm.

The more expensive the metronome, the more bells and whistles you get (and I mean this quite literally!). You can find metronome and tuner combos, tiny in-ear metronomes, as well as deluxe models that allow you to stack rhythms one on top of another. Expect to shell out from $25 to $160, depending upon which bells and whistles suit you best.

Drum machines do everything that metronomes can do, but they're also capable of emulating hundreds of percussion sounds. Most models have presets that instantly give you satisfying jazz, country, funk, and rock backing rhythms, but you can create your own drum sounds as well. Turn it on and set the speed and the preset, and you've got an instant drummer cooking underneath your banjo playing! Many professional players prefer practicing with a drum machine, and if you follow in their footsteps, you'll spend from $180 to $300 for a current model.

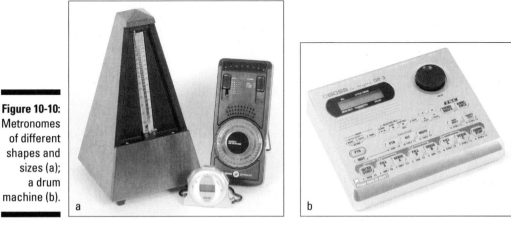

Figure 10-10:
Metronomes
of different
shapes and
sizes (a);
a drum
machine (b).

Playing along with the metronome

I rely on my trusty metronome to assist me in checking my rhythmic accuracy and to help me increase speed. Unfortunately, metronomes don't come with instructions on how to use them, and figuring out how to get started on your own isn't easy. Here's a step-by-step guide to playing with the metronome with examples oriented towards the bluegrass player (for more on bluegrass banjo, see Chapters 4, 5, 6, and 8):

1. **With banjo in hand, set the metronome to around 66 beats per minute.**

   If your metronome has the option of accenting a particular beat, turn this feature off for now.

2. **Start counting in a cycle of four beats, saying one number for each metronome click: one, two, three, four, and repeat.**

3. **Because bluegrass roll patterns have eight notes in them, play two of these roll notes for every metronome click.**

   Pick one note when you hear the click and the second note exactly half way between one click and the next.

4. **Use an alternating thumb roll to get started; continue until you've reached the end of the roll pattern.**

   If you play 3-2-5-1-4-2-5-1 as your string sequence, play the 3rd string at the same time as you hear a metronome click, play the 2nd string between that click and the next, and play the 5th string on the next click. Congratulations! You've successfully played with the metronome.

5. **Now try the same roll pattern, repeating the sequence as many times as you can without stopping while staying with the metronome beat.**

   You want to go from the end right back to the beginning of the roll without missing a beat.

   If the metronome is set too fast for you to keep up, gradually adjust it to a lower number setting until you find a tempo where you can play along. If the metronome is too slow, increase the speed by moving it to the next highest number.

   After you're comfortable playing this first roll with the metronome, try playing other rolls or an easy song that you already know well.

Even the best musicians have trouble following the beat of the metronome. If this happens to you, don't worry. Stop playing, find the beat, and start over again. If you're still having trouble getting started, listen to the beat of the metronome and imagine what your roll pattern should sound like against that beat. After you can hear this in your head, try again.

After you're able to play an exercise or song effectively all the way through at one metronome setting, adjust the tempo to the next highest setting and try it again. This is a great way to gradually increase your speed and accuracy. You will find that there are some tempo settings where you'll hit a roadblock and find it difficult to play what you just played at a slightly slower tempo (and these roadblocks can be different for each song). Just keep practicing and you'll soon be able to move on to the next higher metronome setting.

As you continue to increase speed, the metronome may end up beating so fast that it becomes a frantic distraction at 140 beats per minute or more. At this point, it's a good idea to change the note value that the click equals from two roll notes to four. Because you're now going to play four roll notes instead of two for every metronome click, you need to adjust your metronome accordingly. If you left the metronome setting at the same number as before, you'd now be playing twice as fast, so go ahead and back the metronome down 30 or 40 beats per minute and try playing once again with the metronome in this new way. If you try the alternating thumb roll again, this time you will play *four* notes for every metronome click instead of two.

Because of the banjo's robust volume, you may have trouble hearing the beat of your metronome above the beautiful sounds of your own playing. If you're thinking about purchasing an electronic metronome, make sure it has a headphone jack. You can then use an external set of headphones to more easily hear the beat. Better yet, try hooking up a set of external speakers like you'd find on your computer to your metronome's jack. This way, you get as much sound as you need.

Do you practice near a computer? If so, try using a metronome or drum machine application that can be downloaded for free off the Internet (type the words *metronome* or *drum machine* into an Internet search engine and see what turns up). Most of these programs have just a small learning curve and work about as well as a stand-alone metronome.

Your computer and the banjo

In addition to metronome and drum machine applications (see preceding section), a host of other computer programs and Web sites can enhance your banjo-playing experience. I go into more detail about how your computer can be one of your banjo's best friends in the following sections.

Many valuable banjo resources on the Internet are completely free, including Web sites with tablature, downloadable MIDI files, and lively discussion groups (begin your hunt by checking out www.banjohangout.org and www.bluegrassbanjo.org).

Slow-downer programs

Perhaps the most useful type of computer aid for banjo playing is one of several applications that slow down the tempo of a digital music source without changing its pitch, called a *slow-downer* program. These programs make it easier to play along or to understand a particular piece of music. I use one of these programs all the time when I really want to dig deep into another player's work to get every note and nuance.

Although you can buy a special stand-alone CD player that performs these same functions, you can save $200 or more by going the computer-application route. Two of the most popular slow-downer programs, both of which cost around $50, are Transkriber, available at most music stores, and the Amazing Slow Downer (shown in Figure 10-11), which is available for purchase only via download at www.ronimusic.com. You can also find no-cost options out there as well. Windows Media Player has a slow-downer feature already built into its interface, and several Macintosh freeware programs also do the trick. However, getting a dedicated program with special looping and mixing features that can isolate the specific licks you want to learn is worth the cost.

After opening a slow-downer application, you put a CD into the computer, choose the track you want to work with, and then set the tempo (which is usually expressed as a percentage of normal performance speed). You can also control the pitch of what you're listening to and work with various mixing options to hear the banjo more clearly through your computer's speakers.

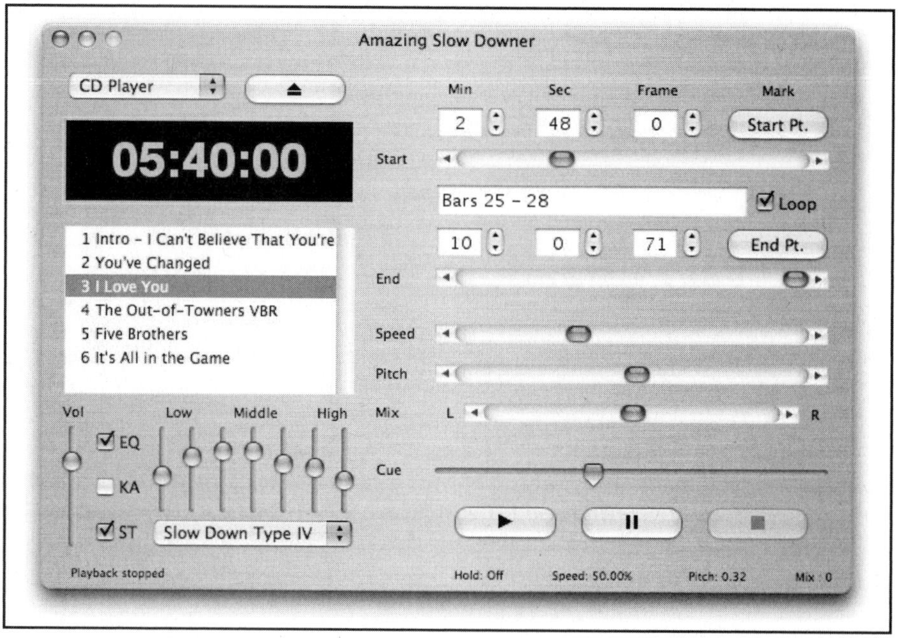

Figure 10-11:
The Amazing
Slow
Downer
is one of
several
computer
applications
that slow
down the
tempo of
the music
without
changing its
pitch.

Recording software

Applications such as Apple's *GarageBand* and *Audacity* allow you to record directly into the computer (so you can hear how good you *really* sound), and programs such as *Band in a Box* (for both Macs and PCs) provide you with a digital bluegrass band accompaniment. *GarageBand* is for Macs only while *Audacity* is available as a free Internet download for either Macs or PCs. *Band in a Box* is available at most music stores, with prices ranging from $100 to $300 depending upon the quality and variety of instrumental sounds you want to add to your accompaniment.

YouTube

Just about everyone by now has seen a talking dog video or two from www.youtube.com. You can also find numerous banjo-related videos at this site, but if you want to avoid watching Harry, the amateur banjo player from northern Minnesota struggling through "Cripple Creek" in his pajamas, be sure to begin your YouTube search by using a particular artist's name. You may still run into some annoying dead ends, but you can also find video jewels from great players such as Pete Seeger, Don Reno, Earl Scruggs, Bill Monroe, and others dating as far back as the 1950s to as current as last weekend's festival appearance.

Swapping Out Parts to Make Your Banjo Sound Better

Because the banjo is put together with nuts, bolts, and screws, exchanging parts on a banjo is easier than on a guitar or mandolin. Not a month goes by without someone bringing to market a new custom part of some kind advertised to give your banjo that extra edge. Although you can replace just about everything on a banjo, you can discover in this section a few of the easiest parts to swap out that can still improve the sound of your instrument.

Don't forget to refer back to Chapter 1 if you run across a banjo part you're unsure of in the following sections.

Bridges

A bridge is a small investment for something that can make a significant difference in the sound of your instrument. The *bridge* is a piece of wood (usually with three contact points, called *feet*) that sits on top of the head and transmits the vibrations from the strings that rest on top of it to the head and the rest of the banjo. The tension of the strings is all that keeps the bridge pressed against the head; glue isn't necessary. To replace the bridge, you can loosen the strings, pull out the old bridge, and install a new one (in Chapter 11, I discuss how to properly place the bridge; several different kinds of bridges are shown in Figure 10-12).

A banjo bridge is conventionally made from hard maple with a strip of ebony glued to the top. These days, builders also offer bridges made from birch, teak, koa, rosewood, and other exotic woods. Bluegrass players especially value bridges made from old growth or submerged wood. Various kinds and densities of wood transmit the vibrations of the strings in different ways and trying a new bridge is one way to noticeably alter the sound of your banjo.

Generally speaking, a bridge made from a dense wood that's lighter in weight will make any banjo sound brighter (but possibly more shrill), while a heavier and less-dense bridge will add bass (but perhaps take away some clarity). Banjo players love to experiment with different kinds and sizes of bridges to find just the right balance of weight and density for their instrument (and then argue about what works best!).

Figure 10-12:
Players often experiment with different kinds of bridges to find just the right banjo tone.

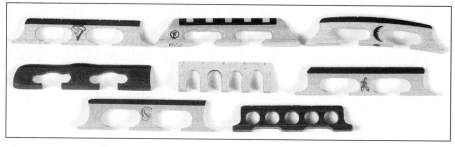

Replacement bridges come in a variety of heights, ranging from ⅝ " to ¹¹⁄₁₆ " or taller. Go with the same height as the bridge that's currently on your banjo unless you're interested in experimenting with slightly higher or lower string action (*string action* refers to the distance that the strings are above the banjo neck and is discussed in greater detail in Chapter 9).

You need to seek out an acoustic retail outlet for the largest selection of custom bridges. Look for prices that range from $15 to $35 from custom builders such as David Wadsworth, Silvio Ferretti (Scorpion), Gary Sosobee, Snuffy Smith, and Rick Sampson, among others.

Heads

Spotting the banjo head is easy: Look for the round, light-colored membrane that's stretched tightly over the banjo pot and acts as the main vibrating surface of the instrument. Because the primary resonating surface is a membrane rather than a piece of wood like on a guitar or mandolin, the head is largely responsible for the beautiful, mind-boggling, piercing tone that says *banjo!*

Every now and then, a head breaks and needs to be replaced. But players also choose to install a particular kind of head in order to get a different sound from their banjo.

Heads were made of animal hide up until the early 1960s when the plastics revolution took over the banjo world in the form of Mylar heads, which proved much more resistant to humidity change and to breakage. Most players now use plastic heads, and that's what comes on most new instruments. However, you can still go retro and get a calf or goatskin head for that "organic" sound. The vintage sound associated with these skin heads is still preferred today by many open-back banjo players and some bluegrass players.

Heads come in varying thicknesses and also have different kinds of spray coatings on their surfaces. Thicker plastic and heavier coatings impart a mellower tone, but skin heads usually give the deepest tone quality of all. Heads with little to no coating make your banjo sound brighter, and if you decide to go this route, you can also choose a clear head or a cool color. Although most synthetic banjo heads set you back from $15 to $30, be prepared to spend $40 to $50 for a skin head.

Banjo heads come in all kinds of diameters to accommodate the various sizes of banjo pots. If you're in the market for a new banjo head, be sure you purchase one that's the same size as the one you're replacing. Especially if you have an open-back banjo, you should take your banjo with you to the music store and ask for assistance to make the correct purchase.

Tailpieces

The *tailpiece* holds the strings to the banjo and is attached to the pot at the opposite end from where the neck is joined. Most bluegrass banjos have adjustable tailpieces that control the tension and angle of the strings as they meet the bridge. Changes in tailpiece height and angle can subtly affect tone and volume.

If a player desires a clearer sound from a banjo, that will often call for an adjustment of the tailpiece *down* towards the banjo head (this puts more pressure on the bridge and eliminates some *overtones,* the frequencies that are present above the basic pitch that color the banjo tone). If a musician wants a more open or full sound, the tailpiece will be adjusted up and away from the banjo head (allowing for more overtones).

Three types of tailpieces (shown in Figure 10-13) include the following:

- ✔ **Presto-style:** Presto is the name of the company that supplied the tailpieces found on many older bluegrass banjos and for this reason is still preferred by some players (the power of tradition is strong!). These tailpieces are lightweight but can be adjusted only up or down in relation to the banjo head.

- ✔ **Straight-line:** Most straight-line tailpieces have adjustment screws that allow for a greater variety of positions in relation to the head. Note how the strings travel in a straight line out from the tailpiece to the bridge (hence the name). Some players feel that the "straight line" of the strings enhances the instrument's tone by putting a more uniform string pressure on the bridge.

✔ **No knot:** These tailpieces are lightweight and small, and are the preference of many clawhammer players. Unlike the other two kinds of tailpieces, the no knot tailpiece accepts both loop- and ball-end strings. Like the Presto-style tailpiece, this tailpiece can be adjusted up or down in relation to the banjo head.

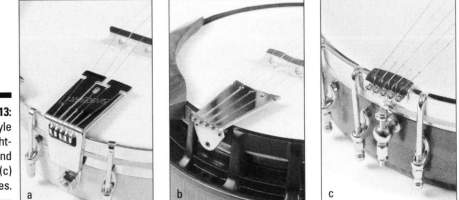

Figure 10-13:
Presto-style (a), straight-line (b), and no knot (c) tailpieces.

Players sometimes swap out a tailpiece on a banjo for the same reasons they may try a new head or bridge: They're looking for that very small, extra edge to their instrument's sound. Prices for a new tailpiece can range from $20 to $80.

"D" tuners

If you've ever heard a banjo instrumental that features the swooping sound of a string being detuned and then magically retuned up to its exact pitch, you've heard the effects of "D" tuners (they are called *"D" tuners* because they can quickly and easily get the banjo into a D-major tuning from G major if they are set properly). These special kinds of tuners are usually used on just the 2nd and 3rd strings by bluegrass players. Two types of "D" tuners include (both are shown in Figure 10-14):

✔ A **cam-type design** that attaches to the peghead. The cam-type tuner applies pressure to the strings at the top of the peghead, with the pitch of the string changed by adjusting levers that are positioned on each side of the peghead that push and pull on each string. One advantage to the cam-type tuner is that *both* strings' pitches can be changed at the same time with this design and the tuners even be used when fretting.

✔ An **internally geared design,** developed in part by banjo innovator Bill Keith, uses two screws on the tuner shaft itself to set high and low stops. With this type of tuner, the pitch is changed through a movement of the tuning peg shaft rather than being pushed or pulled above the peghead. When it's adjusted correctly, the tuner stops when it reaches the desired pitch. The Keith tuners are an especially good investment because they function as excellent regular tuners and can be easily moved from one banjo to another.

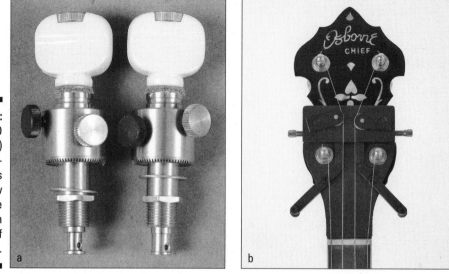

Figure 10-14:
Keith D tuners (a) and cam-type tuners (b) allow precise changes in the pitch of a string.

These tuners can be an expensive addition to your collection of accessories at $170 to $250 per pair, but they're ultimately the only satisfying way to play such instrumentals as "Flint Hill Special" and "Earl's Breakdown," tunes which feature the sound of the banjo's strings being raised and lowered in precise ways.

Chapter 11

Taking Care of Your Baby: String Changing & Basic Maintenance

*B*anjos are the mechanical wonders of the acoustic-instrument world. To the uninitiated, a banjo appears as a complex and intimidating hybrid of wood and metal with a bit of plastic (that would be the banjo head and your tuning peg's buttons, by the way). However, for those of you who know your way around a banjo, the instrument offers endless potential for adjustment and tinkering. Of course, knowing what you're doing before you start going crazy with a wrench and wire cutters is always good!

Part of being a good banjo player is knowing how to keep your instrument in top shape. In this chapter, I start you down the road to becoming a banjo-adjustment expert by introducing several basic things you can do now to keep your banjo sounding its best. You discover how to take off your old strings and put on new ones, how to properly set the bridge so that all the fretted notes stay in tune, and how to adjust head tension. You also figure out how to keep your banjo looking its best, and I discuss when you need to seek professional advice on repairs and maintenance.

The type, quality, and workmanship of the main components of your banjo — the wooden rim, the metal tone ring (if you have one), and the neck — determine the basic sound of your banjo. However, that basic sound can be altered in ways that you can easily hear by using different kinds of strings or by making adjustments to such components as the bridge and head (or replacing them entirely with different parts; see Chapter 10). The art of banjo adjustment, which consists of matching the playability and sound of the instrument to the preferences of an individual player, is called *setup*.

Replacing Banjo Strings

Like checking the oil in your car, shining your shoes, or balancing your checkbook, changing your old banjo strings for new ones is one of those slightly annoying tasks that's always possible to put off for another day. Although you don't do any damage to your banjo by continuing to play with worn-out strings, you'll feel much better about your banjo and your playing after you've installed a slick, shiny set of new strings. Your instrument will sound great and be easier to play, and you may be inspired to practice even harder.

If you've never changed strings on an instrument before, replacing the strings for the first time should take you no more than 30 to 40 minutes if you follow the instructions in this section. After you've gotten the hang of it, you should soon be able to change all your strings in 15 minutes or less. The only tools you need to have on hand are a pencil and a wire cutter. A couple of handy tricks makes string changing a much less onerous task. I cover everything you need to do in the next sections.

Deciding when your strings need a changin'

Some banjo players are able to play on the same set of strings for months at a time, but other players change strings as frequently as once a week. Body chemistry and climate have a lot to do with how fast strings wear out. In either case, the stickier and dirtier the immediate environment for your banjo, the quicker your strings collect dust and grime — and the more frequently you should change them.

Because a set of strings costs about as much as a latte these days, claiming poverty probably isn't a good reason for not keeping them fresh and new. However, if you live in a moderately humid climate, you keep your hands relatively clean when you play, and you wipe your strings down with a soft rag at the end of each practice session, your strings should last for a good, long time. Here are a few telltale signs that you need to think about making a change:

✔ The banjo becomes more difficult to tune; the strings especially sound out of tune when fretted up the neck.

✔ The strings feel rough to the touch, and you can see signs of grit, grime, and corrosion.

✔ A string breaks! You definitely need to replace the broken string. If you haven't changed strings for a while, go ahead and change all of them. (By the way, if the *same* string breaks consistently you could have a problem with your nut or bridge, in which case you should consult your local acoustic music store repairperson.)

Make sure you've figured out whether your banjo is designed to take loop- or ball-end strings (the great majority of banjos use loop-end strings). Take a moment to read up on this topic in the section on strings in Chapter 10 so you can make an informed string purchase. After you're at the store, go ahead and buy more than one set so you have plenty of extra strings on hand (stores often offer a discount on multiple sets too, so don't be afraid to ask!).

Changing strings 1 through 4: A step-by-step guide

Some folks like to place the banjo on a table to change strings, while others simply hold the banjo in a normal playing position. Either way, the process of replacing old strings with new is the same.

The bridge isn't glued to the head. It stays attached to the banjo with the tension of the strings. If you were to remove all the strings at one time, the bridge would come off, and you would have to reposition it while installing your new strings. For this reason, I recommend changing just one string at a time. It doesn't really matter in what order you change strings, as long as you can remember which ones you've changed and which ones you haven't after you've started.

In the following sections, I give you the steps to change your 1st string. Follow the same steps to change the other strings on your banjo — with one important exception. The 3rd- and 4th-string tuners rotate clockwise to raise the pitch of a string and counterclockwise to lower it. This direction is opposite from how the 1st- and 2nd-string tuners raise and lower strings. Remember that all four strings are threaded so that they wrap around each tuning post from the center of the peghead.

Step 1: Meeting your new strings

Your new strings most likely come packaged in a plastic pouch. Inside this pouch, you find each string stored in a separate paper envelope. The five envelopes are labeled either with the numbers 1 through 5 indicating which string is which (1st for 1st string, and so on), or they have numbers indicating the width of the string, measured in thousandths of an inch (0.010, 0.012½, for example). If this is the case, the outside packaging indicates which width goes with which string. The width of the 1st and 5th strings should be the same and are the smallest numbered strings in your set. The 2nd, 3rd, and 4th strings are consecutively larger.

Step 2: Removing the old string

Before you can put a new string on, you have to remove the old one. This step isn't rocket science. Begin by changing the 1st string. Simply turn the 1st string peg counterclockwise until the string is completely slack. Carefully pull the string through the hole in the tuning peg at the headstock to free it from that end of the banjo. Then take a moment to observe how the string is threaded through the tailpiece at the pot end of the banjo before removing it. You retrace these steps when you attach the new string.

Step 3: Attaching the string to the tailpiece

Before you unravel the new string and install it on your banjo, take a sharpened pencil and gently rub its point back and forth a few times in the grooves of both the bridge and the nut, blowing off the excess. The graphite provides lubrication for the string at these two points of contact, which makes keeping the string in tune easier. You can also use the pencil to widen the loop end of the string to secure it to the banjo more easily (both of these steps are shown in Figure 11-1).

You always want to attach the loop end of the string first onto the banjo's *tailpiece* (the claw-shaped object attached to the edge of the head that holds the strings at the opposite end of the banjo from the tuning pegs). Most tailpieces have five finger-like hooks or knobs that are designed to hold this end of the string. Tailpieces on bluegrass banjos often have covers, in which case you need to lift that up to find the attachments. Take note of how the old string is fastened to the tailpiece and install your new string in the same way. Figure 11-2 shows the string fit on two kinds of tailpieces typically found on open-back and bluegrass banjos.

Most bluegrass banjo tailpieces are designed so that the string comes out from under the front edge of the tailpiece. Check to see that you've threaded the string so that it emerges from the tailpiece in the same way.

Figure 11-1:
Using a pencil to lubricate the string slots in the bridge (a) and for preparing a loop-end string to fit securely on the tailpiece (b).

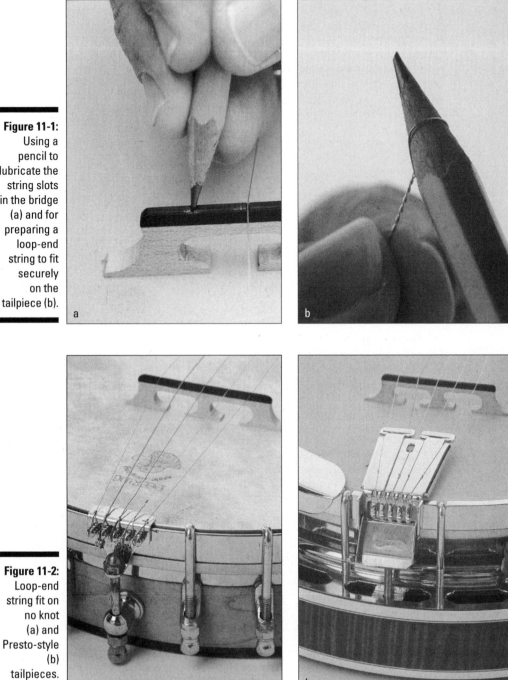

Figure 11-2:
Loop-end string fit on no knot (a) and Presto-style (b) tailpieces.

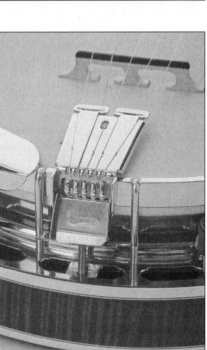

Step 4: Fastening the string to the tuning post

Now you must attach the other end of the 1st string to the tuning peg's post. Note that the post has a small hole in it. Thread the end of the string through this hole from the center of the peghead, pushing the string out through the hole towards the peghead's outer edge. Then pull the string through the hole so that you have just a bit of slack in the string along its entire length — enough for you to wrap around the tuning shaft no more than three or four times. See Figure 11-3 to see how this process looks.

Make sure that the string is seated in the proper 1st-string notch in the bridge. The loop end of the string may occasionally slip out from the tailpiece, so use this time to check that the string is still secure at that end of the banjo.

Step 5: Winding the string around the tuning post

Things get a little tricky with the next two steps. While holding the string with the right hand, use your left hand to create a crease in the excess string pointing towards the center of the headstock (see Figure 11-4). This kink prevents the string from moving back through the post when you begin to tighten it.

Figure 11-3:
Attaching the 1st string to the tuning post from the center of the peghead (a); pulling the slack of the string through the tuning peg hole before winding it around the post (b).

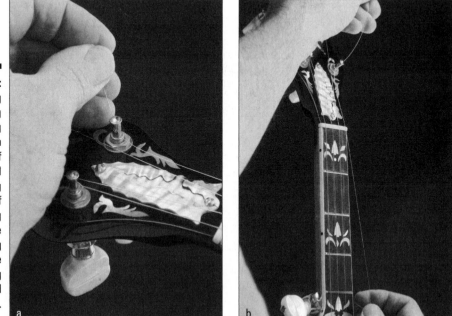

a

b

Figure 11-4:
Kinking the
1st string
towards the
center of the
headstock
to prevent
slippage.

Now tighten the 1st string around the post by turning the peg in a clockwise direction. Try feeding the string through your right-hand thumb and index finger. As you continue to turn the peg with your left hand, guide the string so that it wraps in downward circles around the post, towards the direction of the headstock (see Figure 11-5).

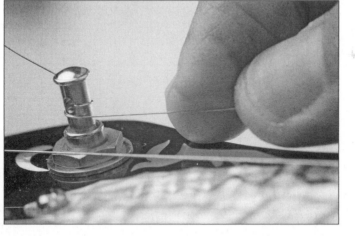

Figure 11-5:
Wrapping
the string in
downward
circles
around the
post while
guiding it
with the
right hand.

Step 6: Securing the string to the tuning post

Remember the crease you put in the string in Step 5? Most of the time, this crease prevents the string from slipping back through the hole in the tuner. However, many players also pin the excess string against the tuning post to insure that the string won't slip back through the hole.

Here's how to do this: Wrap the excess part of the string back around the post towards the center of the headstock and bring it underneath the string just in front of the tuning post. Now pull the excess string up and wedge it between the string and post. As you continue to tighten the string with the tuner, the excess string will be pinned against the post, preventing it from slipping out of the hole (both steps are show in Figure 11-6).

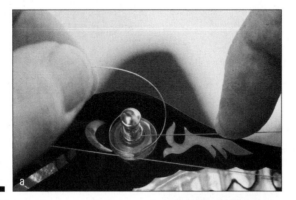

Figure 11-6: Wrapping the excess part of the string back around the post (a) and wedging it against the post to avoid slippage (b).

Step 7: Bringing the string up to pitch

You're almost finished! Continue to turn the peg clockwise to tune the 1st string up to a D note, making sure that the string is sitting in the 1st-string nut slot. Use your electronic tuner to tune the 1st string or use the 2nd string fretted at the third fret as a reference pitch. (For more instructions on tuning, see Chapter 2.)

Trim the excess string as close to the tuning post as you can by using your wire cutters, and you're done!

Replacing the 5th string

Most banjos have a *geared* 5th-string tuning peg, meaning that the tuner has internal gearing to assist in more accurate tuning, like your other tuners. With this kind of peg, the tuning post emerges from the side of the peg, making the string installation process a bit different. Here's a step-by-step guide:

1. **Remove the old 5th string, observing carefully how it is wrapped around the tuning post and attached to the tailpiece.**

2. **Turn the tuning peg so that the hole in the tuning post is parallel to the direction of the other four banjo strings.**

3. **Secure the new 5th string at the tailpiece and thread the string through the hole in the tuning post, leaving just a bit of slack.**

   Check to see that the string is seated in the bridge notch for the 5th string.

4. **Turn the peg counterclockwise.**

   This step also causes the post to move counterclockwise as the string begins to wrap around the tuning post.

5. **Crease the excess part of the string in a clockwise direction and move it around the back of the tuning post and underneath the string to pin it against the post.**

   Doing this after the string has wrapped around the peg with one full revolution may be easier.

6. **Because the 5th string has its own nut or a small spike to guide it to the peg, make sure that as the string tightens, the string is seated in the 5th-string nut.**

7. **Tune the string up to pitch (G for G tuning), and trim the excess string with a wire cutter.**

   And you're done! If you need some help tuning your 5th string, you can use an electronic tuner or check out the tuning instructions in Chapter 2.

A few inexpensive banjos have 5th-string tuners without gears. The big difference between geared and non-geared tuners is that the string's pitch goes up and down much more dramatically with only a slight movement from a tuner without gears. The process of changing the 5th string with a non-geared peg is the same as the steps I outline in this section, except that this time around, you wrap the string counterclockwise around a vertical tuning post (see Chapter 9 for more on geared and friction 5th-string tuning pegs).

Setting the Bridge

Unlike a guitar, the bridge on a banjo is movable. However, the bridge needs to be positioned on just one spot on the banjo head so that your strings sound in tune when fretted up and down the neck.

Even though the tension of the strings usually keeps the bridge firmly in place, over time the bridge may drift from its original position or may even fall over if bumped the wrong way (this scenario is typically a moment of high drama accompanied by a loud cracking sound, but usually no permanent damage is done). You may also decide to try different kinds of bridges on your banjo to see how they affect the sound (for more on this, see Chapter 10).

For these reasons, you need to know how to properly set the bridge. For this procedure, you don't need three hands — just your two ears and the help of an electronic tuner, if you have one. Finding the correct bridge placement involves playing harmonics and comparing the sound of these notes to the sound of a fretted string, which I explain how to do in the following sections.

When in doubt about bridge placement, consult your friends at your local acoustic music store. They should be more than glad to set the bridge as well as get you on the road to making this adjustment yourself without the stress and hassle.

Discovering harmonics

Harmonics (or *chimes*) are one of the natural physical byproducts of a vibrating string. When you pick a string, it vibrates not only along its entire length, but also in fractional sections of ½, ⅓, ¼, and so on. These additional, shorter-length vibrations add color and tone to the sound of the string.

If you very lightly touch a string directly above a fret at one of the points where the string length can be evenly divided and play that string, you hear the bell-like sound of a harmonic. Harmonics are a central feature of such bluegrass favorites as *Bugle Call Rag* and Earl Scruggs's *Foggy Mountain Chimes*. For the 4th to the 1st strings on your banjo, harmonics are found directly above the 5th, 7th, 12th, and 19th frets. Because the 5th string is a different length than your other banjo strings, its harmonics are found at the 10th, 12th, and 17th frets.

It can take some practice (and some time) to get your banjo harmonics sounding good. The key is to find the exact location over the appropriate fret with the left hand and to use the lightest touch possible. Move the finger ever slightly back and forth along the string to find the exact spot that allows the string to ring at its best.

Using harmonics to set the bridge

After you have a feel for how to play harmonics (see preceding section for tips), you can use them to help you set your bridge. Try playing the harmonic that's found at the 12th fret of the 1st string (see Figure 11-7). Remember that creating a harmonic takes a very light touch and that your left-hand finger has to be positioned directly over the fret instead of behind it as you would when normally fretting a note. After you're able to sound the harmonic (you'll know it when you do), you can enhance the bell-like effect by raising your left-hand finger off the string just after you strike it with the right hand.

Compare the pitch of the 12th-fret harmonic to the pitch of the string when fretted at the 12th fret. If your bridge is placed correctly, these two notes should sound the same. However, if you can hear a difference in pitch, you need to reposition the bridge in the following ways:

✔ If the fretted note sounds higher than the harmonic, move the bridge away from the neck, towards the tailpiece.

✔ If the fretted note sounds lower than the harmonic, move the bridge towards the neck, away from the tailpiece.

Figure 11-7:
The 12th-fret harmonic on the 1st string.

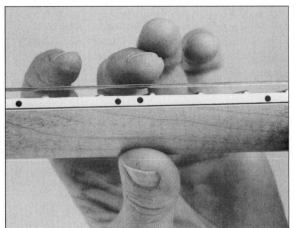

Usually only very small movements — fractions of an inch — are required to find the right position for the bridge. Grab one end of the bridge with each hand and firmly but gently push it just a bit along the head in the proper direction to get the string in tune.

After moving the bridge, you need to retune the banjo and try this procedure again. Getting the bridge in the best position may take several tries to get the harmonic in precise tune with the fretted note (your tuner can help you here).

After you've matched the pitches for the 1st string, try the same exercise on the 4th string. The 4th-string side of the bridge may need to be positioned slightly closer to the tailpiece in order to match the pitch of the harmonic to the fretted note.

Adjusting Head Tension

Tweaking the tightness of the banjo head is another basic skill that makes a difference in the tone and volume of your instrument. The *head* is the drum-like skin that's stretched across the top of your banjo's round pot (to read more on banjo heads, visit Chapter 10). When you play a note, the energy from the moving string is transferred through the bridge to the surface of the head, which amplifies and colors the sound of the string across its entire surface. The tightness of the head affects how bright and loud your banjo sounds and can also contribute to the playability of your instrument along with its ability to stay in tune.

In the following sections, I discuss the relationship between the tightness of your head and your instrument's tone and show you how to make adjustments to the head to bring out the best from your banjo.

Relating head tension to banjo tone

In general, the looser your banjo head is, the mellower your banjo sounds. A looser heads adds more low (or *bass*) tones to the banjo and somewhat reduces the volume of the instrument. Conversely, the tighter the banjo head, the brighter and louder the instrument is. Although adjustments or changes in bridges and tailpieces can also affect the tone of your banjo in similar ways, changing head tension is the best — and easiest — thing you can do to brighten the sound of your banjo (or take a bit of the edge off in order to stop attracting the pets in your neighborhood).

The philosophy of banjo setup is usually to find a middle ground within a range of adjustment to bring out the best tonal qualities of a particular instrument. In regard to banjo heads, when you hear players talk about loose or tight heads, they're usually splitting hairs and talking about small adjustments in head tension. If the head is *really* loose, keeping the banjo in tune would be next to impossible and its tone would be very muddy. If the head is *really* tight, the banjo would sound like a tin can, or the tension may even cause the head to break. Although beauty is in the ear of the beholder, most players feel that a banjo responds best and has the best tone when the head is "medium tight." When pushing against the head with your thumb close to the bridge, a medium-tight head should offer a good deal of resistance against your thumb but should depress slightly against this pressure.

Tightening the head

A new head, whether on a brand-new banjo or as a replacement head on an old instrument, stretches and needs some retightening once or twice in the first couple of weeks of use. For this reason, bringing a new banjo home from a music store with a loose head isn't unusual. After the first weeks of using your banjo, the head should remain stable and only need a slight adjustment once every three to four months or when temperature and humidity significantly change.

The head is stretched tightly across the top of the banjo by the tension hoop, and everything is held in place by the brackets that ring around the pot. Banjos vary in the number of brackets that they have. Most bluegrass banjos have 24 brackets, but minstrel banjos have far fewer brackets and some open-back instruments have even more. Figure 11-8 shows the side view of a bluegrass banjo pot as it appears when looking down on it while playing.

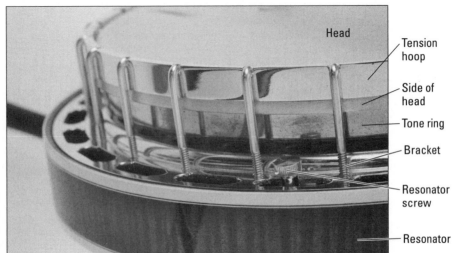

Figure 11-8: The banjo pot.

Head

Tension hoop

Side of head

Tone ring

Bracket

Resonator screw

Resonator

To check to see whether your banjo's head is loose, try pushing against the head near the bridge with your thumb. Does the head bend under this pressure and cause the bridge to sink with it? If so, you need to try tightening it by using the instructions in the following sections.

Using your banjo bracket wrench

Your banjo likely came with a bracket wrench tucked in the pocket of your case. *Banjo bracket wrenches* are sized to fit securely over the ends of the *bracket nuts,* which are the nuts that are attached to the long, slender metal rods (called *brackets*) that hold the banjo head tightly to the pot (see Figure 11-9). Make sure you use the right size wrench for this adjustment. In a pinch, an adjustable conventional wrench works for quick fixes, but this type of wrench can be difficult to work with in the close quarters of the banjo pot — and inadvertently cause you to strip out the bracket nuts. Consult your local acoustic music store or acoustic Internet retailer to find a wrench that's designed for your banjo. They usually cost around $5.

If you have a resonator on your banjo, you need to remove it to find the bracket nuts. Most resonators are attached to the pot with three or four screws that are easily visible and can be unscrewed by hand. Some entry-level banjos use small Philips head screws to hold the resonator. In this case, you'll need to dig through your garage tool kit for a screwdriver that will provide a proper fit.

After the resonator is off your banjo, use your banjo bracket wrench to tighten the head by turning the nuts clockwise, and loosen the head by turning in a counterclockwise motion. For more specific instructions on how tightly or loosely to adjust your banjo head, you can "head" to the next section.

Making small adjustments

The key to having a well-adjusted and happy head is to make gradual adjustments and to keep the pressure as uniform as possible around the tension hoop. Here's a step-by-step guide to tightening the head:

1. **Before you go to work with the banjo wrench, make sure that each bracket is finger tight.**

   Having one or two brackets work themselves completely loose isn't unusual if the head hasn't been adjusted for some time or at least since the banjo was in the showroom. Feel each bracket with your fingers, tightening each one as needed by hand, before tightening with a wrench.

2. **After the brackets are finger tight, fit the banjo wrench onto the end of the bracket that's closest to the neck of the instrument and tighten no more than ¼" of a turn or until the wrench meets some additional resistance; tighten the other brackets in the same way.**

Monitor the resistance you feel in the banjo wrench as you tighten each nut and try to match the tightness of the other brackets as you move around the pot.

Some players tighten *opposite* brackets when installing a new head, moving consecutively to the bracket that's 180 degrees across the rim near the banjo tailpiece and proceeding around the circle in this way. If you're doing only a slight adjustment to the head, you don't need to do this. Just move to the adjacent bracket and go around the circle.

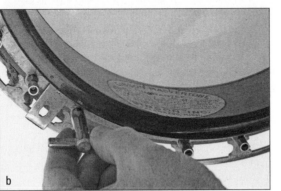

Figure 11-9:
A banjo bracket wrench (a); using the wrench to adjust the bracket nuts (b).

After moving around the banjo pot to uniformly tighten all the brackets, take a moment to retune your instrument and try playing a few chords or tunes. As you tighten the head, you should hear a brighter and clearer tone and more volume, but if the head gets too tight, the sound of the banjo becomes thin and wiry. If your head was very loose to begin with, the bridge should rise in response to the tighter head, causing the string action to become higher (in this case, your banjo is likely closer to factory specifications).

Maintaining uniform tension is key to having a good banjo sound, whether your preference is for a mellow or a bright tone. Take a moment to visually inspect the tension hoop; it should appear level around the pot and parallel to the tone ring and the top of the rim. If the tension hoop has one side pulled lower than the other at any point around the circle, the hoop is providing uneven pressure to the head. In this situation, loosen the head to even the pressure and begin the tightening process again.

Keeping Your Banjo Looking Its Best

Keeping your banjo looking sharp should be a part of your regular maintenance routine. Banjo players tend to go off the deep end in everything that they do related to the instrument, including cleaning. I try to practice moderation in this aspect of banjo maintenance. With a brand-new banjo, I try to keep it clean and shiny for a while, but sooner or later, especially after the first weekend festival of the summer, the plating inevitably begins to show signs of wear.

At that point, I resort to spot cleaning the banjo every now and then when the mood strikes me, leaving a complete and thorough polishing of the metal parts for those times (maybe once every couple of years) when I have the banjo disassembled (to install a new head, for instance).

If you keep up with regular cleaning rituals, your instrument will be easier to play, you'll have to change strings less often, and you'll preserve the wood finish and metal plating longer. So be sure to follow these few simple maintenance guidelines:

- **Rub the strings down with a cloth after each playing session to dramatically increase the life of your strings.** A cloth diaper or flannel rag is just right for this job.

- **After cleaning off the strings, gently rub the back of the neck with the cloth to remove smudges and hand oil from the neck.** Keeping the wooden surfaces of your banjo free from dirt and hand oil preserves the finish and keeps your banjo shining for years to come.

✔ **Take a moment to wipe off fingerprints, smudges, and whatever else may have accumulated on the metal plating of your banjo.** If your banjo has nickel plating (which is silver in appearance), that cloth diaper or soft rag can once again work wonders.

Even the softest rags can scratch fancy gold plating. For gold, try an eyeglass cleaning cloth and spray. Together, they remove smudges without scratching the delicate plating.

✔ **Wipe off your armrest with a soft cloth to remove any sweat or other grime and dirt.** The plating on your armrest is especially susceptible to tarnishing. Sooner or later, you'll likely just give up and let the power of biochemistry take its course, but some extra attention with the cloth keeps nature at bay for a while.

Wearing a wristband on your right arm while playing is an even better solution if you want to keep your banjo in like-new condition for as long as possible. You may look a little silly, but you'll have the cleanest armrest in town!

✔ **Every month or two, use a guitar polish to bring luster back to the wood finish on the resonator and neck.** Most high-quality polishes are applied by using a damp soft cloth and are buffed using a clean and dry soft cloth. If your banjo has a resonator, take it off the banjo to make polishing it easier.

When cleaning plated parts, use the softest cloth you can find and don't apply too much pressure when cleaning. The idea here is to gently remove stains from the surface of the plating, not to rub off the plating itself! Some folks recommend using silver polish every now and then on nickel- or chrome-plated parts (never use silver polish on gold plating!). I stopped doing this kind of housekeeping on my banjo some years ago when I realized that what was left on my polish cloth used to be the plating that was on my banjo! Although metal polishes such as Simichrome Polish can make the metal parts of your banjo shine like nothing else can, keep in mind that metal polishes are actually removing your plating in very small increments to create that shine. Metal polishes are best for very occasional use (once or twice a year).

Sooner or later, I always forget to move my belt buckle to the side, and I put a few scratches into the back of the resonator. No big deal! Your banjo is meant to be played and a scratch here and there or some tarnished plating isn't going to hurt your instrument or make it sound worse. The point is to have fun playing and not spend too much time worrying about keeping your banjo in showroom condition.

Knowing When to Consult a Professional

You may have gotten the impression from the discussion in the preceding section that a banjo is a delicate flower of an instrument, susceptible to damage by just breathing the wrong way on it. Of course, nothing could be further from the truth. Banjos are hardy creatures, and if you have a well-made instrument, it should provide years of enjoyment with no significant repairs of any kind needed.

However, you may have occasions when consulting a repairperson for help on things that you shouldn't try to fix yourself is your best option. These problems include the following:

- Cracks in any part of the wood or metal — anywhere on your banjo, inside or out.

- Severely twisted or bowed neck.

- Worn frets. Over time, the frets develop gouges where they come into contact with the strings. A repairperson will first even out the frets (this is called *dressing the frets*). This gives them a couple of years of additional use, at which point you will want to replace your old frets with new ones (called *refretting*).

- Broken head. After you've been playing a while, you'll learn how to install a new head yourself. For now, leave this task to your trusted repairperson.

- Tuner, tailpiece, or nut problems. With more experience, you can fix some of the problems that arise from these parts. For now however, consult a repairperson before replacing or working on any of these parts yourself.

Chapter 12

Networking into Banjo Culture

*P*laying the banjo isn't intended to be a solitary experience. Although you may feel that you're the only person in town who has ever even *heard* of a banjo (much less *like* one), I can assure you that hundreds of thousands of other people who share your passion for the instrument are out there. I know this may be hard to believe, but these folks are just as nuts as you are about everything to do with the banjo.

This worldwide community is just waiting for you to find them, and in this chapter, you can figure out how to connect with other players who can help you on your banjo journey. I discuss how to find a good teacher, how to locate other musicians in your area who play your kind of music, and what to expect at your first jam session. You also discover how workshops, camps, and festivals can heighten your banjo-playing experience.

Most people become interested in the banjo because they love the sound of the instrument. Most players *stay* interested because of the new friendships and experiences that come from their involvement with the banjo and with bluegrass and old-time music. Whatever your ability level, becoming a part of banjo culture is one of the most important things you can do to become a better player and increase your knowledge of the instrument.

Taking Private Lessons

One-on-one lessons from a skilled teacher are the best way to learn how to play the banjo. However, if you've never studied with a teacher before, recognizing a good instructor from a not-so-good one and gathering up enough nerve to go in for a lesson can be intimidating. This section unlocks the process of finding a teacher and getting comfortable with lessons by using a little psychology and a little detective work.

Overcoming lesson anxiety

The thought of music lessons may dredge up negative experiences you've had with music teachers in the past or other not-so-successful attempts at learning an instrument (I still remember my childhood piano teacher and her ruler — ouch!). Or you may feel that you're too old (or too young) to start serious study with a teacher. The bottom line is that everyone experiences fear of failure in their lives. Try your best not to let these kinds of thoughts limit you from doing everything within your power to find a banjo teacher in your area and start taking lessons.

Another reason that many folks don't take lessons is that they think they aren't yet good enough to get together with a teacher. They convince themselves that they'll contact a teacher after they've taught themselves the next section in that book or DVD that came with the banjo or after they've finally figured out how to get the banjo in tune!

Stop a minute and examine this way of thinking. Seems illogical, doesn't it? However, I've met many folks who have talked themselves out of lessons because they don't want to waste the teacher's time. I've talked myself out of everything from tennis lessons to subjecting my dog to obedience training with this kind of thinking. (Okay, it really *would* be a waste of the dog trainer's time, but that's a story for another time.)

Most professional teachers love working with students who have no playing experience. Brand new players don't have bad habits to unlearn and are often more fun (and less work) to teach than someone who already plays banjo. You aren't going to be wasting a teacher's time if you don't know the first thing about playing. That's the reason you're starting lessons! Teachers want to help you and welcome you just as you are. Also, don't worry if you're starting as an adult. Most new banjo players are middle-aged or older. I've known many people who begin to play banjo in their 70s!

Finding just the right teacher

After you make up your mind to take lessons, you have to go about the process of locating a good teacher. Sound like a headache waiting to happen? Don't stress it. With the advice in this section, you can be well on your way to finding an A+ teacher.

If you're new to the banjo, my best advice for finding a teacher is to start close to home. However, if you've already played for a few years, you may have to cast a wider net to find a teacher who can take you to the next level.

Using local and online resources

Your regional acoustic specialty store is the best place to find out about banjo teachers in your area. This store may even have an instructor who teaches in-house. If the store is some distance away, you should still place a phone call to inquire about teachers closer to home. This kind of store has contacts over a wide area and can probably connect you with teachers in your immediate area who the folks at your local all-purpose rock 'n' roll music store may not know.

The Internet has also made finding a good teacher easier. Type the key words *banjo teacher (your city and state)* or *banjo teacher directory* into an Internet search engine and see where it leads you. You may also be able to find a state or regional bluegrass club or association that sponsors events in your area, and its members should have the scoop on area instructors. Try conducting a search using *bluegrass association (your state)* as key words and see what comes up.

You can also post to one of several Internet banjo community Web sites to inquire about teachers in your area. You can get a response within hours! A few sites with good teacher directories include www.banjohangout.org and www.angiesbanjo.com.

The first stages of your search for a banjo teacher are going to be the most difficult. Don't get discouraged. Depending on where you live, finding someone in your area who can help you takes some persistence. One person may lead you to another who may lead you to then another before you've located the right person to teach you. If over time you have real trouble connecting with other players, consider attending a banjo camp (I discuss camps later in this chapter).

Choosing the right teacher

After you've uncovered a couple names of teachers (see preceding section), you need to decide which one to visit first. Try taking a lesson with each instructor who seems qualified and sounds interesting. Here are some of the most important questions to ask your prospective teacher:

- ✔ **Does the teacher actually play banjo?** The answer to this question may seem like a no-brainer, but many, if not most, "banjo" teachers play something else — usually the guitar — as their primary instrument. Although the person who offers lessons in guitar, mandolin, autoharp, violin, bass, piano, drums, glockenspiel, hurdy gurdy, theremin, *and* banjo may actually be a fantastic banjo teacher, approach this kind of lesson situation with caution. A few pointed questions should quickly reveal your prospective teacher's depth of knowledge.

  If you're a total beginner and can't find anyone else, this kind of teacher can at least help you to fret chords and get you started with right-hand technique, which is better than nothing! However, you soon want to move on to an instructor who really can play banjo.

- ✔ **Does the teacher play clawhammer or bluegrass?** Be sure to ask up front about this important aspect of teaching. Most teachers feel more comfortable giving lessons in one approach or the other, but if you find an instructor who is capable of teaching you both clawhammer and bluegrass, all the better (if you want to learn both ways of playing)!

- ✔ **Does the teacher welcome all levels of students?** Most dedicated, professional-level banjo teachers accept all levels of students. If a teacher accepts only beginning students, this may indicate that she may not be a very skilled player. If you're looking for lessons for a child, be sure to ask about the teacher's experience and comfort level with kids. Also feel free to ask how many banjo students the teacher is currently teaching. This number gives you a good idea of how serious this person is about teaching banjo.

- ✔ **How are lessons put together?** Does the teacher instruct everyone in the same way or are lessons tailored to fit the individual needs of students? Does the teacher use tablature, or will you be learning by ear (either is fine — the quality of teaching in either area is what counts)? Is the teacher willing to instruct you on accompaniment skills? Does he have a lesson plan? You want to be sure your prospective teacher is flexible enough to match your learning style, and the answers to these kinds of questions give you an idea of the instructor's willingness to shape lessons to what's best for you.

- ✔ **How often, and how much?** Weekly lessons, with travel time to and from your teacher's studio, can be difficult to work into an adult's busy schedule. However, if your lessons are too far apart in time, staying focused in your practice is difficult. In my experience of teaching hundreds of students over the last 30 years, most adults can make good progress on the banjo with a one-hour lesson every two to three weeks.

Kids (teenagers and younger) need more structure and a weekly half-hour lesson is just about perfect for them. Discuss scheduling with your teacher up front to see what's going to work out best for both of you.

Lesson prices can range from $25 to $80 or more per hour, depending on where you live and your individual teacher's scale. Better teachers cost more — this truth is the way of the world! However, even if you're a beginning-level player, I recommend splurging on at least one or two lessons from the very best teacher that you can find in your area, regardless of price. You can avoid months of frustration if you use this opportunity for an expert player and teacher to fine-tune your overall technique and help you with your sound at the initial stages of your banjo journey.

Connecting with a great teacher is the easiest way to make quick progress on the banjo, but you must determine how many lessons you need, the type of teacher you want, and how long to stay with a teacher. Some players study with the same teacher for many years, while others are more comfortable setting out on their own after only a few lessons. If your primary goal is to just get familiar with a few chords to strum along with others, you don't want or need many lessons. However, if you're interested in becoming a real bluegrass or old-time banjo player, you can expect to work with your teacher for six months to a year on the basics before spending another year or more on advanced tunes and techniques. Sound like a long time? It won't be if you're having fun with a good teacher.

Playing Music with Others

One of the greatest pleasures you experience playing banjo is when you make music with others. These days, connecting with other acoustic musicians is easier than ever before. Whether you're a beginner or a more experienced player, you make faster progress on the banjo if you take the opportunity to make music with other musicians as often as you can.

The primary way that amateur bluegrass and old-time musicians get together to make music is via a jam session. At a *jam session,* musicians at a variety of different skill levels come together to share tunes. Each musician gets an equal chance to be featured, but you aren't expected to know every tune that's played. One of the best things about jams is getting to hear and try your hand at new songs. Most jam sessions provide a welcoming environment for just about all levels of players (I note some exceptions in the following sections).

Jam sessions are common in other styles of music such as jazz, folk, blues, and even rock, but they play an especially important role with the kinds of music you play on the banjo. Bluegrass and old-time music are participatory art forms, and if you're a serious fan, you're more than likely a musician as well. Jamming is a primary way to become a better banjo player as well as get connected to your local music scene.

In the following sections, you unlock the secrets of how musicians are able to miraculously play together in a jam session. You also figure out how to match a jam session to your ability level and become familiar with how musicians interact with one another to make the music flow more smoothly. By observing good jam etiquette, you can be a welcome participant at any musical gathering that needs a banjo!

Finding a good jam

In most urban areas, the amateur acoustic music scene is based around free weekly jam sessions in music stores, cafes, coffeehouses, churches, and private homes. Your acoustic specialty store, banjo teacher, local music association, or the Internet should be able to point you in the direction of the most appropriate local sessions for your ability level.

Be sure to investigate *slow jams* or *jam classes* in your area. Both are relatively new phenomenon on the acoustic music scene and are ideal ways for newer players to start making music in a group context. The following describes what these kinds of jams are all about:

- **Slow jams** are led by one or two professional teachers and are designed for brand-new or beginning-level players to get accustomed to playing with other musicians by following along on bluegrass and old-time standards played *slowly*. The instructors lead you in playing simple tunes to give you a chance to use the capo, play in different time signatures, and become familiar with many different bluegrass and old-time standards. Slow jams have no limit in size, and they provide an easy and painless way to begin developing the techniques you need to play music with others in real jam sessions.

- **Jam classes** bring together one or two people on each ensemble instrument (banjo, guitar, fiddle, mandolin, dobro, and bass) to make music in a way that's a lot like playing in a real band. With the help of one or two professional teachers who are at the ready to provide comfort and aid to the jam afflicted, you work with other players to arrange tunes, work out vocal harmonies, and divide up the instrumental solos. You have the first-hand opportunity to experience what works (and what doesn't) when playing banjo with others. Jam classes are usually designed for musicians who have played six months to a year or more and already have many of the skills they need to get out and play with others.

Both slow jams and jam classes are often structured as weekly classes that run in eight- to ten-week sessions. In addition, many larger bluegrass festivals around the country also host slow jams or jam classes as part of their programming. In this case, these classes may take place before the festival actually begins, so be sure to check schedules (for more on festivals, see the section "Heading to a Bluegrass Festival" later in this chapter). As a complement to private lessons, both slow jams and jam classes are great ways to expand your playing horizons and help you get ready for a real jam.

Getting ready for a jam session

The egalitarian attitude shared by most bluegrass and old-time musicians is one of the most remarkable aspects about the communal experience of playing music with others. At a bluegrass festival, you may see professional players showing a song or lick to a young novice or see people from all walks of life (and all musical ability levels) joining together in an impromptu jam session around a festival campfire. The accessibility of the music's most skilled performers and the willingness of practically all players to share knowledge are unique to bluegrass and old-time music.

However, you don't want to just walk up to any jam session, take out your instrument, and start to play. Before you consider joining a real jam, you need to have mastered the following skills on the banjo:

✔ **Keeping your banjo in tune.** All participants in a jam session must be in tune with one another for the music to sound pleasing — nothing is less welcome than an out-of-tune banjo! You need to be able to tune your banjo by using either an electronic tuner or by getting a reference pitch from a guitar player. If you're a beginner, ask for tuning help from others instead of continuing to play out of tune. (For more on tuning, see Chapter 2.)

✔ **Fretting the G, C, and D or D7 chords and playing along to a simple chord progression by using basic right-hand techniques.** Hundreds of songs use just these chords. If you're comfortable fretting these chords and moving from one to another, you're well on your way to being able to play along with many tunes.

In slow jams, an instructor calls out the chords, but in a regular jam session, you're expected to figure out the chord progression as you play. This may seem like an impossibly difficult skill to master, but as you become familiar with more songs, you'll start to hear how one piece is similar to another. You'll soon be able to quickly figure out new chord progressions by using your ear. Asking other musicians for assistance is fine if you're having trouble figuring out any chord progression (for more on fretting, chords, and chord progressions, see Chapters 2 and 3).

✔ **Maintaining good rhythm as you play.** Rhythm is the most important organizing factor in making music with others because all the musicians participating in a jam session need to play a song at the same tempo. If they didn't do this, everyone would quickly be at a different place in the same song and *that* would really sound interesting!

Banjo players have the unfortunate reputation for wanting to play faster than everyone else. The secret to playing in good rhythm with others is to calm down, take a deep breath, and listen to what other musicians are playing, and then you can adjust your own playing to match what you hear other musicians doing. If you stop playing, everyone else is going to keep going! Figuring out how to play in good rhythm is a lifelong process, but finding and staying in the groove with others is one of the most fun parts of making music. (For more on rhythm, see Chapter 3.)

In reality, this list is just the bare minimum set of skills you need to keep your head above water in a real jam session. You should also know a wide variety of chords both in first position and up the neck and be comfortable with accompaniment techniques such as *vamping* (a bluegrass banjo rhythm technique that uses up-the-neck chords and allows you to play on faster songs). In addition, you should know how to use the capo and be able to play songs in the keys of C and D.

Keep in mind that a jam session isn't a private banjo lesson. Although other players or the jam leader are usually willing to help you with some aspects of a song, such as showing you a new chord or assisting you with the capo, you're essentially on your own after a tune begins. Unless the jam is specifically advertised as a slow jam (see preceding section), musicians play tunes up to speed and won't slow down or stop for you.

Joining in a jam

Whether you're wandering around the campground at a bluegrass festival or heading to an evening session at the local acoustic music store, deciding if, when, or how to join a jam session can be difficult and awkward. Each jam session is a bit different from any other one, and many factors can affect your decision whether to join in. You may see that a banjo player (or two) is already part of the group, or maybe they're playing faster than what you're used to. So how do you know whether you should take out your banjo and join in? And how do you best start to play with others in a session?

Although the group dynamics of a jam session can be subtle, you need to consider two important things before joining in:

✔ **What is the general ability level of the jam session?** If the skill level of the other players seems to be significantly above your capabilities, the better decision is probably to leave the banjo in the case and spend some time watching and listening. However, if you've found a session where the other players are just *slightly* better than you are, you may have found an ideal jam to take part in.

If you join in a jam session where the players have less experience than you do, keep your playing at their level. The other players will appreciate your generosity and may even say good things about you behind your back after the session is over. (And who wouldn't like that?)

✔ **How many other banjo players are already playing?** In a more advanced-level bluegrass jam, many musicians prefer to take part in a session where just one player, or two at most, is on each instrument — just like you see in a band playing on stage. By adding your banjo to the mix, you could disrupt the musical dynamic that's already been established. On the other hand, if the jam is large and everyone seems to be having a good time just playing along (and making a racket!), that's a good indication to join right in!

Closed jams: A time to listen

Although you never see a sign indicating a jam session is closed, you may find some jam sessions where you aren't welcome, regardless of your playing level. *Closed jams* take place for a variety of reasons that have absolutely nothing to do with you: perhaps an annual reunion of old friends who travel long distances to a festival just to play music with one another or a band is showing off its stuff for fans in an informal setting. Exercise great caution and a lot of common sense before joining in on what sounds like a very high-level jam session around a private RV, featuring just one other banjo player. This session is likely private!

Look for signs from the other musicians to gauge how welcome you may be to their session. Players often sit or stand in a circle and if that circle opens up right where you're standing, that's an unspoken invitation to join in. If one of the other banjo players, or the person who seems to be leading the jam, invites you to play, you've also just been given the green light.

When one of these signals occurs, you still need to figure out whether you can hold your own on the banjo with these folks. But at least you now know you're welcome to play along if you choose to do so. By the way, turning down an invitation to join in is fine if you'd rather listen.

Observing good jamming etiquette

After you've been accepted into a jam circle, it's time to play! These first moments can be stressful as you figure out your role (as well as remember your rolls) in the session. Here are a few tips to make yourself a welcomed guest after you've started playing:

- ✔ **Play conservatively to get comfortable.** If you've been asked to be a part of a jam that's already started, begin by playing quietly and simply, taking cues from the other musicians as to when to take a solo. You want to give room to the other banjo players in the session, especially with backup.

- ✔ **Strive to make the group sound good.** The best jams happen when all the participants try their best to make the entire group sound good. Showing off can be considered bad form, especially if you're the newcomer in a session. Don't use an introduction to a new group of players as an opportunity to put on display everything you know, played at excessive speed.

- ✔ **Keep good rhythm.** Nothing spoils a jam session for other musicians than someone who rushes the tempo, slows down, or starts and stops while playing. Although missing a chord change or even blowing your solo is alright, bad timing truly disrupts everyone in the session. If you can't keep up, you'd be better off not to play.

✔ **Use good dynamics.** For banjo players, good dynamics translates into not playing too loudly. Tone it down when playing behind another instrumental solo or a singer who sings quietly. 'Nuff said!

✔ **Be ready to contribute a song.** In most jams, everyone gets the opportunity to play one or more songs he chooses. Have several songs worked up well enough so you can lead others through the song by telling them the chords and directing the order of solos.

✔ **Make sure that your song choice is appropriate and everyone knows it.** Don't suggest "Stairway to Heaven," "Take Five," or "Smoke on the Water." Fit your song choices to the kinds of tunes that have already been played in the session. If everyone is having fun playing traditional songs with three chords, suggest another tune of this type. If more than one or two folks are hesitant about playing with you on your tune, choose something else that the other players can quickly catch on to as the song is being played.

Sitting out a particularly challenging song in a jam is perfectly fine, but if you find you're sitting out on almost every song, you may want to put the banjo back in the case. One strategy that works in many sessions is to stay outside the primary circle of pickers and follow along quietly by mirroring what other banjo players are doing, but being careful not to disturb the inner circle of players as you play.

Attending Workshops and Camps

A fantastic way to jumpstart your banjo playing is to attend a workshop or camp. Both events allow you to leave the rest of the world behind for a while and focus on nothing else but playing banjo. You also get the chance to hang out with legendary players and teachers as well as connect with other musicians from not only your own part of the country but also all over the world. If you're interested in this type of experience, keep reading the following sections.

The most common excuse I hear from folks who don't attend workshops and camps is that they feel that they aren't "good enough" to benefit from these kinds of experiences or that their own playing skills are so marginal that they will drag the other players down. Don't be a needless victim of workshop anxiety syndrome! These events are designed to help each and every banjo player move to the next level in their playing. You can't find a "best" player or a "worst" player in these situations. Each musician has a personal and unique set of strengths and weaknesses and all participants — teachers and students alike — come to a workshop or camp ready to help others.

Workshops: Fine-tuning your techniques

A *workshop* is usually a one-day event, lasting from a couple hours to a full day of instruction. Often, your area acoustic music store sponsors a weekday evening or a weekend afternoon workshop when a well-known player passes through town or when the local teacher wants to present a session on a particular topic, such as working up solos, banjo setup, or playing backup.

Workshops present a great opportunity to network with other local players as well as provide an opportunity to experience different teachers' perspectives on playing. Plus, hanging out with a famous player for a couple of hours and hearing this musician demonstrate techniques and play tunes in an intimate setting is a whole lot of fun.

Most workshops are geared towards intermediate- to advanced-level players. However, don't let that dissuade you from attending a workshop if you're a beginning player — especially if the featured teacher is one of your banjo heroes. Audio and video taping is usually encouraged at workshops, so if you don't understand everything that's covered right then and there, you can come back to this material later on when you're ready for it.

Workshops are group instruction sessions, so don't expect to receive much individual attention from the instructor in this kind of learning environment. On the other hand, you also won't be asked to play for the teacher or the rest of the class, so you don't need to worry about trying to impress everyone with your playing.

You can expect to spend from $25 to $80 on a workshop, depending on the number of hours of instruction and the notoriety of the teacher. Don't forget to bring extra money to buy some of the instructor's CDs, books, and DVDs!

Catching the workshop bug

Although workshops on topics related to the banjo are naturally of greatest interest to us, don't pass up sessions that cover subjects such as harmony singing, music theory, arranging songs, or developing good listening skills. The more general music knowledge you can absorb, the stronger a banjo player you'll be in the long run. General workshop sessions also provide a chance to meet local folks who play other instruments, and these new friendships can result in new jamming opportunities or even the formation of a new band — featuring you on the banjo!

To find workshops in your area, check with your local acoustic music store as well as your regional folk or bluegrass music association. Don't forget to also take a look at your favorite performers' or teachers' touring schedules, which can quickly be accessed via their Internet homepages. In addition, many festivals sponsor workshops as part of their programming at no extra charge. Be sure to take advantage of these opportunities.

Banjo, bluegrass, and old-time camps: Rubbing elbows with the pros

Camps are more intense experiences than workshops (see preceding section), because they involve living from two to five days or more with 50 to 200 other music enthusiasts of all ages from all over the world who share your passion for the banjo, bluegrass, and old-time music. Imagine spending time and getting to know such banjo legends as Sonny Osborne, Mike Seeger, Tony Trischka, Bill Keith, Pete Wernick, and Alan Munde — and even getting the chance to play music with them and share a meal (or a game of hoops). As the television commercial says, that's priceless!

Well, not exactly. Camps are big investments, and after you factor in transportation costs, you can easily spend $600 to $1,500 or more for this kind of experience. Choosing a camp that matches your ability level, your musical interests, and your personality is important. Camps are experiments in communal living, and you also want to make sure you've selected an event that fits your tastes in food, accommodations, and overall comfort level.

The biggest decision to make in choosing a camp is whether to attend a *banjo camp* that's designed just for banjo players or a *bluegrass* or *old-time camp* in which the banjo class is part of a larger event that provides instruction on all of the different instruments in the bluegrass and old-time ensemble (such as guitar, mandolin, fiddle, bass, and dobro). Each type of camp has its own strengths and advantages, so consider the points in the following sections as you shop for a camp that's a good match for you.

Banjo camp

The great thing about banjo camps is — you guessed it — they're all about banjos! You get small-group instruction in clawhammer and bluegrass styles in an all-banjo, all-the-time environment where you play banjos, talk about banjos, eat and sleep banjos, and maybe even take a few of them apart and put them back together. Plus, you'll never run across a more interesting bunch of folks in your life than those you meet at a banjo camp — you'll love it.

The main advantage of a banjo camp is that you soak in more banjo at this event than you can at an all-purpose bluegrass camp. The larger banjo camps have teaching staffs of up to 20 professional players with class offerings that encompass a wider variety of styles than what you might encounter at a blue-grass or old-time camp with fewer banjo teachers.

Most banjo camps offer instructional tracks designed for beginning-level play-ers, with some camps even offering classes for those who are picking up a banjo for the very first time. Even if you're an advanced-level player, plenty of great class topics are available for you to choose from. Read up on the types of classes offered by each camp and the level of student that typically attends.

A few banjo camps I recommend include the Midwest Banjo Camp in Lansing, Michigan (www.midwestbanjocamp.com); Banjo Camp North in the Boston, Massachusetts area (www.mugwumps.com/bcn.html); the American Banjo Camp near Seattle, Washington (www.langston.com/ABC); Pete Wernick's Winter Banjo Camps in Boulder, Colorado (www.drbanjo.com); and my own NashCamp Fall Banjo Retreat near Nashville, Tennessee (www.nashcamp.com).

Bluegrass and old-time camps

Bluegrass camps offer instruction in bluegrass banjo style while *old-time camps* focus on clawhammer and pre-bluegrass finger-picking techniques. Some camps, such as the California Bluegrass Association's Music Camp in Grass Valley (www.cbaontheweb.org), offer instruction in both styles at the same time. Other sponsors, such as the Augusta Heritage Center's camps in Elkins, West Virginia (www.augustaheritage.com) hold separate bluegrass and old-time events at different times.

The advantage of a bluegrass or old-time camp that offers instruction in all the instruments is that your jamming possibilities are much broader with an event of this type. Many bluegrass camps put you together with other musi-cians at your ability level to form a real (if temporary) band. The music you make in this context can be the most rewarding and memorable experience of your week at camp.

In addition to several hours per day of small-group instruction on banjo, you spend the afternoons during the week practicing with your bandmates and getting help from professional instructors as you work up a song or two to play on stage for the other campers at the end of the week. You come away from this kind of camp being more comfortable playing with other musicians and having a greater understanding of the role of the banjo in a band.

In addition to the bluegrass and old-time camps I mention previously, other great camps to check out include Camp Bluegrass in Levelland, Texas (www.campbluegrass.com); NashCamp's Bluegrass Weeks near Nashville, Tennessee (www.nashcamp.com); Bluegrass at the Beach outside of Portland Oregon (www.bluegrassatthebeach.com); and the Swannanoa Gathering near Asheville, North Carolina (www.swangathering.org) for old-time music.

Room and board

Food and accommodations are usually included in the price of a music camp. I bet you thought your days of sharing a bathroom with several other hall mates in a college dorm and eating at the cafeteria were behind you, right? Not so — at least not at a banjo camp! Many camps utilize college campuses or actual summer camp venues to host their events to keep tuition prices as reasonable as possible. Don't be surprised to share a room with one or two other people at most camps.

Living in such close quarters to other aspiring musicians is usually a highlight of the camp experience for most students. You aren't at camp long enough for this living arrangement to be a hassle. However, if dormitory life and shared bathrooms prove to be a bit too much for you, you can arrange for private lodging at a local hotel during your camp stay.

A few camps, such as my own event, the NashCamp Fall Banjo Retreat held each fall near Nashville, Tennessee (www.nashcamp.com), offer bed-and-breakfast style accommodations with gourmet meals. You pay a higher tuition for such extravagances, but if your creature comforts are a primary concern, be sure to check out the fine print regarding food and lodging for your camp as you make your decision on which camp to attend.

Heading to a Bluegrass Festival

The most popular way to experience bluegrass and old-time music and find others to play music with is to attend one of the several thousand annual outdoor bluegrass festivals that are held all over the United States each year as well as in Japan, the United Kingdom, and Europe. At a festival, you hear renowned performers on stage as well as participate in jam sessions that take place at all hours in campsites throughout the festival grounds. People flock from all over to be a part of the fun, and you can too! In the following sections, I break down what's so great about bluegrass and old-time festivals and help you find one near you.

Discovering what festivals are all about

A bluegrass festival can be one of the highlights not only of your banjo-playing experience, but also your year. These festivals are designed for musicians and their families to temporarily be part of a community who enjoys and plays bluegrass and old-time music. The outdoor setting provides a perfect context for down-home music making.

You can find bluegrass festivals of all shapes and sizes. Some bluegrass festivals, such as Hardly Strictly Bluegrass in San Francisco, California (www.hardlystrictlybluegrass.com); MerleFest in Wilkesboro, North Carolina

(www.merlefest.org); the Telluride Bluegrass Festival in Colorado
(www.bluegrass.com); or the Grey Fox Bluegrass Festival in upstate New
York (www.greyfoxbluegrass.com) attract large international audiences
numbering 100,000 or more that travel to hear the most well-known performers in bluegrass and acoustic music today. Contrast this kind of event to a
local bluegrass or old-time festival held at a nearby county fairground with
around 300 to 400 people in attendance or a regional contest held out in the
country that attracts the best amateur musicians from a wide region.

Most festivals last from two to five days and are held outside, but a few cold
weather events, like Wintergrass in Tacoma, Washington (www.acoustic
sound.org) and Bluegrass First Class in Asheville, North Carolina (www.
bluegrassfirstclass.com), are held indoors at a hotel or convention
site. Very few festivals are free of charge, and most events charge up to $100
or more for a full weekend adult ticket (which really isn't bad for a full weekend of music). Children's admission prices are frequently much less than an
adult ticket price, which allows the entire family to attend.

A bluegrass festival is different in several ways from a rock, jazz, or classical
music festival, and you can have more fun if you keep the following guidelines
in mind:

- ✔ **Bring the whole family.** Bluegrass festivals offer a secure and safe environment for the entire family to have a good time. Your kids are soon
  playing with new friends, and you're playing music with the folks you've
  just met at the campsite next door. And although you should bring the
  spouse and the kids, remember that most festivals don't allow pets.

- ✔ **Pack your camping gear.** You enjoy a bluegrass festival more if you camp
  out at the festival site for the weekend. Bring all the equipment that you
  would normally bring with you to a drive-in campground (or bring your
  RV if you have one). You can buy a variety of food from festival vendors
  or bring your own. Don't forget sunscreen, insect repellant, rain gear,
  and a flashlight (which you use to walk from one midnight jam session
  to another without falling over a tent stake).

- ✔ **Take your instruments.** Don't forget your banjo! At a larger festival, you
  have many opportunities to play with others in campground jam sessions at virtually all hours of the day (and night). Also don't forget extra
  strings, picks, and even an audio recorder to preserve a hot jam session
  or a new tune.

  A festival is also a great opportunity to get other members of your family
  interested in playing, so be sure to pack extra instruments and bring these
  with you. Don't be surprised if someone in your family starts playing a
  new instrument by the end of the weekend.

- ✔ **Remember your earplugs . . . and aspirin.** Your adrenalin keeps you
  going until about Saturday afternoon at a three- or four-day festival.
  Sooner or later, you need to catch up on your sleep and recover a bit from
  whatever overindulgences you may have committed the night before.

Finding a festival that's right for you

Although seeing legendary performers at a large mega-festival is thrilling, you may have just as much fun and get the chance to play more music by attending a smaller event closer to home. Many of my favorite bluegrass festivals, like the California Bluegrass Association's Father's Day Bluegrass Festival in Grass Valley (www.cbaontheweb.org) and the Gettysburg Bluegrass Festival in Pennsylvania (www.gettysburgbluegrass.com), lie somewhere between the two extremes. Make sure you choose a festival that's large enough to attract the best musicians in your region, but small enough to still easily allow lots of opportunities to make music with others in a safe environment.

So how do you find just the right bluegrass festival? The Internet once again is a great resource in finding the right music festivals for you in your area and beyond. Visit www.bluegrassfestivalguide.com for a national database of bluegrass and old-time festivals. You may also want to check out *Bluegrass Unlimited* (www.bluegrassmusic.com) and *The Old Time Herald* (www.oldtimeherald.org) magazines, because each publishes an annual festival guide in their spring issues.

The Web site of your regional music association, the bulletin board of your local acoustic music store, and the calendar listings provided by your local bluegrass radio DJ can also point you in the right direction towards the best area festivals. And don't be afraid to ask other musicians what festivals they like to attend — word of mouth is important too!

A wide variety of festivals around the country these days use the name *bluegrass* to describe their programming. Some of these events hire bands popular with younger audiences, while others attract mostly retired folks. Other festivals include a wide variety of music in their programming. The kinds of bands hired to play at different festivals are a good indication of what kind of audience will be in attendance. Make your decisions based on which festival looks like the most fun for you and your family.

Part V
The Part of Tens

The 5th Wave   By Rich Tennant

"So you're attempting to learn how to play the banjo, but your wife hates bluegrass music... Go on..."

In this part . . .

Every *For Dummies* book ends with top-ten lists, and this one is no exception. I present ten suggestions to make your practice time more fun and productive, and I include a select list of ten important banjo players who are well worth the listen.

Chapter 13

Ten Tips to Make Practicing More Fun

. . . .

In This Chapter

▶ Making the most of your practice time

▶ Discovering practical tips to make you a better player

. . . .

*P*ractice. Ugh. For many people, just the word itself conjures up bad memories of traumatic mandatory childhood music lessons. You already know by now that if you're going to make progress on the banjo, you have to practice just about every day if you can, but I don't want you to view this as a chore. Practice should be something that you look forward to every time you pick up the instrument. You gotta do it, so try to find ways to make it as fun as possible.

In this chapter, you find practical and useful tips you can use right now that will keep you coming back time and time again . . . to practice!

Listen Actively

Actively listening to your favorite banjo music on CD or to other musicians at concerts and jam sessions makes you a better player. Before you even start to work on a new song, find a recorded version of it first and try to pick up the song by ear. As you listen to great playing, you're internalizing what the banjo is supposed to sound like, the finer details of the style you're learning, and how the instrument fits in a group setting. Active listening also helps you to remember a song's chord progression and gives you ideas on how to accompany others when you aren't taking a solo.

Keep in mind that there's a time and a place for active listening. To keep the peace at home, carve out time when you can listen alone or in a way that doesn't disturb others (here's where headphones can come in handy). If you feel compelled every once in a while to expose your friends to your favorite banjo music, be aware that they may not want to listen to "Whoa Mule" 20 or 30 times in a row (I'm not sure why however. . .).

Set Goals

Setting short-, medium-, and long-range goals keeps your practice routine on the right track and helps you to assess your overall progress. Your goals are unique to you. If you've never played a stringed instrument before, your first goal may be to successfully play a few simple songs for your friends. A little farther out in time, you may aspire to hold your own in a beginners' jam session. If you're feeling even more ambitious, someday you may want to play in a local amateur band or organize your family to make music together.

Your long-range goals (where you want to be one to three years out in time) determine your medium-range goals (6 to 12 months out in time). These medium-range goals help you to focus on what you should be practicing in the next one to two weeks (your short-term goals). Adjusting your goals every once in a while is fine. They're there to inspire you to keep scaling to ever-greater banjo-playing heights, not to take all the fun out of playing.

If you're taking lessons, work with your teacher to create a set of realistic, achievable goals that you can put in writing. You can even do this on your own. After you write down your goals, check back every month or two to see whether you're still on track.

Practice Regularly

Regular daily practice, even if each session is for a short amount of time, leads to quicker progress than cramming in long sessions on your days off from work. When my daughter Corey was learning to play piano a few years ago, she came up with an interesting practice regimen: She would play for five or ten minutes three or four times almost every day, approaching the piano to play whenever the urge struck her. Similarly, when he's at home, banjo virtuoso Béla Fleck also practices several times a day in short intervals.

If you can play for a little while almost every day *and* find one or two days a week where you can stretch out and play for a couple of hours at a time, all the better. Keep in mind that the more skilled you are as a player, the more practice time you need to advance to the next level.

Take the banjo out of its case and keep it on an instrument stand in your practice area (but out of the way of dogs, cats, and young children who may inadvertently tip it over). Then, when you're ready to spend a few minutes playing, your instrument is right there waiting for you.

Warm Up

Athletes warm up with stretching routines, and you can do the same in your practice sessions. Warming up is a very important part of your overall practice as it prepares you mentally and physically for what comes next. When you warm up, work on aspects of your playing that you don't have time to think about after you start playing faster.

For instance, you can devise warm-up exercises to isolate and work on specific right-hand picking patterns or left-hand techniques apart from songs. Your warm up is also the time for you to focus on your tone, your rhythm, and the clarity of your left-hand fretted notes, making adjustments when necessary. Try playing a few of your favorite songs, listening carefully to the clarity and fullness of each note and checking your overall technique as you play. Chapters 4 and 5 cover the fundamentals of banjo technique and contain excellent exercises for your warm up.

Although some players may need to warm up for only a few minutes before they're ready to move on (which is the case with some experienced players), you may want to stay in this warm-up mode for up to 30 minutes or more before moving on to work on specific tunes. That's fine! Practicing "within your zone" is better than wasting time playing things that are too difficult for you.

Use Tablature Sparingly

Although _tablature_ (written music) is a wonderful resource that allows quick access to hundreds of tunes and also allows you to study closely the subtleties of a master player, use it in small doses. Tablature is great for showing you the left and right mechanics of how something is done, but don't confuse the ability to read and play tab with really being able to play banjo. Try to internalize the _sound_ of what you're playing as quickly as possible so that you're concentrating on what you're hearing, rather than what your eyes are following on the tab page. (For more tips on how to read tab, see Chapter 3.)

Using tab in a jam session can be a significant breach of custom. You can begin to break the tab habit now by working on your accompaniment skills and playing with other musicians at your level as much as possible. Think of tablature as a road map, not a destination! (For more ideas on accompanying others, see Chapter 4.)

Get the Right Hand First

For adult learners, one of the most difficult aspects of banjo playing is putting the right- and left-hand techniques together and using both hands at the same time to play smoothly without interrupting the even flow of notes. If you're also experiencing this problem, try playing the right-hand part by itself on the banjo's open strings. After you have the rhythm and the mechanics of the right hand down, begin to add the left-hand techniques, bit by bit if necessary. Using this building-block approach may feel a bit mechanical at first, but it can cut your learning time in half. Plus, this method is a good way to check whether you're playing something correctly.

Your right-hand technique communicates a lot about you as a player — your tone, your rhythm and drive, your volume, and even your mood! When playing with others, staying in rhythm is much more important than getting every note fretted correctly. Great players spend a lot of time working on right-hand technique. If you do the same, you'll be a great player some day too!

You can get the basics of right- and left-hand techniques in Chapter 4; for more in-depth coverage, check out Chapters 5, 6, and 8 for bluegrass banjo and Chapters 5 and 6 for clawhammer banjo.

Gradually Increase Your Speed

Playing slowly until you master a technique or song is a tough guideline for banjo players to remember, because they all want to play as fast as they can as soon as possible. However, if the song doesn't sound right when played slowly, the tune isn't going to get any better when played fast (trust me on this one!). After you're warmed up, use your practice time more efficiently (and enjoy it more in the process) by practicing at a slow enough speed where you're still in control of what you're playing. Keep in mind that this tempo could be different for each piece you're working on.

After you're comfortable playing at a slower pace, you may decide that you want to crank the speed up a notch. Regular practice with a metronome can help you to play faster. First, find a tempo where you're playing a song well and get comfortable playing along without getting out of sync. Now try increasing the tempo on the metronome to the next highest setting and start playing again. The increase in speed is sometimes so gradual that you may not notice a difference in the tempo at first. However, sooner or later you'll hit a bump in the road where you find one or two parts of a tune that give you problems. Work on just those sections at the new tempo, and after you've mastered them, start playing the entire tune again. You'll soon be playing effectively at a faster tempo. (See Chapter 10 for more on metronomes.)

Be patient with your progress in this area — speed is a function of time spent with your instrument and is measured over months or even years. Especially if you're an older player or if you've never played a fretted instrument before, speed may be the last element that falls into place as you're learning to play. Banjo music is virtuosic stuff — think of it in the same way as you would approach a piece by J. S. Bach or Charlie Parker if you were an organist or a sax player. You wouldn't expect to pick up *that* kind of music overnight would you? Just keep playing as much and as often as you can, and you will reach your goals.

Take Songs One Measure at a Time

Tablature enables you to play a song from beginning to end without really knowing what you're playing. However, when you go to actually internalize something that you just played from tab, you need to work on memorizing each note and phrase and be able to move comfortably from one part to the next without stopping. The best way to do this is to start at the beginning (hey, what a concept!) and play the first measure or two over and over until you've got it without looking at the tab. If you're learning by ear, you want to be able to play these measures by hearing them first in your head.

Listen to the sound of several measures played together and try to identify the musical phrases of your song (think of a musical phrase like you would a line of verse from a lyric — a *phrase* is a complete musical thought that usually consists of a couple of measures of music). After you've mastered the first phrase, move on to the second phrase. After you've got the second phrase down, spend a few moments playing the first and second phrases together, remembering not to rely on the tablature. Keep building out in this fashion to the end of the song, remembering to work each new phrase into the entire tune as you go along.

You'll likely encounter some repetition along the way, so after you have the first section of a tune down pat, the second section usually takes less time. (See Chapter 3 for an introduction to the anatomy of a song.)

Play the Right Repertoire

If your goal is to play music with others, work on the tunes that they like to play. Luckily, almost all bluegrass and old-time musicians learn a basic shared set of tunes at one time or another. The musicians at your local jam session may also play a few personal favorites, including some tunes that may be unique to your part of the country. Keep in mind that more advanced players share a different set of tunes than beginning-level players, bluegrassers have a different repertoire than old-timers, and younger musicians may play some different tunes than the older folks play.

In Chapter 6, you can play four tunes that are jam standards, using both blue-grass and clawhammer techniques. These examples give you a good place to start in terms of building up your repertoire. After you've mastered a few basic pieces and you feel you're ready to try a beginner's jam session, find out what tunes these musicians like to play. Attend the session and make a list of the songs you hear or (with the permission of the other musicians) bring a tape recorder along to record the pieces you don't know, so that you can work on them at home.

The Internet can also be of assistance as you search for tunes. Banjo player Pete Wernick has lists of bluegrass jam session favorites at www.drbanjo. com. You can also find several archives of old-time music; visit the homepage of the Friends of Old Time Banjo (www.oldtimebanjo.com) for links to the Digital Library of Appalachia at Berea College and other archival resources.

Keep Track of Your Progress

Most players keep a tune list in the front pocket of their music notebook. You can group tunes in any way you like. Some players group by key or tempo, while others create a list of tunes they already know, a list of tunes they're working on right now, and another list of tunes they want to learn in the near future. A tune list comes in handy when you're comparing what you know with another musician, but you suddenly can't recall a thing about any of the tunes you know (believe me, it happens, even with professional players).

If you're working hard at building up speed with the metronome, write the tempo settings down in pencil for each tune you're working on so that you know at what tempo to start at your next practice session. You may also want to maintain a practice diary where you can keep some brief notes about some of the things you worked on that day and also remind yourself about what needs more work the next time your pick up the banjo, which will be either just after you put down this book today or tomorrow at the latest, right?

Chapter 14

Ten Banjo Players You Need to Hear

This chapter presents ten players (more if you care to count) who have made a difference in the world of the banjo. They're not only the best at what they do, but they have also been among the most influential upon other banjo players. Some have expanded the musical potential of the banjo, while others are responsible for bringing new audiences to the instrument. I end this chapter with a list of other great players you should check out if you have the time.

Earl Scruggs (b. 1924)

You can't possibly overstate Earl Scruggs's influence on the world of the banjo. His three-finger technique is the most emulated banjo style in the world and is the important defining characteristic of bluegrass music (for more on bluegrass banjo, see Part II and Chapter 8). After raising the banjo within country music from a simple accompaniment instrument played by comedians to an instrument capable of the highest levels of virtuosity in the 1940s, Scruggs helped popularize the banjo and bluegrass music with a large national audience in the 1950s and '60s through television appearances (*The Beverly Hillbillies*) and movie soundtracks (Earl's unforgettable show-piece "Foggy Mountain Breakdown" was featured in *Bonnie and Clyde*).

Hundreds of thousands of banjo players cite him as a primary influence. Check out *The Essential Earl Scruggs* (Columbia) for a good overview of his music and career. Scruggs's early 1960s instrumental masterpiece *Foggy Mountain Banjo* (Copper Creek Roots/Columbia) is the best bluegrass banjo instrumental album of all time.

Pete Seeger (b. 1919)

In the 1940s through the 1960s, Pete Seeger placed the banjo front and center in the American folk song revival as part of a long and prolific career as a singer, songwriter, author, and political and environmental activist. Pete's 1948 book *How To Play The Five-String Banjo* was the first instructional book on American folk banjo styles. This book reveals his musical eclecticism, with chapters also devoted to blues and Spanish and South American music in addition to clawhammer, old-time, and bluegrass playing techniques. (For more specifics on banjo techniques, check out Parts II and III of this book.)

On the head of his trademark long-neck banjo is written "This Machine Surrounds Hate and Forces It to Surrender." You may want to check out his CD *Darling Corey and Goofing Off Suite* (Smithsonian Folkways) for a taste of Seeger's wide-ranging musical sensibility.

Béla Fleck (b. 1958)

Béla Fleck emerged from the progressive bluegrass scene in the 1980s to blaze trails and set new standards for the banjo within contemporary rock, jazz, classical, and world music. He's the premiere banjo player in the world today, bringing a staggering technical ability and lyrical musicality to the music he creates with his band, Béla Fleck and the Flecktones, and through collaborations with such diverse artists as Chick Corea, Zakir Hussein, Edgar Meyer, Tony Trischka, and others. I recommend listening to the bluegrass-oriented *Tales from the Acoustic Planet* (Warner Brothers), the classical recording *Perpetual Motion* (Columbia), and the Flecktones's *The Hidden Land* (Columbia) to learn more about today's most influential player.

Tommy Jarrell (1901–1985)

Some of the best traditional clawhammer banjo playing in the world originates from the Round Peak, North Carolina and Galax, Virginia areas. Although Tommy Jarrell is more celebrated as a fiddler, his drop-thumb clawhammer banjo playing, usually on a fretless banjo, has influenced many of today's finest players, including Paul Brown, Bruce Molsky, Brad Leftwich, and Kirk Sutphin. Simultaneously intricate and hard driving, Jarrell's music, along with other clawhammer players such as Wade Ward, Kyle Creed, Fred Cockerham and Matokie Slaughter, served as a bridge connecting the music's late 19th century rural Southern roots to the modern old-time music revival. For more on Jarrell, check out *The Legacy of Tommy Jarrell Volume 3: Come and Go With Me* (County), a recording featuring Tommy's solo clawhammer playing.

Bill Keith (b. 1939)

The banjo's innovative Renaissance man, Bill Keith helped to develop the melodic style of banjo playing, enabling banjo players to play scales while still using familiar three-finger roll patterns. This widely adopted technique empowers the player to reproduce note-for-note versions of everything from a fiddle tune to a Bach invention and has significantly enhanced the banjo's musical potential. (For more on the melodic style, see Chapter 8.)

Keith is also responsible for the Keith "D" tuner, which allows the player to quickly and accurately move from one pitch to another within a song. To dive in deeper to Keith's music, you can explore *Something Auld, Something New* (Rounder) for Bill's ingenious playing on bluegrass and jazz tunes.

Mike Seeger (b. 1933)

Mike Seeger (Pete's half brother) has devoted his life to singing, playing, and documenting traditional music made by American southerners before the media age. With over 25 field recordings to his credit, Mike has helped to preserve the diversity of southern folk banjo styles while exposing historically important players such as Dock Boggs to a wider audience.

As a player, Mike uses old-time music as a wellspring for his own creative and personalized fusions, forming a model for contemporary artistic expression within this genre that has influenced hundreds of other old-time players. *Southern Banjo Styles* (Smithsonian) is essential listening if you want to get a feel for what Mike Seeger is all about.

Uncle Dave Macon (1870–1952)

Nicknamed the "Dixie Dewdrop," Dave Harrison Macon was the most popular banjo player in the first decades of commercial country music (from the 1920s to '40s) and the early Grand Old Opry's biggest star. With musical roots in 19th century minstrel, folk, and vaudeville music, Macon, whose folksy performing style earned him the nickname of "Uncle Dave," brought a dizzying array of banjo playing techniques to the sound of early country music. His outrageous humor and showmanship often obscured his considerable banjo playing skills, which are on fine display on the recording *Go Long Mule* (County).

J. D. Crowe (b. 1937)

Considered the most influential banjo player of bluegrass music's modern age (1970s to the present), J. D. Crowe brings a forceful right-hand attack and a bluesy intensity to his Scruggs-based bluegrass banjo playing. With crisp, aggressive pull-offs and ideas borrowed from early rock 'n' roll and country guitar, Crowe is also a superb and influential band leader. The mid-1970s version of his band, The New South, featuring mandolin player Ricky Skaggs, guitarist Tony Rice, and dobro player Jerry Douglas, set the standard for the sound of modern bluegrass, absorbing contemporary country and folk influences. *J.D. Crowe and the New South* (Rounder) and *The Bluegrass Album Band, Vol. 1* (Rounder) are essential discs for any banjo player's music collection.

Don Reno (1927–1984)

Around the same time Earl Scruggs was learning to play in nearby North Carolina, Don Reno developed his three-finger approach to banjo playing in South Carolina. As his professional performing career blossomed in the 1950s and '60s, Reno separated himself from Scruggs's sound by bringing a new set of playing techniques to bluegrass banjo, adopted from his extensive knowledge of country guitar playing. From jazzy chordal licks to virtuosic single-string runs and an innovative right-hand technique, Reno's playing offered an alternative to Scruggs's approach within bluegrass and has inspired several successive generations of bluegrass banjo players. Reno's *Founding Father of the Bluegrass Banjo* (CMH) is a compilation of some of his best late-career work. (See Chapter 8 for an introduction to Reno's single-string playing technique.)

Sylvester (Vess) Ossman (1868–1923)

This classic banjo performer recorded almost a thousand cylinder and disc recordings at the dawn of the recording era, from 1893 to 1917, and was probably America's most well-known banjo player at the beginning of the 20th century. Ossman had spectacular fingerpicking technique and a wonderful rhythmic feel to his playing. He was usually accompanied by piano, band, or orchestra. The immense popularity of ragtime in the early 1900s is reflected in Ossman's repertoire, which included marches and popular music of the day as well as music composed for the banjo (see Chapter 7 to play two early 20th-century classic banjo pieces).

You can listen to some of Ossman's recordings online by visiting the following Web sites:

- ✔ www.archive.org/details/VessLossman
- ✔ cylinders.library.ucsb.edu

Alison Brown (b. 1962)

Count this Nashville-based banjoist at the top of the list of today's most influential progressive players. Combining influences from jazz, folk, Latin, bluegrass, Irish, and world music, Brown's work on electric and acoustic banjo is lyrical, warm, and virtuosic — all at the same time (a rare accomplishment on this instrument)! She fronts the Alison Brown Quartet, a jazz-tinged ensemble featuring drums, piano, and bass, and she also heads up her own record label, Compass Records. Check out *Stolen Moments* (Compass) for the acoustic side of Brown's playing and *Out of the Blue* (Compass) for a listening adventure in jazz fusion.

Tony Trischka (b. 1949)

Tony's reputation as the first avant-garde bluegrass player was established in the 1970s through a series of groundbreaking recordings filled with startling original compositions. Luckily, the rest of the banjo world has finally caught up to him. Today, in addition to being at the forefront of the boldest of banjo explorations, Tony is known as a master of a wide variety of traditional banjo styles, including Scruggs-style bluegrass banjo. He's a complete player who's at home in any kind of music played on the banjo. Tony is also known an outstanding instructor who has influenced thousands of players through his books, DVDs, and private teaching. Count such players as Béla Fleck, Chris Pandolfi, and yours truly among his dedicated students. Check out *Double Banjo Bluegrass Spectacular* and *World Turning* (both on Rounder Records) for a sampling of music from this very influential player.

Other Banjo Players You Should Hear

If you want to go a little further in your exploration of the ever-expanding universe of banjo sounds and styles, I've provided the following lists of banjo players I think you need to check out:

- **Clawhammer and old time:** Virgil Anderson, Danny Barnes, Riley Baugus, Mac Benford, Carroll Best, Dock Boggs, Laura Boosinger, Hank Bradley, Kate Brislin, Paul Brown, Samantha Bumgarner, Gaither Carleton, Bob Carlin, Maybelle Carter, Fred Cockerham, John Cohen, Cousin Emmy, Mary Z. Cox, Kyle Creed, Rufus Crisp, Dwight Diller, Cathy Fink, Dan Gellert, Alice Gerrard, Roscoe Holcomb, Mark Johnson, Grandpa Jones, Buell Kazee, Walt Koken, Jens Kruger, Lilly May Ledford, Frank Lee, Brad Leftwich, Dan Levenson, Bertram Levy, Charlie Lowe, R. D. Lunceford, Joel Mabus, Reed Martin, Michael Miles, Bruce Molsky, Lynn Morris, Molly O'Day, Tom Paley, Ken Perlman, Charlie Poole, Dirk Powell, Olla Belle Reed, Dink Roberts, Ivan Rosenberg, Mark Schatz, Lee Sexton, Morgan Sexton, Wayne Shrubsall, Matokie Slaughter, Will Slayden, Hobart Smith, Jody Stecher, Kirk Sutphin, Molly Tenenbaum, Suzanne Thomas, Odell Thompson, Leroy Troy, Stephen Wade, Abagail Washburn, Doc Watson, Oscar Wright

- **Bluegrass:** Tom Adams, Eddie Adcock, Danny Barnes, Terry Baucom, Ron Block, Dennis Caplinger, Cia Cherryholmes, Pat Cloud, Noah Crase, Charlie Cushman, Doug Dillard, Steve Dilling, Joe Drumright, Ben Eldridge, Tony Ellis, Bill Emerson, Emily Erwin, Tony Furtado, John Hartford, Casey Henry, Murphy Henry, John Hickman, Steve Huber, Snuffy Jenkins, Courtney Johnson, Vic Jordan, Jens Kruger, John Lawless, Greg Liszt, "Little Roy" Lewis, Keith Little, Rudy Lyle, Ned Luberecki, Rob McCoury, John McEuen, Jim Mills, Lynn Morris, Alan Munde, Mike Munford, Alan O'Bryant, Sonny Osborne, Chris Pandolfi, Herb Pedersen, Noam Pilkelny, Don Wayne Reno, Butch Robins, Kristin Scott Benson, Sammy Shelor, Allen Shelton, Avram Siegel, Craig Smith, Fred Sokolow, Ralph Stanley, Ron Stewart, Don Stover, Dave Talbot, Bobby Thompson, Scott Vestal, Eric Weissburg, Pete Wernick

Part VI
Appendixes

"Okay — I'll front the band. But I want someone other than Dopey on banjo."

In this part . . .

1 provide a helpful chord digest. You can never know enough chords. I also include some instructions about the CD that accompanies this book.

Appendix A

Banjo Chords and Notes

Chords

In the next two figures, A-1 and A-2, I give you 57 chord diagrams for the major, minor, 7th, and minor 7th chords found in the first position on the banjo neck (frets one through five) along with five chord shapes used for 6th and 9th chords.

I've included a movable banjo chord position chart, Figure A-3, which shows the positions of the G, C and D movable major, seventh, minor, and diminished chords on the first 12 frets of the banjo. A movable chord position requires the left hand to fret strings one through four of your banjo. The advantage of movable chords is that they can be easily shifted up and down the neck to fret new letter name chords.

To find other letter name chords using these same positions, shift the movable chord position up or down according to the order of notes listed below:

   G   G♯/A♭   A   A♯/B♭   B   C   C♯/D♭   D   D♯/E♭   E   F   F♯/G♭   G

For example, if you fret the F-shape G chord that's found at the fifth fret (and shown on the upper left chart on the movable banjo chord positions page), and if you move this chord up two frets, you'll now be playing an A chord. Note that the A note is located two notes above the G note, as shown in the list above. Each adjacent note corresponds to a one fret change up or down on your banjo neck.

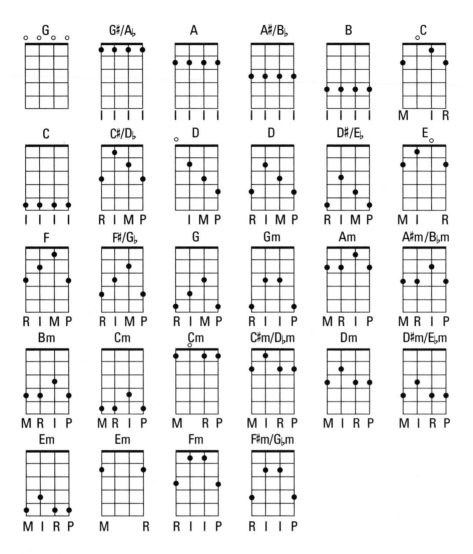

Figure A-1: First position major and minor chords.

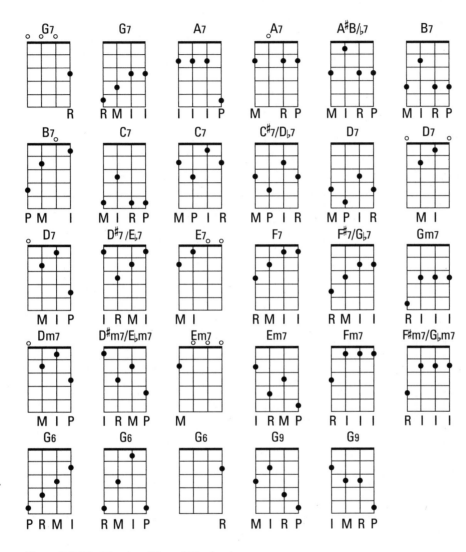

Figure A-2: 6th, 7th, minor 7th, and 9th chords.

F-shape: ●
D-shape: ■
Barre-shape: ◆
□ =not necessarily fretted, but may be

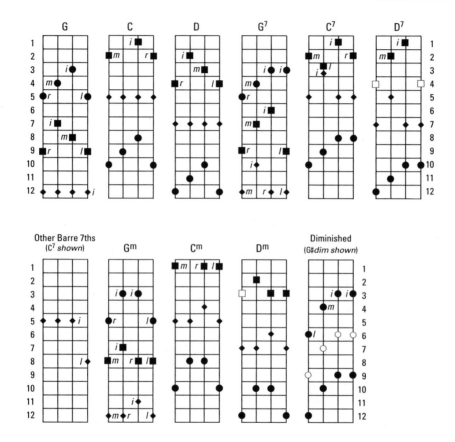

Figure A-3: A movable banjo chord position chart.

Notes on the Banjo in G Tuning

Figures A-4 through A-8 show you the names of the notes on the banjo finger-board in G tuning. Knowing these names can be useful in building chords and for locating melody notes on your banjo. Each figure lists the names of the notes on an individual string.

There are often two notes (for example, G♯/A♭) at the same fret. Called *enharmonic equivalents*, these notes have the same pitch but are called either by one letter name or the other depending upon what key you are playing in.

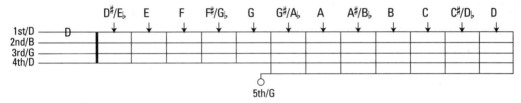

Figure A-4: 1st string: Open D.

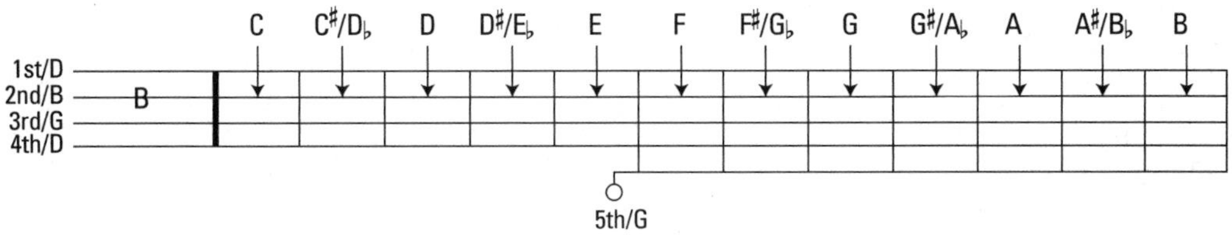

Figure A-5: 2nd string: Open B.

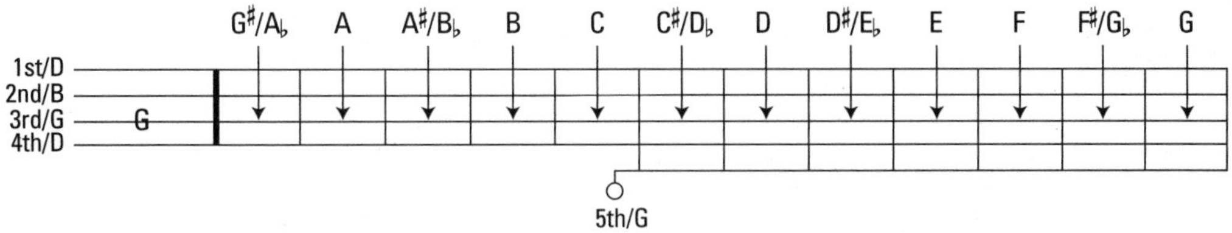

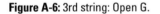

Figure A-6: 3rd string: Open G.

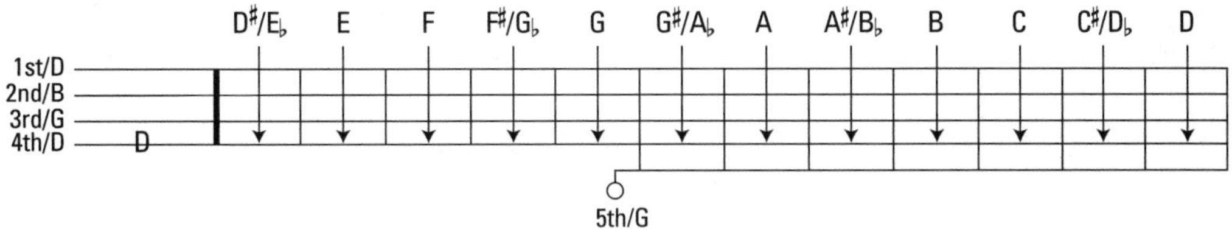

Figure A-7: 4th string: Open D.

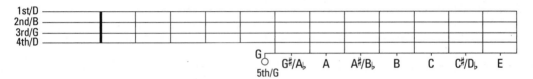

Figure A-8: 5th string: Open G.

Appendix B

About the CD

● ●

*T*he CD that accompanies this book contains a whopping 94 tracks. Each of these tracks contains musical examples that you can listen to and practice as much as you need to in order to improve your banjo playing.

A fun way to use *Banjo For Dummies* is to scan the chapters for the On the CD icon. In every instance, the text flagged by this icon refers to a musical example that not only appears as written music, or tablature, but also is presented as an audio track on the book's CD. When you see an example that seems interesting, skip to the corresponding track on the CD and give it a listen. Maybe you can even play along.

Relating the Text to the CD

Throughout the book, the text contains musical examples that you can play and practice over and over again. These musical examples most often come in the form of tablature. If a piece of tablature appears on the CD, the CD's track number appears in the tab's caption. Just use the track-skip buttons on your CD player to move to whatever track you want to listen to.

System Requirements

For many of you, all you're going to do is pop the CD in your CD player and skip around to the tracks you want to hear and play along with. Others may want to load the CD onto a computer. This section helps you do both.

Audio CD players

The CD included with this book will work just fine in any standard CD player. Just pop it in and press play or use the track-skip buttons to jump to whatever tracks you want to explore.

Computer CD-ROM drives

If you have a computer, you can insert the CD into your CD drive to access the MP3 files of all the CD tracks. Make sure your computer meets the minimum system requirements shown here:

- ✔ A computer running Microsoft Windows or Mac OS
- ✔ Software capable of playing MP3s and CD audio (such as iTunes or Windows Media Player)
- ✔ A sound card (almost all computers these days have the built-in ability to play sound)
- ✔ A CD-ROM drive

Using the CD

To install the items from the CD to your computer's hard drive, follow these steps:

1. **Insert the CD into your computer's CD-ROM drive. The license agreement appears.**

   Note to Windows users: The interface won't launch if you have autorun disabled. In that case, click Start⇨Run (For Windows Vista, Start⇨ All Programs⇨Accessories⇨Run). In the dialog box that appears, type D:\Start.exe. (Replace D with the proper letter if your CD drive uses a different letter. If you don't know the letter, see how your CD drive is listed under My Computer.) Click OK.

   Note for Mac Users: The CD icon will appear on your desktop; double-click the icon to open the CD and double-click the Start icon.

2. **Read through the license agreement, and then click the Accept button if you want to use the CD.**

   The CD interface appears. The interface allows you to install the MP3 files onto your hard drive with just a few clicks.

3. **If you would like to install the MP3 files of the CD audio tracks onto your computer, click the MP3 button.**

   You can now copy the MP3 files from the CD to your hard drive.

The Tracks on the CD

The following table lists all 94 tracks on the CD along with the corresponding tablature numbers from the chapters in the book.

All the audio tracks have been stored on the CD in the MP3 format, which means that if you follow the steps in the preceding section, you can copy the MP3 files from the CD onto your computer. From there, you can listen to the MP3s with your audio software or even copy them onto your portable MP3 player.

Track Number	Tab Number	Track Description
1	–	G tuning reference notes (Chapter 2)
2	–	Strumming G, C, and D7 chords (Chapter 2)
3	3-1	"Red River Valley" singing & handclaps
4	3-2	"Red River Valley" singing & strumming
5	3-3	"Boil Them Cabbage Down" strumming
6	3-8	Tab rhythm exercise
7	3-9	Pinch patterns with G, C, and D7 chords
8	3-10	"Red River Valley" with pinch-pattern accompaniment
9	3-11	"Boil Them Cabbage Down" with pinch-pattern accompaniment
10	4-1	Clawhammer melody-note exercise #1
11	4-2	Clawhammer melody-note exercise #2
12	4-3	Clawhammer brush exercise
13	4-4	Clawhammer brush and 5th-string exercise
14	4-5	Basic clawhammer technique exercise #1
15	4-6	Basic clawhammer technique exercise #2
16	4-7	Clawhammer technique with G, C, and D7 chords
17	4-8	"Red River Valley" singing with clawhammer accompaniment

(continued)

Track Number	Tab Number	Track Description
18	4-9	"Boil Them Cabbage Down" singing with clawhammer accompaniment
19	4-10	Bluegrass right-hand thumb note exercise
20	4-11	Bluegrass right-hand index and middle-finger exercise
21	4-12	Bluegrass alternating thumb roll with G, C, and D7 chords
22	4-13	Bluegrass forward-backward roll with G, C, and D7 chords
23	4-14	Bluegrass forward roll with G, C, and D7 chords
24	4-15	"Red River Valley" singing and guitar with forward-roll accompaniment
25	4-16	"Boil Them Cabbage Down" singing & guitar with mixed-roll accompaniment
26	5-1 to 5-3	(0:00) 3rd-string slides / (0:25) 4th-string slides / (0:44) 1st-string slides
27	5-4	Open-string hammer-ons
28	5-5	Fretted hammer-ons
29	5-6	Open-string pull-offs
30	5-7	Fretted pull-offs
31	5-8	Heavy metal lick
32	5-9	Choke / choke and release / pre-choke
33	5-10	Basic clawhammer technique with G, C, and D7 chords
34	5-11	Bluegrass roll review: alternating-thumb, forward-backward, and forward rolls
35	5-12	Clawhammer 3rd-string slides
36	5-13	Clawhammer 1st-string slides
37	5-14	Clawhammer 4th-string slides
38	5-15	Clawhammer open-string hammer-ons
39	5-16	Clawhammer fretted hammer-ons
40	5-17	Clawhammer 4th-string pull-offs

Track Number	Tab Number	Track Description
41	5-18	Clawhammer 3rd-string pull-offs
42	5-19	Clawhammer 1st-string pull-offs
43	5-20	Clawhammer special pull-off
44	5-21	Clawhammer with tenth-fret chokes
45	5-22	Bluegrass alternating thumb rolls with slides
46	5-23	Bluegrass forward-backward rolls with slides
47	5-24	Bluegrass forward rolls with slides
48	5-25	Bluegrass alternating-thumb rolls with hammer-ons
49	5-26	Bluegrass forward-backward rolls with hammer-ons
50	5-27	Bluegrass forward rolls with hammer-ons
51	5-28	Bluegrass alternating-thumb rolls with pull-offs
52	5-29	Bluegrass forward-backward rolls with slides & pull-offs
53	5-30	Bluegrass forward rolls with hammer-ons & pull-offs
54	5-31	Bluegrass forward rolls with chokes
55	–	G-major scale (Chapter 6)
56	–	D-major scale (Chapter 6)
57	–	G-major scale, beginning on open 4th string (Chapter 6)
58	6-1	Frere Jacques
59	6-2	"Red River Valley" banjo melody notes with guitar accompaniment
60	6-3	"Red River Valley" clawhammer melody with guitar accompaniment
61	6-4	"Red River Valley" bluegrass melody with guitar accompaniment
62	6-5	"Red River Valley" clawhammer melody using left-hand techniques, with guitar accompaniment
63	6-6	"Red River Valley" bluegrass melody using left-hand techniques, with guitar accompaniment

(continued)

Track Number	Tab Number	Track Description
64	6-7	"Boil Them Cabbage Down" clawhammer melody with guitar accompaniment
65	6-8	"Boil Them Cabbage Down" bluegrass melody with guitar accompaniment
66	6-9	"Cripple Creek" clawhammer melody with guitar accompaniment
67	6-10	"Cripple Creek" bluegrass melody with guitar accompaniment
68	6-11	"Goodbye Liza Jane" clawhammer melody with guitar accompaniment
69	6-12	"Goodbye Liza Jane" bluegrass melody with guitar accompaniment
70	6-13	"Ground Hog" clawhammer melody with guitar accompaniment
71	6-14	"Ground Hog" bluegrass melody with guitar accompaniment
72	7-1	"Pompey Ran Away" African banjo tune
73	7-2	"Juba" 19th-century minstrel banjo tune
74	7-3	"Hard Times" 19th-century minstrel banjo tune
75	7-4	"Colorado Buck Dance" early 20th-century classic banjo piece
76	7-5	"Banjoisticus" early 20th-century classic banjo piece
77	8-1	Bluegrass roll patterns: alternating thumb / forward-backward / forward / forward-reverse / Foggy Mountain / backward roll / middle leading roll / index leading roll
78	8-2	8 G licks (a through h)
79	8-3	4 C licks (a through d)
80	8-4	4 D licks (a through d)
81	8-5	4 G fill-in licks (a through d)
82	8-6	Creating a bluegrass solo using licks, G-C-D7 chord progression

Track Number	Tab Number	Track Description
83	8-7	"Everyday Breakdown" bluegrass banjo with guitar and mandolin accompaniment
84	8-8	"Shortening Bread" bluegrass banjo with guitar and mandolin accompaniment
85	8-12	"Banjo Cascade" melodic banjo with guitar and mandolin accompaniment
86	8-13	"Turkey in the Straw" melodic banjo with guitar and mandolin accompaniment
87	8-14 to 8-16	Single-string right-hand exercises (a through c)
88	8-17 to 8-20	Single-string scale exercises (a through d)
89	8-21	D scale
90	8-22	"Arkansas Traveler" banjo with guitar accompaniment
91	8-23	"Reno's Rag" banjo with guitar accompaniment
92	8-24	"Winston's Jig" banjo with guitar accompaniment
93	8-25	"Meadows of Dan" banjo solo
94	8-25	"Meadows of Dan" full-band track

Troubleshooting

If you have trouble with the CD, please call the Wiley Product Technical Support phone number at 800-762-2974. Outside the United States, call 1-317-572-3994. You can also contact Wiley Product Technical Support at `http://support.wiley.com`. John Wiley & Sons will provide technical support only for installation and other general quality control items. For technical support on the applications themselves, consult the program's vendor or author.

Wiley Publishing, Inc.
End-User License Agreement

READ THIS. You should carefully read these terms and conditions before opening the software packet(s) included with this book "Book". This is a license agreement "Agreement" between you and Wiley Publishing, Inc. "WPI". By opening the accompanying software packet(s), you acknowledge that you have read and accept the following terms and conditions. If you do not agree and do not want to be bound by such terms and conditions, promptly return the Book and the unopened software packet(s) to the place you obtained them for a full refund.

1. **License Grant.** WPI grants to you (either an individual or entity) a nonexclusive license to use one copy of the enclosed software program(s) (collectively, the "Software") solely for your own personal or business purposes on a single computer (whether a standard computer or a workstation component of a multi-user network). The Software is in use on a computer when it is loaded into temporary memory (RAM) or installed into permanent memory (hard disk, CD-ROM, or other storage device). WPI reserves all rights not expressly granted herein.

2. **Ownership.** WPI is the owner of all right, title, and interest, including copyright, in and to the compilation of the Software recorded on the physical packet included with this Book "Software Media". Copyright to the individual programs recorded on the Software Media is owned by the author or other authorized copyright owner of each program. Ownership of the Software and all proprietary rights relating thereto remain with WPI and its licensers.

3. **Restrictions on Use and Transfer.**

   (a) You may only (i) make one copy of the Software for backup or archival purposes, or (ii) transfer the Software to a single hard disk, provided that you keep the original for backup or archival purposes. You may not (i) rent or lease the Software, (ii) copy or reproduce the Software through a LAN or other network system or through any computer subscriber system or bulletin-board system, or (iii) modify, adapt, or create derivative works based on the Software.

   (b) You may not reverse engineer, decompile, or disassemble the Software. You may transfer the Software and user documentation on a permanent basis, provided that the transferee agrees to accept the terms and conditions of this Agreement and you retain no copies. If the Software is an update or has been updated, any transfer must include the most recent update and all prior versions.

4. **Restrictions on Use of Individual Programs.** You must follow the individual requirements and restrictions detailed for each individual program in the "About the CD" appendix of this Book or on the Software Media. These limitations are also contained in the individual license agreements recorded on the Software Media. These limitations may include a requirement that after using the program for a specified period of time, the user must pay a registration fee or discontinue use. By opening the Software packet(s), you agree to abide by the licenses and restrictions for these individual programs that are detailed in the "About the CD" appendix and/or on the Software Media. None of the material on this Software Media or listed in this Book may ever be redistributed, in original or modified form, for commercial purposes.

5. **Limited Warranty.**

   (a) WPI warrants that the Software and Software Media are free from defects in materials and workmanship under normal use for a period of sixty (60) days from the date of purchase of this Book. If WPI receives notification within the warranty period of defects in materials or workmanship, WPI will replace the defective Software Media.

   (b) WPI AND THE AUTHOR(S) OF THE BOOK DISCLAIM ALL OTHER WARRANTIES, EXPRESS OR IMPLIED, INCLUDING WITHOUT LIMITATION IMPLIED WARRANTIES OF MERCHANTABILITY AND FITNESS FOR A PARTICULAR PURPOSE, WITH RESPECT TO THE SOFTWARE, THE PROGRAMS, THE SOURCE CODE CONTAINED THEREIN, AND/OR THE TECHNIQUES DESCRIBED IN THIS BOOK. WPI DOES NOT WARRANT THAT THE FUNCTIONS CONTAINED IN THE SOFTWARE WILL MEET YOUR REQUIRE- MENTS OR THAT THE OPERATION OF THE SOFTWARE WILL BE ERROR FREE.

   (c) This limited warranty gives you specific legal rights, and you may have other rights that vary from jurisdiction to jurisdiction.

6. **Remedies.**

   (a) WPI's entire liability and your exclusive remedy for defects in materials and workman- ship shall be limited to replacement of the Software Media, which may be returned to WPI with a copy of your receipt at the following address: Software Media Fulfillment Department, Attn.: *Banjo For Dummies,* Wiley Publishing, Inc., 10475 Crosspoint Blvd., Indianapolis, IN 46256, or call 1-800-762-2974. Please allow four to six weeks for delivery. This Limited Warranty is void if failure of the Software Media has resulted from accident, abuse, or misapplication. Any replacement Software Media will be warranted for the remainder of the original warranty period or thirty (30) days, whichever is longer.

   (b) In no event shall WPI or the author be liable for any damages whatsoever (including without limitation damages for loss of business profits, business interruption, loss of business information, or any other pecuniary loss) arising from the use of or inability to use the Book or the Software, even if WPI has been advised of the possibility of such damages.

   (c) Because some jurisdictions do not allow the exclusion or limitation of liability for conse- quential or incidental damages, the above limitation or exclusion may not apply to you.

7. **U.S. Government Restricted Rights.** Use, duplication, or disclosure of the Software for or on behalf of the United States of America, its agencies and/or instrumentalities "U.S. Government" is subject to restrictions as stated in paragraph (c)(1)(ii) of the Rights in Technical Data and Computer Software clause of DFARS 252.227-7013, or subparagraphs (c) (1) and (2) of the Commercial Computer Software - Restricted Rights clause at FAR 52.227-19, and in similar clauses in the NASA FAR supplement, as applicable.

8. **General.** This Agreement constitutes the entire understanding of the parties and revokes and supersedes all prior agreements, oral or written, between them and may not be modified or amended except in a writing signed by both parties hereto that specifically refers to this Agreement. This Agreement shall take precedence over any other documents that may be in conflict herewith. If any one or more provisions contained in this Agreement are held by any court or tribunal to be invalid, illegal, or otherwise unenforceable, each and every other pro- vision shall remain in full force and effect.

Index

• *N* •

• T •

Notes

Notes

Notes

Notes

Notes

Notes

SPORTS, FITNESS, PARENTING, RELIGION & SPIRITUALITY

0-471-76871-5

0-7645-7841-3

Also available:
- Catholicism For Dummies
  0-7645-5391-7
- Exercise Balls For Dummies
  0-7645-5623-1
- Fitness For Dummies
  0-7645-7851-0
- Football For Dummies
  0-7645-3936-1
- Judaism For Dummies
  0-7645-5299-6
- Potty Training For Dummies
  0-7645-5417-4
- Buddhism For Dummies
  0-7645-5359-3

- Pregnancy For Dummies
  0-7645-4483-7 †
- Ten Minute Tone-Ups For Dummies
  0-7645-7207-5
- NASCAR For Dummies
  0-7645-7681-X
- Religion For Dummies
  0-7645-5264-3
- Soccer For Dummies
  0-7645-5229-5
- Women in the Bible For Dummies
  0-7645-8475-8

TRAVEL

0-7645-7749-2

0-7645-6945-7

Also available:
- Alaska For Dummies
  0-7645-7746-8
- Cruise Vacations For Dummies
  0-7645-6941-4
- England For Dummies
  0-7645-4276-1
- Europe For Dummies
  0-7645-7529-5
- Germany For Dummies
  0-7645-7823-5
- Hawaii For Dummies
  0-7645-7402-7

- Italy For Dummies
  0-7645-7386-1
- Las Vegas For Dummies
  0-7645-7382-9
- London For Dummies
  0-7645-4277-X
- Paris For Dummies
  0-7645-7630-5
- RV Vacations For Dummies
  0-7645-4442-X
- Walt Disney World & Orlando
  For Dummies
  0-7645-9660-8

GRAPHICS, DESIGN & WEB DEVELOPMENT

0-7645-8815-X

0-7645-9571-7

Also available:
- 3D Game Animation For Dummies
  0-7645-8789-7
- AutoCAD 2006 For Dummies
  0-7645-8925-3
- Building a Web Site For Dummies
  0-7645-7144-3
- Creating Web Pages For Dummies
  0-470-08030-2
- Creating Web Pages All-in-One Desk
  Reference For Dummies
  0-7645-4345-8
- Dreamweaver 8 For Dummies
  0-7645-9649-7

- InDesign CS2 For Dummies
  0-7645-9572-5
- Macromedia Flash 8 For Dummies
  0-7645-9691-8
- Photoshop CS2 and Digital
  Photography For Dummies
  0-7645-9580-6
- Photoshop Elements 4 For Dummies
  0-471-77483-9
- Syndicating Web Sites with RSS Feeds
  For Dummies
  0-7645-8848-6
- Yahoo! SiteBuilder For Dummies
  0-7645-9800-7

NETWORKING, SECURITY, PROGRAMMING & DATABASES

0-7645-7728-X

0-471-74940-0

Also available:
- Access 2007 For Dummies
  0-470-04612-0
- ASP.NET 2 For Dummies
  0-7645-7907-X
- C# 2005 For Dummies
  0-7645-9704-3
- Hacking For Dummies
  0-470-05235-X
- Hacking Wireless Networks
  For Dummies
  0-7645-9730-2
- Java For Dummies
  0-470-08716-1

- Microsoft SQL Server 2005 For Dummies
  0-7645-7755-7
- Networking All-in-One Desk Reference
  For Dummies
  0-7645-9939-9
- Preventing Identity Theft For Dummies
  0-7645-7336-5
- Telecom For Dummies
  0-471-77085-X
- Visual Studio 2005 All-in-One Desk
  Reference For Dummies
  0-7645-9775-2
- XML For Dummies
  0-7645-8845-1

HEALTH & SELF-HELP

0-7645-8450-2

0-7645-4149-8

Also available:
- Bipolar Disorder For Dummies
  0-7645-8451-0
- Chemotherapy and Radiation
  For Dummies
  0-7645-7832-4
- Controlling Cholesterol For Dummies
  0-7645-5440-9
- Diabetes For Dummies
  0-7645-6820-5* †
- Divorce For Dummies
  0-7645-8417-0 †

- Fibromyalgia For Dummies
  0-7645-5441-7
- Low-Calorie Dieting For Dummies
  0-7645-9905-4
- Meditation For Dummies
  0-471-77774-9
- Osteoporosis For Dummies
  0-7645-7621-6
- Overcoming Anxiety For Dummies
  0-7645-5447-6
- Reiki For Dummies
  0-7645-9907-0
- Stress Management For Dummies
  0-7645-5144-2

EDUCATION, HISTORY, REFERENCE & TEST PREPARATION

0-7645-8381-6

0-7645-9554-7

Also available:
- The ACT For Dummies
  0-7645-9652-7
- Algebra For Dummies
  0-7645-5325-9
- Algebra Workbook For Dummies
  0-7645-8467-7
- Astronomy For Dummies
  0-7645-8465-0
- Calculus For Dummies
  0-7645-2498-4
- Chemistry For Dummies
  0-7645-5430-1
- Forensics For Dummies
  0-7645-5580-4

- Freemasons For Dummies
  0-7645-9796-5
- French For Dummies
  0-7645-5193-0
- Geometry For Dummies
  0-7645-5324-0
- Organic Chemistry I For Dummies
  0-7645-6902-3
- The SAT I For Dummies
  0-7645-7193-1
- Spanish For Dummies
  0-7645-5194-9
- Statistics For Dummies
  0-7645-5423-9

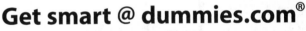

Get smart @ dummies.com®

- **Find a full list of Dummies titles**
- **Look into loads of FREE on-site articles**
- **Sign up for FREE eTips e-mailed to you weekly**
- **See what other products carry the Dummies name**
- **Shop directly from the Dummies bookstore**
- **Enter to win new prizes every month!**